'Gripping, witty and enlightened, this book is unique. It is a must-buy for anyone wanting to stop working so hard for their money and start making their money work hard for them … without doubt the best book I've read in the last five years.'

Emma Kane, CEO of Newgate Communications and Chair of
Target Ovarian Cancer and the Barbican Centre Trust

'One of the City's great failings is the widespread use of complex and elitist language. *How to Own the World* takes the reader on an educational and inspirational journey through the world of investing, written in plain English. A triumph.'

Ian Peacock, Managing Director, IG Group plc

'Accessible, actionable and fun. Lifts the veil on the often impenetrable world of finance and investing. The City will probably hate it.'

Tim Price, Award-winning Fund Manager

'If you want just one book on investment from the cacophony, you couldn't do much better.'

Professor Michael Mainelli, author of
The Price of Fish

'How refreshing to find a book which clarifies the sometimes arcane world of investment for the layman. The next time you talk to your financial adviser they will be impressed with your insights. This book will guide you towards a better financial life experience.'

Steve Thomas, Professor of Finance and Associate
Dean for the MBA Programme at Cass Business School

'This book is the simplest and easiest method for becoming smarter about money. *How to Own the World* should be a must read for anyone with a bank account. No hype or conjecture, just plain English on money, investing and finance.'

Michael Killen, author of *From Single to
Scale* and founder of Sell Your Service

Andrew Craig believes that you owe it to yourself to learn about money and investment because doing so is life-changing. He has worked in the City of London for over twenty years and in 2011, he founded the personal finance website, plainenglishfinance.co.uk to help people improve their finances. Since then he has appeared in numerous publications including: *Mail on Sunday, CityAM, The Spectator, Shares, MoneyWeek, YourMoney, This Is Money* and *Money Observer*. He has been interviewed on Bloomberg and Shares Radio and on IG TV, was featured in Russell Brand and Michael Winterbottom's 2015 film *The Emperor's New Clothes* and interviewed by Eamonn Holmes for the Channel 5 programme *How the Other Half Live*.

How to Own the World

A plain English guide to thinking globally and investing wisely

ANDREW CRAIG

First published as *Own the World* in Great Britain in 2012 by Plain English Finance Limited
This revised and updated edition published by John Murray Learning in 2019.
An Hachette UK company.

British Library Cataloguing in Publication Data: a catalogue record for this title is available
from the British Library.
ISBN 978 1 473 69530 6
eISBN 978 1 473 69532 0

5

The publisher has used its best endeavours to ensure that any website addresses referred to
in this book are correct and active at the time of going to press. However, the publisher and
the author have no responsibility for the websites and can make no guarantee that a site
will remain live or that the content will remain relevant, decent or appropriate.
The publisher has made every effort to mark as such all words which it believes to be
trademarks. The publisher should also like to make it clear that the presence of a word in
the book, whether marked or unmarked, in no way affects its legal status as a trademark.
Every reasonable effort has been made by the publisher to trace the copyright holders
of material in this book. Any errors or omissions should be notified in writing to the
publisher, who will endeavour to rectify the situation for any reprints and future editions.

Typeset by Cenveo® Publisher Services.
Printed and bound in Great Britain by Clays Ltd, Elcograf S.p.A.
John Murray Learning policy is to use papers that are natural, renewable and
recyclable products and made from wood grown in sustainable forests. The logging and
manufacturing processes are expected to conform to the environmental regulations of the
country of origin.
Carmelite House
50 Victoria Embankment
London EC4Y 0DZ
www.hodder.co.uk

Contents

Foreword by Sir Roger Gifford

Everyone can benefit from talking about what she or he does in terms people can actually understand, and this perhaps applies to those who work in financial services above all.

And yet, despite the greater wealth and education that modern Western society enjoys, one of the great challenges we still face is to increase and broaden financial literacy, enabling people to take greater control of their finances and their lives. Over the last decade a succession of academic publications and surveys has provided evidence for what many people know intuitively to be true: that real financial literacy is poorly distributed throughout the general population.

This reality has wide-reaching implications because it raises serious questions about the traditional economic theory still taught at most universities throughout the world. This prevalent economic thought assumes that people are 'rational' and have 'perfect information'. The truth is that the majority of people know little about financial markets and are often 'irrational' as a result, at least as far as their economic behaviour is concerned.

This goes a long way to explaining why the economics profession has been found so wanting in the financial crises of the last few years. Andrew Craig, the author of this book and a former colleague, sees widespread financial literacy as a sort of 'silver bullet' that can go a long way towards helping resolve many important issues in society – and I agree with him.

For individuals, possessing real financial literacy can help them move away from poverty and towards being comfortably off, and can even bring the possibility of substantial wealth on to their horizon, should that be desired. Even more important, however, is what financial literacy can do for society as a whole, helping people to participate in the market mechanisms that provide the capital for the solution to real human problems. These can include building better infrastructure, more efficient houses and modes of transport, weaning us off fossil fuels, and helping us develop our economies more responsibly – or even finding the capital our biotech and pharmaceutical industries need to help them get ever closer to curing diseases like cancer or dementia.

Andrew and I share a passion for changing the status quo to achieve this reality. Those of us in financial services need to communicate far more effectively about what we do – in clear and accessible language. People need to understand the enormous social good that financial services can provide. Andrew has set out to do exactly that with this excellent and much-needed book.

The City of London is the world's pre-eminent international financial centre. English is its *lingua franca* as well as its *Umgangssprache*. Financial literacy can pay enormous dividends for you and me as individuals and for society as a whole. Let's make finance as widely understood and as widely useful as we can by reading Andrew's book and by passing on the messages it contains.

Sir Roger Gifford, former Lord Mayor of London

Who I am – and why I think I can help you

Before we get into the meat of this book, it is entirely natural for you to want to know why I feel qualified to help you, and why I am different from the rest of the finance industry. There are a huge number of people working in finance who promise the earth and then fail to deliver – why should I be any different?

Well, the most fundamental difference between any financial adviser and me is that my goal is for *you* to learn how to look after *your* money. In terms of why I feel qualified to help you achieve this goal, obviously the traditional approach would be to tell you about my educational and professional background in order to establish my credentials, and I will get to that in a moment. Before I do, however, I want to make this point – it is my fervent wish that, as you read what follows, you will find the material sufficiently compelling in its own right that it won't really matter to you who I am or what my background is. The information in this book should appeal so strongly to your common sense that you won't really care who wrote it.

That said, for the sake of tradition I will now say a bit about why I felt qualified to write this book. Feel free to skip ahead if you are bored by 'about the author' pieces.

I started taking an interest in economics, economic history, politics and finance from what might be considered a freakishly young age. My father might not thank me for writing this, but it is not an exaggeration to say that he used to take me through magazines like *The Economist* and through the financial pages of the Sunday papers.

Perhaps inevitably, I chose to study Economics and International Politics at university, graduating in 1997. The day after my final exam, I left for Washington, DC to work as an intern for a US congressman (the American equivalent of an MP).

Rightly or wrongly, the chief of staff in my congressional office was convinced that a half-British, half-Irish person like me was inherently better at writing than any of the Americans on her payroll, despite my tender years. This was fantastic news and meant that I gained rapid promotion from '"executive" intern in charge of opening mail and getting coffee' to actually writing policy speeches for the congressman, almost from day one. As you can imagine, this was an incredible experience. My time in DC gave me an early idea of how important politics and politicians can be when thinking about finance and investment.

Happily, my stint with the US Congress meant that I was lucky enough to be asked to interview by the vast majority of the companies I applied to back in London: investment banks, management consultants and accountancy firms, as well as the Civil Service. I eventually accepted a job with what was then SBC Warburg (now UBS Investment Bank). Since then I have spent nearly 20 years working for various finance firms in London and New York. These include the aforementioned UBS, CA Cheuvreux, the European equity arm of Crédit Agricole (France's biggest bank), SEB (one of Sweden's leading banks) and now a boutique investment bank where I am a partner. I started my career in the bond market at UBS before moving into equities (shares). I will make the point later in this book that many finance professionals become highly specialized very early in their careers, often from day one. Although I am by no means unique, it is nevertheless reasonably rare to have worked in both bonds and equities, and it means I don't have quite the cat vs dog approach to people who work in another branch of the industry that many finance professionals do.

Perhaps even more importantly, however, when I moved into equities, my area of specialism was called 'pan-European small and mid-caps'. Although something of a mouthful, this simply meant that I dealt with companies from all over Europe and the UK that were worth less than about £2–3 billion. This meant that I was able to travel around Europe and the US and meet with the CEOs, CFOs and chairpeople of several hundred companies from every sector imaginable. I was involved with the stock market flotation (Initial Public Offering, or 'IPO') of dozens of high-profile companies, including Burberry, Campari, EasyJet, HMV, lastminute.com, Carluccio's and the Carbon Trust.

Working with 'smaller' companies meant two things. First, I was granted high-level access to the top management teams, which was an incredible learning experience, as you might imagine. Second, the price of these companies tends to be more volatile than the bigger household names in the FTSE 100 such as M&S, BP, Shell and Vodafone. I witnessed many companies appreciate in value by dozens – even hundreds – of per cent; and, equally, I saw others lose a huge percentage of their value, sometimes overnight.

This experience was key to developing my belief in the amazing possibilities of investment. I saw first hand how much money the very best investors were able to make, something very few members of the general population ever do. I was also in the front row when certain investors lost a great deal of money very quickly, which developed a keen desire to work out how to avoid this if at all possible. My reaction was to read widely about investment and to start investing my own money. Thanks in great part to the returns afforded by those investments, I have been able to spend around five of the last 20 years outside of conventional employment (i.e. not having to earn a conventional salary). This gave me the time to read a huge number of books on finance, trading, economics, history and economic history.

In fact, if you were to ask me the number-one reason why I feel qualified to present you with what follows, it is the bibliography at the end of this book and the fact that I have read dozens of emails about finance and economics nearly every day for more than two decades. More than my degree or years of working in banking, it is the time I have spent reading the best material on investment and economic history that has enabled me to put this book together.

I first came up with the idea for this book in November 2007. While on holiday, I found myself having yet another conversation with someone who was extremely bright and had a great job but who went to great lengths to tell me they had no clue about finance and investment – and were too scared and distrustful of the industry to ever invest their money in anything other than property. For the umpteenth time, I thought what a tragedy it was that so few people realize that it is relatively easy to learn how to look after your money. I decided there must be something I could do about this.

I spent another three years working; by mid-2010 I had enough saved to give me the financial security I needed to take a couple more years off work in order to write the first edition of this book.

You can be the judge of whether the result is that I am able to bring you information that you will find useful, even life-changing. I very much hope you will.

Andrew Craig

Introduction to the third edition

You may or may not know that the book you currently hold in your hands, or are reading on your Kindle, iPad or other fabulous tool of the modern age, is actually no less than the third version of this book.

As I explained in the 'Who I am ...' section above, I decided to take some time out of conventional employment from July 2010 to January 2013. Initially, this was with a view to creating a website aimed at helping people with their finances. During 2011 and 2012 I wrote something like 100,000 words of content for that website, www.plainenglishfinance.co.uk. Through a lucky series of events, those 100,000 words morphed into the first edition of this book, then called *Own the World* – which was self-published as an ebook using Amazon's Kindle platform in September 2012 and in print using Amazon's CreateSpace platform a few months later in January 2013.

To my surprise and delight, *Own the World* started selling reasonably well. Pretty soon we had something like 50 reviews on Amazon and 90 per cent or more of them were five stars (not all of which were written by my mother). The ideas in the book seemed to resonate with people and strike a chord. Through 2013 and 2014 our audience grew, and the book and the site began to take on a life of their own.

By the beginning of 2015 the Plain English Finance team and I (for we now had a team – a merry band of folk passionate about improving people's finances) decided that it was time to significantly upgrade and improve the book and produce a second edition which we snappily entitled *How to Own the World*.

The second edition was still a self-published affair, but we spent a bit of money engaging the services of a professional publishing company and did a great deal of work to tighten up certain sections and improve on the look and feel. There were also a number of subjects

I found myself keen to address or expand on since researching and writing the first edition in the second half of 2011 and first half of 2012. As you might expect, no matter how many times you proofread a book or think about the message you want to impart to readers, there will always be things that occur to you (along with a robust slap to your forehead) after the thing has gone to print.

On top of this, there was all the feedback from readers to consider. After publishing the first edition of the book, I was lucky enough to hear from hundreds of people from all over the world. Feedback included the incredibly moving ('you've quite literally changed my life'; 'after reading your book, I have decided to go back to university'), the highly complimentary (thanks in particular are due to all those who took the time to post five-star reviews on Amazon) and, as you would expect, the critical, with one reader accusing me of possessing 'naive theories of monetary inflation', for example.

The critical feedback was of particular use, as it showed me where I needed to do a better job of explaining a concept, or where I perhaps needed to provide more evidence.

We were proud of the new edition (justifiably I think) – which was a significant, sleek, black upgrade to the lurid-blue home-brew product that was our first edition. Happily, that new version sold even better than the first edition. It wasn't long before it was an Amazon bestseller, reaching the top spot in personal finance. At the time of writing, if you type 'investing' into the search bar of Amazon.co.uk, the book appears at the top of the page above Ben Graham's classic *The Intelligent Investor*, one of the best-known finance books of all time – written by Warren Buffett's great mentor.

By the beginning of 2018, this success attracted the attention of one of the largest publishers in the world, Hodder & Stoughton, who approached me with a view to producing this third edition. I was delighted with this development and set about working on the version you now hold in your hands, eager to see *How to Own the World* in the same stable as the likes of J. K. Rowling, John Grisham, Stephen King and Charles Darwin!

That having been said, it wasn't long before my excitement and delight in the opportunity to produce a third edition of the book with a leading publisher were tempered somewhat by the realization of just how hard it was going to be. I would like to think that I'm not the only author in history to discover that the production of a new edition of a book may very well actually be harder than starting with a blank sheet of paper and writing a brand-new one from scratch – particularly when the subject matter is as diverse and dynamic as finance. It certainly has felt that way as I've approached this new edition.

The reason for this is actually quite simple: three years have passed since the last edition (six years since the first edition) and there are new things to say. Yet, as I have written in the past, one of my key wishes when writing the book was that as much as possible of the content would be 'timeless'. Many of the key things you need to understand about finance haven't changed in decades (such as the importance of diversification) or even centuries (the sheer power of compound interest, for example). The 'set and forget' investment strategy outlined in the 'keeping it simple' chapters of the last two editions of the book is as relevant today as it was when I first suggested it back in 2012, seeing that it is designed to preserve and grow your wealth regardless of what the economy and financial markets are doing and through the economic and business cycles.

These points aside, there are still things that have happened since the last edition which need to be acknowledged at the very least. Set against this fact, however, is a natural reluctance to tamper with what has, to date, apparently been something of a 'winning formula'.

On the one hand: 'If it ain't broke, don't try to fix it.' On the other, I have wondered if things like Trump, Brexit and the explosion of interest in crypto assets and blockchain technology should put in an appearance.

Addressing this conflict has been a struggle, and the devil has been very much in the detail. Overall, however, what I have tried to do in this third edition is to continue to work everything backwards from the most fundamental end goal of the book: giving you, the reader, the confidence to invest your hard-earned savings and the tools to do something tangible and practical to make a huge difference to your finances and, as a result, to your entire future and ability to really enjoy life.

As such, in what follows you will find sections where I have left examples in place that may seem a little out of date but which I have kept because they still do a perfectly good job of illustrating the relevant point and nothing that has happened in the last three years has changed the relevance of that relevant point (as it were). This especially applies to some of the graphs, although I have also occasionally added new ones where these reinforce my argument.

Elsewhere, there are a few entirely new sections – not least on bitcoin, crypto assets and blockchain in Chapter 7, given how much focus this space has had in the last year or two.

I very much hope that you get a great deal out of this new, third edition and that it continues to achieve the goal of the last two editions: to provide you with a world view and a toolkit to give you the confidence to get your financial affairs humming once and for all and genuinely change your life as a result ...

Happy reading and even happier investing!

PART I

The big picture: why should you care?

- What is going on in the world economy today?
- Why do we feel poor when the world is getting richer?
- What are some of the myths about investment, inflation, wealth and the economy?

I

Why you can and should invest your money

'There is an essential life skill that has never been and still isn't taught to the masses: how to manage, control and invest money to protect and provide for your financial future.'

Mark Shipman, *Big Money, Little Effort*

Mark Shipman, a UK hedge fund manager and the author of *Big Money, Little Effort*, retired at the age of 35. What I mean by 'retired' in this context is that by this age he was making enough money from his money that he was free to do whatever he wanted to do. He could spend his days playing golf and going on cruises, and be comfortable for the rest of his life or do something considerably more meaningful. Either way, the key message is that it is entirely realistic for you to control your wealth, make a lot of money doing so, and become financially free as a result.

As you read on, I will present a framework for transforming your wealth based on eight fundamental truths of finance.

How to own the world's fundamental truths

1 No one is better placed than you to make the most of *your* money.
2 You have significant and inherent advantages over many finance professionals.
3 Making money from your money (investing) is far easier than you've always thought. If you managed to learn how to drive, you can look after your money. It is no harder.
4 You can make far more from your money than you ever thought possible.
5 It is realistic for you to target making more from your money than from your job. This is the money secret understood by virtually every rich person in history.
6 Achieving the above is possible almost no matter how much you currently earn.
7 The good news: doing this today is easier than ever before. The tools available to you are the most powerful and the cheapest they have ever been.
8 The bad news: it has never been more important to take charge of your financial affairs. If you are under the age of about 50, there is no chance that you will receive a government-funded pension you can actually live on after retirement.

Perhaps the best definition of a truly wealthy person is that they are able to live on the money they make from their money, rather than the money they make from working. If you are contributing to a pension, you are already planning to do this – it's just that you are aiming to get to this point in your fifties or sixties rather than any sooner.

There are two problems with this traditional approach to money. As we shall see, the first is that the vast majority of people in the UK are not making nearly enough of their pension and other investments in order to end up with a decent income once they retire. Unless you are in the small minority, it is extremely likely that you will have a very low income in retirement – not the most enticing of prospects, and something we will address later in this book.

Secondly: wouldn't it be preferable to get to the point of making a meaningful amount of money from your money a decade or two before traditional retirement age? Can you imagine the quality of life you could enjoy if you were able to create true financial freedom a great deal sooner than your fifties or sixties?

The best news is that this is actually possible. You just need to decide right now that you are willing to put a little time in, understand a bit more about investment, and take the steps required to optimize your financial affairs. If you do, you have a far better chance than you ever realized of enjoying genuine financial freedom and doing so in less time than you think.

I think it is worth noting that this is true even if you are already at or near retirement age. It is never too late to implement the ideas that follow.

The fundamental truths stated above might seem far-fetched to many people. Nevertheless, I am confident that you will find sufficient evidence in the pages that follow to back them up. As you read on, your common sense alone will be enough for you to see the inherent truth in the book's message.

The information in this book and the accompanying website (plainenglishfinance.co.uk/) will:

- Make you confident in your ability to get your financial house in order
- Help you learn how to make serious money from your money – no matter what your financial background or what happens in the future
- Ensure that you take the steps required to make the changes you need to make
- Do all of the above in language everybody can understand: plain English.

Why you must understand what is happening in the world today

We will deal with each of our fundamental truths in turn. In the fine tradition of bad news first, let's get the depressing stuff out of the way as quickly as possible and look at the last of them immediately: namely that it has never been more important for you to take charge of your financial affairs.

> I am deadly serious when I say that if you do not have a solid grasp of what is happening in the world at the moment, then it is very likely you are becoming poorer, and this process is only set to accelerate.

The good news is that understanding what is happening and what to do about it is not nearly as difficult as you might think.

Those of us alive today are living through a complete change in how the world economy is structured – and particularly as this relates to the pension situation for those of us lucky enough to live in the developed world. This has far-reaching consequences for our ability to survive and thrive in the years ahead.

What was generally described as a 'financial crisis' a decade or so ago was just part of a huge structural – that is to say, inherent – change in how the world's economy works. This is not some temporary, cyclical blip; it is not just part of a normal business cycle. Things are not going to return to 'normal' and the economy is not going to 'recover', at least not to the way it was between about 1945 and 2007.

What is actually happening is that we are experiencing nothing less than a complete paradigm shift in finance and economics and in how money works. The seeds for this change were sown in the early 1970s. Since then, a combination of the actions of politicians and central bankers and the impact of rapid technological change has driven us to where we are today. We will look at these ideas in more detail later.

For now, it is enough to understand that this game change in finance and economics has already had a huge impact on politics and society, and the pace of change is only going to increase. If you aim to survive and thrive in the years ahead, you will need to get to grips with what is going on and you will need to take action.

I acknowledge that financial forecasting is never easy. However, I would argue that if you have a basic grasp of economic history and a real understanding of what is happening in the world today, you can be reasonably convinced that certain things have a higher probability of happening in the future than others. You can then invest your money accordingly.

As an example: if it is a statement of fact that government, corporate and private debt levels are the highest they have ever been, this information can be used to make assumptions that give us a better chance of investment success. Economics is not rocket science, despite what some economists would like you to think, and history provides us with plenty of examples of change similar to what we are experiencing now. On the basis that history 'rhymes', as Mark Twain noted, we can use this knowledge to help us run our money more successfully.

Conventional wisdom holds that no one predicted the 'global financial crisis' of 2007–8. This is simply not true. A brief look at the bibliography section at the end of this book reveals plenty of people who saw what was going to happen, made a great deal of noise about it and, in many cases, made a great deal of money as a result. We might call these folk the 'smart money'. The goal of *How to Own the World* is to give you the best chance possible of being on the side of the smart money in the years ahead.

As you read what follows, I hope you will find that it intuitively makes sense. It is also crucial to understand that the genie is out of the bottle – and absolutely cannot be put back in. The changes you see around you cannot be reversed. Things have gone too far and the implications are with us for good. The only sensible action you or anyone else can take is to make the little effort required to get to grips with what is going on and make the very best of it. You can only play the hand you are dealt.

Don't panic! Crisis equals opportunity

Thankfully, and perhaps somewhat ironically, many of the very same forces that have caused the global financial meltdown you are living through can be harnessed to help you most effectively navigate it.

There has never been a better time for those who do understand what is happening to turn this knowledge to their significant financial advantage. The great news is that the road to gaining this understanding is not as long or as scary as you might think. You just need to sit down for a few minutes a day and go through what follows. The information should make sense to you as you go along. At the end of the book you should be genuinely excited about making the positive changes that will help you ride out the storm and end up in a stronger position than ever before.

You may know that the Chinese word for 'crisis' is made up of two symbols, one of which can signify 'opportunity'. Throughout history, it has always been the case that those who make an effort to understand what is going on around them have come out on the other side better off – and certainly far better off than those who don't make such an effort.

Reading this book and taking action will place you in a minority of people who stand to weather the incredible economic, financial and social storm breaking around us. Anyone who does not get to

grips with our current predicament is likely to see a truly horrendous erosion of their wealth and standard of living over the next few
decades. This is not some pie-in-the-sky academic argument. This
is a statement of cold hard fact, as you will see. Millions of people
in the world are already feeling the painful consequences of what is
happening. You can see this every time you watch the news. You may
even be one of them.

So let's get started. Get comfortable and commit to making meaningful changes to your understanding of what is going on in the
world and what you can do about it. I have every confidence that
you will find it easier than you previously thought and that you will
find the results inspiring.

Why you must understand your finances today

There are two specific reasons why it has never been more important
to understand finance: inflation and poor state pension provision.

The real inflation story

> By a continuing process of inflation, governments can confiscate, secretly
> and unobserved, an important part of the wealth of their citizens ...
> There is no subtler, no surer means of overturning the existing basis of
> society than to debauch the currency. The process engages all the hidden
> forces of economic law on the side of destruction, and does it in a
> manner which not one man in a million is able to diagnose.
>
> John Maynard Keynes,
> *The Economic Consequences of the Peace*

Real inflation today is far higher than you think it is, and this is
destroying your ability to become wealthy. I will explain this in more
detail later but for now you absolutely must understand that the
'inflation' numbers produced by many governments are highly misleading. This is bad news for your wealth.

Many people think they understand what inflation is, but few truly grasp how significant *real* inflation is, just how negative an effect this can have on your real wealth, or how misleading published numbers such as CPI and RPI are.

At the time of writing this new edition of the book, nearly every major stock market index in the world is at or near an all-time high. The same is true of numerous property markets all over the world: London, New York, Hong Kong, Singapore, Sydney, Vancouver – the list goes on and on. Although some of these are beginning to show signs of running out of steam, they are all nevertheless at or close to an all-time high – something that is key to the point I am making here.

These numerous share and property markets have all gone up dozens or, in some cases, even hundreds of per cent in the last few years, yet government inflation numbers have consistently been in the low single digits and the press constantly talks about 'low inflation'.

As another illustration of just how far removed from reality published inflation numbers are, Figure 1.1 is a chart showing the price

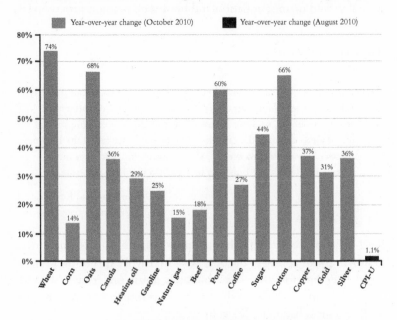

FIGURE 1.1 The real cost of living
Source: Casey Research (2010)

increases in a number of commodities in the year 2010. Crucially, check out the column furthest to the right, which is an official government inflation number (consumer price inflation or CPI – one of the key measures of inflation). How can it be 1.1 per cent when everything else has increased by so much more? I concede that this chart is now almost a decade old and many of the commodities have seen price falls since, but I would argue this doesn't matter. In no way does this alter the point I am making here: how can there be such a big difference between price increases in so many of the things that we need to buy versus government inflation numbers that are supposed to be a fair reflection of those changes?

I fully concede that the price of many of these commodities is extremely volatile and does not go up in a straight line. Nevertheless, the general trend of the last several decades is very discernibly up. Despite such large increases in the prices of share and property markets and the large majority of things you or I might want to consume, government inflation numbers on both sides of the Atlantic continue to come in as low single digits. These government numbers are bad enough to destroy your wealth, but the real picture is far worse. I will explain why this is the case and why many financial analysts, journalists and politicians appear not to understand what the real numbers are.

As a statement of fact, with relatively few exceptions (consumer electronics, for example), the price of nearly all of the things you actually need in your life – food, fuel, shelter, medical care, insurance, education and so on – is going up in leaps and bounds, and by substantially more than is suggested by what I would call the 'science fiction' inflation numbers (CPI or RPI) published by authorities on both sides of the Atlantic.

Property, financial markets and 'things' have been getting more and more expensive in terms of most of the paper currencies on the planet, which means that, unless your salary is going up by at least as much or you're making money from investments, in reality you are getting poorer every day.

This is only going to get worse. Any money you have is gradually being destroyed. If you have any savings in the bank, you are losing real wealth every day, and losing more than you think. This is one of the many reasons people are feeling poorer without really understanding why.

Taking the richest 1 per cent of people in the USA and Britain out of the numbers, the remaining 99 per cent have been getting poorer in real terms for nearly 40 years. In the USA, the average salary peaked in 1973. The UK is no different. Today the richest 1 per cent of Americans are worth more than the bottom 90 per cent. This is one of the reasons why over 45 million Americans are currently living on food stamps, a situation actually worse than the Great Depression. In the UK, it is estimated that over 1 million people are currently relying on food banks to help them find enough to eat (both of these numbers were true at the time of writing the last edition of this book in 2015 and are still true today). You need to understand this, and you need to act on it.

Pension systems all over the world are essentially bankrupt

This is a controversial statement but completely factual nevertheless. With very few exceptions (Norway and Australia, for example), wherever you live in the world today you absolutely cannot count on being able to live on handouts from your government for the rest of your life when you stop working. It just won't happen, yet most people are relying on just such handouts.

Nearly every Western government is effectively bankrupt. As we shall see, this includes the USA and the UK as well as the more obvious countries you have read about in recent years such as Greece, Ireland, Spain, Italy and Portugal. (Debt per capita in the USA was $44,215 compared to $39,937 in Greece at the time of writing the first edition of this book and US debt is even worse now – but how often do we see the American or British press examine this reality?)

All of these countries are totally incapable of funding the pension and medical needs of the hundreds of millions of people set to retire in the next few decades. This is a mathematical inevitability, not some grey area to be debated. National debts in all of these countries are now so high that many governments can't afford their interest payments without printing money, let alone paying back the entire loan.

Once in this position, the only way governments can repay what they owe is by creating money out of thin air (sometimes called 'quantitative easing'). But when governments *invent* money, it causes inflation, which is precisely what I described in the previous section.

Western governments have mismanaged things to such an extent that they can't provide for your retirement, but at the same time people themselves have made completely inadequate private provision for their old age. In the UK, over 50 per cent of the adult population have no effective private pension at all. They are relying on a state that categorically cannot afford to pay for them.

Sadly, the vast majority of the other 50 per cent have made no adequate pension provision, such that they will find their standard of living in retirement likely to be far lower than it was during their working lives, particularly given the real level of inflation.

Amazingly, this group even includes those who have made serious amounts of money in their lives. Estimates vary, but there are at least 150 ex-professional footballers currently in prison in the UK. Despite earning tens or even hundreds of thousands of pounds a week for at least a few years of their lives, these individuals failed to make any provision for life after football and then turned to crime when their career ended, usually drug dealing, in a bid to sustain their lifestyle. This is a tragedy when you consider that a small amount of relatively uncomplicated information could have easily set them up for a truly wealthy life. My point here is that this is often not even a problem of income, it is a problem of financial literacy.

Most people, even a decent proportion of former Premiership footballers, are looking at a retirement lived, quite literally, in complete poverty. The average British adult has about £50,000 saved by retirement (that is around £25,000 for women and just over £73,000 for men according to pension provider Aegon). This is enough to buy them a pension income of about £2,500 a year at current annuity rates. That is just over £200 a month. I would imagine that you would like to have a great deal more than £200 a month plus a tiny – or, more likely, completely non-existent state pension to live on for the last 30 or 40 years of your life.

This disastrous situation is true in nearly every single country in the world. As you might imagine, the ramifications are pretty frightening. History has taught us time and again that an impoverished population is an unstable one. We have seen this reality play out in North Africa and the Middle East in recent years, and closer to home in places like Greece, Spain, Russia and even Canada. At worst, the pension situation all over the world could very well be a 'blood in the streets' problem before too long – there are compelling arguments, for example, that one of the key causes of the Arab Spring in 2010 was inflation, primarily in food prices.

I fervently hope this does not end up being the case, but the only way we can deal with the problem effectively is if as many people as possible take personal responsibility for their own financial situation right now. This book will empower you to do just that.

To put things in perspective: if you want to have a pension income equivalent to the average British salary of roughly £27,000 per year, you will need to have saved up a pension pot of over £500,000 when you retire rather than the £50,000 mentioned above.

Although this might seem rather frightening, the good news is that sorting it out is actually far easier than you think, almost no matter what you earn. You can do it. You just need to know how and you need to get started. The sooner the better.

What this book is *not* about

Crucially, what follows is absolutely not about trusting some 'guru' to show you an 'incredible system' to make money. This is not a 'get rich quick' scheme – though you will get rich. Instead, *How to Own the World* will show you that making a good return on your money, and becoming truly wealthy as a result over time, is easier than you ever thought. The necessary information is not particularly complicated, but it is incredibly poorly distributed throughout the general population.

In my opinion, *true* financial literacy should be taught as a compulsory subject in every secondary school in the country. Though there are signs that this might happen in the future, for now, the reality is that it is only really taught at major investment banks, as well as in the best investment and hedge funds. As with most things, the knowledge is available in books for those willing to seek it out (see the bibliography for more detail) but there is obviously a fair amount of ground to cover. I have done my best to cover that ground for you and save you a great deal of time by presenting only the most relevant and actionable information.

If most people understood the message of this book, financial crises would be far less likely to happen. We can focus on greedy bankers and corrupt or incompetent politicians all we like, but none of them would have been able to land us in our current predicament were it not for another key ingredient: financial illiteracy on the part of the great majority of people. Year after year, there are literally millions of individuals all over the world making bad personal decisions about their finances. 'Bankers' have only been paid big bonuses because the financial industry has been selling bad products with high costs for decades. If the car industry consistently sold us terrible cars that broke down all the time but still cost an arm and a leg, we wouldn't buy them. But we have allowed many of our financial service providers to do just that, ever since financial products were first invented.

Why has this been the case and how have we let them get away with it? I believe the answer is quite simply that it is because the vast majority of people have never taken the time to understand finance or financial products in anything more than an incredibly simple way. To go back to my car analogy: many people are interested in cars. They buy magazines about them and do a reasonable amount of homework before they buy one. If people did the same before buying financial products, including property, we wouldn't be where we are today. Sadly, most people do not undertake such homework, as a result of a dangerous combination of fear and boredom and because they were never taught the basics at school. As the ancient Roman philosopher Seneca would have it: 'It is not because things are difficult that we dare not venture. It is because we dare not venture that they are difficult.'

This is what I want to change. Like anything you know nothing about, once you spend a little time on finance you will find it much easier and much more interesting than you expected. It is also worth highlighting that if you can be bothered to apply the same effort to buying financial products as you do to buying cars, it won't be long before you are buying very nice cars and quite possibly doing so without using any debt.

The reason so few people optimize their finances and become wealthy is because they never spend any time researching and never properly try their hand at investment. There is a very high correlation between understanding finance and being wealthy. If you read on, you will see very quickly that with a relatively small amount of effort you can do a superb job with your money – and quite possibly a better job than many professionals you might have turned to in the past.

What this book *is* about

This book will have succeeded when you have a number of 'eureka' moments and find that you 'get it'. You won't need to trust me or think I'm particularly clever. You will feel confident in your own ability to arrange your financial affairs in a way that makes a huge and lasting difference to the rest of your life. Your minimum goal should be to build a pot of at least £1 million by the time you retire. Actually, a far better target would be to achieve this sort of number before you reach retirement age, and significantly more by the time you retire, so that you can start enjoying your wealth much sooner. A million is a pretty arbitrary goal, after all. As you will see, this is entirely possible.

All you have to do for this to happen is read on and …

1 Realize that finance is easier than you ever thought – and understand why most people never work this out. The reason is extremely obvious: most people never spend any time at all learning about it. This is one of those strange aspects of human nature. Learning how to run your own financial affairs is a life skill which must rank up there as one of the very best for having a positive impact on all other areas of your life, yet most of us invest our time learning about a vast range of other, far less useful life skills and totally neglect finance.

2 Learn two amazing facts about finance (Chapter 3).

3 Understand two crucial investment themes for today (Chapter 4).

4 Take simple steps to arrange your financial affairs and start making money from your money.

In summary

After you have finished this book, optimizing your financial affairs will very possibly take you less time than you wasted the last time you watched a bad film. It will certainly take less time than it took you to learn how to drive a car. Apologies if I'm labouring the automotive analogy a little, but I think the point stands.

As repetition is the mother of all learning, let us end this chapter by repeating the quote from Mark Shipman:

> There is an essential life skill that has never been and still isn't taught to the masses: how to manage, control and invest money to protect and provide for your financial future.

I firmly believe that if we can change this, not only can you personally make a huge difference in your own life but you can also make a huge difference to the fortunes of the society you live in. Good luck. I know that reading what follows and acting on it will do nothing less than change your life.

2

Why you will do better than many professionals

'No one cares more about your money than you do. With a basic understanding of the investment process and a bit of discipline, you're perfectly capable of managing your own money ... By managing your own money, you'll be able to earn higher returns and save many thousands ... in investment costs over your lifetime.'

Alexander Green, *The Gone Fishin' Portfolio*

Most people do not have confidence in their ability to invest their own money.

Be honest – did you spend more time researching the purchase of your last car (or pizza delivery or pair of jeans for that matter) than you have ever spent learning the best way to look after your money or reading a solid 'how to invest' book? Do your eyes glaze over when you hear words like 'bond', 'equity' and 'commodity'?

If you answered 'yes' to the above questions, don't worry. You are in good company. In my experience, this is true of the vast majority of people. Crazy as it might sound, this includes many financial advisers and people who work in financial services, for reasons we will examine shortly.

This is a huge shame given that the number-one secret of nearly all truly wealthy people throughout history is that they *do* understand money and how they can make more from it.

Over time, it is actually far easier, quicker and less hassle to have your money (capital) make you money than it is to make money from your work (labour). Whether we like it or not, we live in a capitalist era. One of the fundamental truths of capitalism is that capital makes a great deal more money than labour; it should be pretty obvious to you that people who *own* businesses tend to make far more money than people who work for them. This is truer today than at any other time in history, primarily because capital is more mobile than ever before. Recent figures show that capital's share of the world's overall wealth relative to labour is the highest it has ever been – something that was the subject of one of the most famous books on economics of the last few decades, Thomas Piketty's *Capital in the Twenty-First Century*. This is one of the reasons why the rich who own businesses are richer than ever, relative to people who work for those businesses.

The great news – and what so few people realize – is that the stock market and other forms of investment are fundamentally just fantastic innovations that enable anyone to become a business owner – potentially of one of the best businesses in the world – almost no matter how little money they have to start with. In addition, it has never been easier to invest, thanks to inexpensive and powerful online tools that have emerged in the last decade or so.

The fact that making money from money is ultimately easier than making money from work is entirely logical when you consider that *you* only have a limited number of hours in which to work. On the other hand, your money 'never sleeps', as the old saying is quite right in telling us. Money will also breed like rabbits if you know what you're doing. Even multimillionaire actors, businesspeople and rock stars have often made vastly more money from their money than from their performance fees, salaries or record sales.

It is not an exaggeration to say that virtually every very wealthy person in history has accrued far more money from their investments than from being paid for their work. It is also worth noting that they have invariably spent far less time making money from their money than they have pursuing their career or passion. Once your money starts making you money, you will find yourself with the freedom to do anything you want – whether you get paid for your time or not. To become rich, you need to get into this mindset.

The fact that most people do not understand this is a tragedy and the main reason so many of the population struggle financially. Because they have never studied it, most people have unfortunate, incorrect and limiting beliefs about how money works: 'the stock market is a casino'; 'investment is risky'; 'cash is safe'. All three of these statements are inherently untrue in one way or another, a fact that is often well understood by the rich. (I would add that the dictum 'money is the root of all evil' is a similarly unhelpful statement – and one which has caused a great deal of misery for people who believe it to be true, in my own view.)

You might find it hard to believe, but 'you can't go wrong with bricks and mortar' is also a dangerous statement. Many people throughout history, including in the past few years, have gone horribly wrong with bricks and mortar, and many more will do so in the future. We will look at this in more detail in Chapter 5. It is also fair to say that cash is nowhere near as safe as you might think, given what is happening in terms of *real* inflation these days.

The reason many people have come to believe the stock market is a casino is simply that most people know nothing at all or incredibly little about it. Amazingly, this includes many of the people investing in it.

I have lost count of the number of people I have met over the years who buy and sell shares without understanding almost any of the things that you should know before investing in the stock market. This is why 'average' investment performance numbers are of no use to you and you should ignore them. A top sprinter who can run the 100 metres in under ten seconds doesn't care that the 'average' adult human can run it in tens of seconds. The fact that there are large numbers of slow people bringing down the mathematical average has no impact at all on the professional athlete's ability to run at his or her speed. We forget this logic when we decide that investment is difficult because the 'average' return is only x per cent. This number includes a vast number of people who have no clue what they are doing.

The efficient market hypothesis

Those who studied finance or economics at university, or work in financial services, may have read the last few paragraphs and disagreed with my argument. They might refer to something called the 'efficient market hypothesis' in order to suggest that what I have said above is incorrect. Given this possibility, I must digress briefly to deal with just such an objection.

The efficient market hypothesis (EMH) is a theory about financial markets that has been around for many years and has been extremely fashionable (arguably with disastrous results). The basic idea is that no one can outperform the stock market by choosing the right investments. That is to say that averages *are* important in financial markets, and no matter how much training you get you will never be able to beat them. This is precisely the opposite conclusion to the one I drew with my professional sprinter example.

The idea is that the price of any asset will always be exactly where it 'should' be because there are lots of intelligent, professional people involved in any given market who are reacting to a wealth of reliable information about where that asset 'should' trade. The hypothesis then proposes that no investor will ever be able to gain an edge or advantage such that they might buy a given asset and make a greater return than the market as a whole.

There are still many folk who believe in the EMH. Everyone is entitled to their opinion, but I feel strongly that the theory has been widely discredited (as do many of the best investors in the world). There is a vast amount of evidence and academic work demonstrating that the theory simply doesn't hold up. As with many of the topics we will cover in this book, there has been a great deal written about the EMH and we don't want to waste time going into any great level of detail.

I would simply hope to strengthen my contention that it is entirely possible for you to be a 'professional sprinter' among investors by giving you a couple of brief examples. Hopefully, these will make sense to you whether you have a financial background or not.

Asymmetric information

The main reason that the EMH doesn't work in reality (and why you can hope to make great returns on your money) has to do with human nature and the existence of what is called 'asymmetric information'. The key point here is that people involved in markets demonstrably do *not* have perfect information about the things they are investing in, as the EMH would have you believe. Some people have far more information than others – that is to say, information is 'asymmetric'. As I have already said, many people who are investing have almost no idea what they are doing. I would argue that it is this reality more than anything else that led to the dot-com boom and bust, to the subprime housing crash and to all other boom-and-bust events in human history.

Example 1: The dot-com boom

In Chapter 7 we will learn the basics of how to value a share. If you can grasp notions such as 'P/E ratios', 'dividend yield' or 'book value', then you can get a good idea of when a share is 'cheap' and therefore more likely to be worth buying or when it is 'expensive' and, therefore, a better idea to sell. Of course, you can never have 100 per cent conviction that you are correct in your analysis, but if you do understand these things you have a huge advantage over those who don't.

The smart money understands these 'valuation techniques'. A large number of people investing in the very same market do not. This meant, for example, that in the dot-com boom, when dot-com shares were trading at prices light years more expensive than any shares had ever traded in the two-century history of stock markets, the smart money really did understand this to be the case and knew that those prices were entirely unsustainable. The amateur investor who was buying technology shares because a friend told them a share was 'hot' did not. Many people lost a great deal of money as a result. As ever, their loss was the smart money's gain. I would argue that the same or worse is happening in the world of cryptocurrency and blockchain technology at the time of writing. There is more on this later in the book in Chapter 7.

In the previous edition of this book, more than three years ago, I wrote the following: 'To my mind, the stock market flotation of Facebook gives us another example of this sort of mania. The stock market valuation of the company equated to a very high multiple of the profits and sales it is forecast to make in the years ahead (which is the main method of valuing a company). In the long run, these sorts of multiples are almost never sustainable. The share is just too expensive. The main reason Facebook is able to achieve such a valuation is because a huge number of people investing in it simply do not understand valuation multiples. There are also plenty of professional investors putting money into the share because they are second-guessing the impact that the herd will have. This is a dangerous game and, arguably, gambling rather than investing – although it is fair to say that some people do play this game successfully, at least for a while.' Since I wrote this, Facebook has gone up massively (although it was hit recently by the Cambridge Analytica scandal). I am more than happy to hold my hands up and admit to being guilty of being completely 'wrong' on the price of Facebook shares.

Nevertheless, I stand entirely by the point I was making. Facebook (and a tiny handful of other shares such as Amazon and Netflix) have made lucky investors exceptional returns (up to this point at least – I don't think Facebook is going to disappear any time soon, but it is perhaps worth remembering that lots of people would have said the same about MySpace in 2008). But this doesn't in any way change my argument – that, *most of the time*, fundamentally expensive shares are more likely to lose you money than make you money and, most importantly, you will do well to understand how to work out whether a share is expensive or not before investing.

I stand by what I said about Facebook even though it has gone up massively since I said it, and the reason for this is because, for every Facebook, there are dozens or even hundreds of companies that were once too expensive and are now worth massively less as a result or, in many cases, worth zero. To name just a few that are now worth zero or 80 per cent or more less than what they were worth in the past: Enron, Lehman Brothers, Worldcom, boo.com, Webvan, pets.com, Ericsson, Nokia, eToys, GeoCities, Nortel, Lucent, Palm Inc, RIM (the makers of Blackberrys), Cisco, Qualcomm, JDS Uniphase – the list goes on and on. A great recent example of what I'm talking about is Snapchat, which has fallen from $27 in March of 2017 to $9 a share at the time of writing.

Successes like Facebook, Amazon and a tiny handful of others are very rare exceptions. At the very least, it is far more difficult to invest in massively overvalued companies and get it right. As another example to illustrate this point, Apple has consistently been more sensibly valued than Facebook and is an even bigger company at the time of writing. It is possible to make money in massively overvalued companies but far harder and far riskier.

The phenomenon of foolishly overvalued companies suits the finance industry because their fees are basically a percentage of a company's value, but it is very bad for the small investor who is pinning their retirement hopes on something that is highly likely to become cheaper in the years ahead (and therefore lose them money). It is worth noting that if enough people who do not understand valuation fundamentals keep buying a company, the price may continue going up for some time (as is the case with Facebook at the time of writing). All those people will then think they've done the right thing and have made a solid investment. As a result of human nature, other people (who don't understand share valuation either) will see the price going up and decide they need to jump in too so they don't miss out. This pushes the share price from very expensive to crazily expensive, which is exactly what happened during the dot-com boom and what is happening – some commentators argue – again as I write.

This strongly illustrates what a weak theory EMH is in the real world. The stock market has its own gravitational pull and the long-term end result of a share being crazily expensive is inevitable. What goes up (beyond sensible levels) must, inevitably, come down.

If you look at many decades of stock market data, it is abundantly clear that, in the long run, no company should ever be worth 25 times the value of its sales or a few hundred times the value of its profits. Any that do trade at these levels are doing so because there are a sufficient number of investors who do not understand this truth. The share will eventually come back to earth, losing most of them a lot of money. Buying these sorts of companies simply isn't investment. It is gambling. People who are informed investors, therefore, tend to leave these companies alone, given that there are thousands of others for which a sensible analysis can be made and an informed decision reached. We will look in some detail at how to do this in Chapter 10.

This phenomenon is even more pronounced in the bitcoin/cryptocurrency/blockchain space which I will discuss in Chapter 7.

Example 2: The subprime crisis

The subprime crisis shows us how asymmetric information can lead to one group of people making a killing and another group losing their shirts. Probably the best-selling book about the subprime crisis – and well worth a read – is *The Big Short* by Michael Lewis, which was made into a big-budget Hollywood film since I wrote the last edition of this book. This tells the story of a group of smart investors whose detailed research gave them better information than most people had about certain financial products (mortgage-backed securities) in the subprime market. Their research told them that these products were completely the wrong price. As a result, they were able to make thousands of per cent on their money in a few years – in some cases making literally billions of dollars betting against these financial assets. This is another glaring example of market inefficiency and asymmetric information, and of the EMH simply not holding true. It is also worth noting that wealth is never destroyed, merely transferred to the smart money from the 'less smart money' (to put it politely).

I could fill a book with examples of why the EMH, while an elegant theory, simply doesn't hold up in the real world of investment but hopefully this will suffice for now.

The most important point here is that investing in financial markets without knowing what you are doing is like driving on a motorway before you have learned how to drive.

You might be lucky and arrive safely at your destination, but it is more likely that you will have a nasty crash and then tell everyone how dangerous driving is. It is only because so many people involved in financial markets do not know what they are doing that so many lose money and come to believe it is 'risky' or 'a casino'.

Six reasons why you can do better than the professionals

There are a number of very good, inherent reasons why you can do a better job with your money than many finance professionals. Obviously, there are a large number of areas of your personal finances where, traditionally, you might have sought professional advice. These would include: arranging a mortgage; buying a type of insurance product such as life or contents insurance; critical illness; and accident and sickness cover. You might also have gone to a financial adviser to discuss inheritance tax or making a will.

In what follows, however, I will discuss how useful financial advice is when it concerns *investment* – that is to say, when it concerns *growing* your money as effectively as possible. As you have already seen, the whole thrust of *How to Own the World* is that you must look after your finances. Once you feel confident in doing so, you may still wish to outsource the more peripheral areas of your personal finances such as those listed in the previous paragraph, if only to save you time, but these are much less important than getting *investment* right.

For what it is worth, my personal feeling is that it is increasingly easy to take care of nearly all of these more peripheral financial products yourself. In recent years, we have witnessed a proliferation of online resources, such as financial comparison websites, that enable people to arrange their own will or buy good-value insurance products very easily, for example.

Whether you choose to go down that route or to use a financial adviser for these sorts of decisions is obviously entirely up to you. My hope is that after you have read this book you will at the very least feel empowered to make your own *investment* decisions. Ultimately, doing the best job with investment is the most fundamental building block of your personal finances. Saving money is certainly crucial (more on this later), but I would stress that most wealthy people focus at least as much, if not more, on *investing* and growing their money than they do on cutting costs – small ones at least. Coupon-clipping misers, or the stereotypical dad who turns the heating down in winter, are far less likely to ever become truly wealthy than folk with a more positive and abundant attitude to money. At the simplest level, this is because three hours spent learning about and sorting out your investments will have a much greater impact on your long-term financial situation than three hours spent shaving £20 off your car insurance, phone or heating bill. Sadly, too few people think this way.

1 A significant conflict of interest and lack of knowledge

One of the key reasons why you may find it easy to do a better job with your money than a professional can is concerned with the traditional structure of the whole finance industry in the UK.

Because most people do not feel confident making their own investments, they will tend to seek the services of a financial adviser of one kind or another. To see why this can be problematic, we need only consider the training traditionally received by most UK financial advisers and the way in which they have been paid historically. One of the best things about investment today is that there is a vast range of things you can invest in: bonds, equities (shares), commodities, currency (foreign exchange), real estate (property) and funds, to name a few.

Each of these types of investment has very different qualities and, as we shall see when we look at them in greater depth in Chapter 7, the successful investor should ensure they are using the right mix of all – or at least most – of them. Arguably the most important reason why many people fail at investment is that they fail to own a sufficiently wide range of investment products. Having a wide range of shares from all over the world, as well as property, bonds and commodities, gives you the best chance of consistent success. Very few people do this, even those who work in financial services.

Few financial advisers are likely to recommend this sort of mix. Almost all traditional advisers want you to invest in funds or insurance products of some kind, and very little else. This is entirely logical (for them) for two reasons:

- Most financial advisers have traditionally been paid a cut of the products they sell, and the only two main product groups where this has been practicable are funds and insurance products.

- Many financial advisers have little or no understanding of any of the other products. This is hardly surprising, since they struggle to make any money from them.

To elaborate: for the last several decades, most financial advisers have been paid on a commission basis. That is to say, they are paid a percentage of whichever product they suggest you buy.

As you can imagine, this has led to a worrying conflict of interest. You may be aware that the Financial Conduct Authority (FCA – formerly the Financial Services Authority, or FSA) is the body tasked with looking after consumers' rights in the UK finance industry. One of the organizations that the FCA uses to examine people who work in finance is called the Chartered Institute for Securities and Investment (CISI) and the CISI themselves acknowledge: 'There are incentives for the intermediary (adviser) to recommend a product that offers the highest commission rates.'

In June 2006, aware of this problem and in the wake of a number of mis-selling scandals you may have read about (endowment mortgages, payment-protection insurance, etc.), the (then) FSA published a review of how financial products are sold to UK consumers, concluding that:

> Many consumers rely heavily on advisers ... and there can be a
> misalignment of advisers' interests with those of consumers. [Consequently
> there is a] risk that substantial consumer detriment will occur.

In plain English: even the government body in charge of regulating the financial services industry freely admits you are at risk of getting bad financial advice from many financial advisers. This is certainly borne out by my experience and the experiences of many people I have spoken to in the decade I have spent asking the question. While I acknowledge that this is anecdotal, the subject matter here will no doubt resonate with many of you.

This state of affairs is pretty incredible when you think about it, and it is one of the reasons so many people have had a bad experience with investment over the last few decades. The good news, however, is that once we understand this reality we are equipped to do something about it.

So the traditional model for financial advice in the UK means that there is a risk that financial advisers might recommend products that pay them the highest commissions rather than those best suited to your needs.

While this might seem bad enough, I would argue that there are even more serious structural flaws in the industry. For example, many financial advisers have traditionally been described as 'tied' or 'restricted'. This means that they are only in a position to sell you the products of one company or a small group of companies (to whom they are tied).

This is generally the case if you look for financial advice from a high street bank, for example. If, as many people naturally do, you go into a high street bank looking for investment advice, their staff will often only be able to suggest products offered by that bank.

As a result, you will only be able to choose an investment from a laughably minuscule subset of what is on offer in the world of investment as a whole. In addition, you will often end up paying higher fees than you need to, as these products tend to be inherently expensive. It is entirely possible for a tied adviser to do the very best they can within the constraints of the product range they have at their disposal and for you still to end up with a poor result for your financial affairs compared to what is possible.

All of the above might seem bad enough, but regretfully I would go even further and say that another general problem with financial advice in the UK is that many of the people in the industry have a woefully inadequate understanding of finance as a whole. In the past, someone could become qualified as a 'financial adviser' without having any detailed understanding of the wide variety of financial markets that exist or about the history of how those markets came about.

Many tied financial advisers have only ever been trained on the products their employer sells and have quite literally no knowledge about the thousands of other investments that might be better for your purposes, let alone any understanding of how to value a share or a bond. At my first ever meeting with a 'financial adviser' in a high street bank, the person I spoke to wasn't even aware that products existed other than the ones their firm sold. Truly astonishing (and this was at a major high street bank in Moorgate – that is, right in the middle of the world's biggest financial centre, the City of London. Unbelievable!).

As an example of how problematic this can be (as we shall see in more detail shortly), many of the smartest investors in the world advocate holding a meaningful percentage of your wealth in gold. To see why this might be a good idea have a look at Table 2.1 which shows gold's performance in most of the world's large currencies over the last 15 years. Have a look in particular at the performance in pounds sterling (GBP).

TABLE 2.1 The performance of gold in the some of the world's key currencies (2003–18)

Gold Price Performance: % Annual Change						Monday, 31 December		
	USD	AUD	CAD	CHF	CNY	EUR	GBP	INR	JPY
2003	19.7%	-9.5%	-0.4%	7.7%	19.7%	0.5%	8.6%	13.6%	7.7%
2004	5.3%	1.8%	-1.9%	-3.4%	5.3%	-2.7%	-2.3%	0.6%	0.7%
2005	20.0%	28.9%	15.4%	37.8%	17.0%	36.8%	33.0%	24.2%	37.6%
2006	23.0%	13.7%	23.0%	14.1%	19.1%	10.6%	8.1%	20.9%	24.3%
2007	30.9%	18.3%	12.1%	21.7%	22.3%	18.4%	29.2%	16.5%	22.9%
2008	5.6%	31.3%	30.1%	-0.1%	-2.4%	10.5%	43.2%	28.8%	-14.4%
2009	23.4%	-3.0%	5.9%	20.1%	23.6%	20.7%	12.7%	19.3%	26.8%
2010	29.5%	13.5%	22.3%	16.7%	24.9%	38.8%	34.3%	23.7%	13.0%
2011	10.1%	10.2%	13.5%	11.2%	5.9%	14.2%	10.5%	31.1%	4.5%
2012	7.0%	5.4%	4.3%	4.2%	6.2%	4.9%	2.2%	10.3%	20.7%
2013	-28.3%	-16.2%	-23.0%	-30.1%	-30.2%	-31.2%	-29.4%	-18.7%	-12.8%
2014	-1.5%	7.7%	7.9%	9.9%	1.2%	12.1%	5.0%	0.8%	12.3%
2015	-10.4%	0.4%	7.5%	-9.9%	-6.2%	-0.3%	-5.2%	-5.9%	-10.1%
2016	9.1%	10.5%	5.9%	10.8%	16.8%	12.4%	30.2%	11.9%	5.8%
2017	13.6%	4.6%	6.0%	8.1%	6.4%	-1.0%	3.2%	6.4%	8.9%
2018	-3.0%	2.6%	2.9%	-1.3%	-3.1%	0.3%	-1.0%	3.0%	-5.4%
Average	9.6%	7.5%	8.2%	7.3%	7.9%	9.1%	**11.4%**	11.7%	8.9%

Source: Goldprice.org

To illustrate the point another way, Figure 2.1 shows the pounds sterling price of gold looking back 20 years. It has gone from £6,000 pounds a kilo to over £30,500 per kilo.

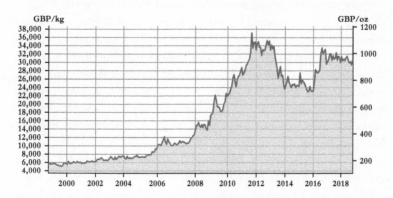

FIGURE 2.1 The price of gold in pounds sterling (1998–2018)
Source: Goldprice.org

Owning gold will have made a strong contribution to your wealth over the last two decades, yet for all the reasons outlined in this chapter, few financial advisers in the UK would have suggested you invest in gold. Many would have had no idea how to do it, and even those who knew which vehicle would give you exposure to gold would have had little incentive to suggest it as a product as they would not earn any commission from doing so.

As we shall soon see, one of the key things that differentiates the very smartest and most successful investors in the world from everyone else is their understanding and use of *all* the main asset classes. If you walk into a high street bank today and ask to see one of their advisers, it is not an exaggeration to say that you have virtually no chance whatsoever of speaking to someone with this level of knowledge. Sadly, the same is also true of many independent financial advisers.

Remember, this isn't just my opinion. The FCA itself has identified these very issues in recent years (one might suggest not a moment too soon). To quote the CISI's *own* examination materials again: 'Those providing advice can do so with relatively little training and testing when compared to other professions.'

This point is especially well made when you consider that an accountant must endure three years of study and professional exams in order to gain their qualification; a financial analyst at an investment bank or investment fund will often have had to complete the Chartered Financial Analyst (CFA) qualification, which also takes at least three years and is famously difficult; and a lawyer will have had, at the very least, to complete a degree in law or a conversion course and further years of professional training before they are able to practise. (Let's not even get into brain surgeons or rocket scientists for now. You get the point.)

For what it is worth, those in charge of regulating UK financial services have attempted to address some of these issues. Since 1 January 2013 financial advisers have had to demonstrate far more knowledge about investment and financial markets than they had to previously and have had to pass much more rigorous exams. As a result, there are estimates that as many as 40 per cent of financial advisers will leave the industry in the next few years.

Having already passed these exams, I would argue that there is still a significant gap between the subject material examined and the knowledge required to understand the investment methods used by the world's best investors (which we will look at in this book). It took me six months to complete the new exams, and I could have completed them a good deal more quickly had I not been writing the first edition of this book. Compare this with the several years of study other professions have had to complete.

That said, as with any profession there is obviously a wide range of ability among financial advisers. I stand by the arguments I have made so far in this chapter and I am strongly of the opinion that the market for financial advice in the UK has many inherent flaws, which increase the risk of you receiving suboptimal financial advice. Nevertheless, there are financial advisers who are perfectly competent and will do a good job for you – if you know how to find them. At the very least, then, reading this book will equip you to identify the best financial advisers, fully understand their charging structure (key), and get the best value out of them as a result.

Many readers are simply too busy to take care of their own financial affairs, and if this describes you then a good financial adviser is certainly worth paying for. *Good* financial advisers (*not* the expensive old-school tie, golf-club know-nothings or the clueless twenty-somethings found in high street banks who were the target of my original ire in previous editions of this book) can actually add a great deal of value by getting you into the right funds at a better price than you can as an individual – as well as taking care of the time-consuming administration that can be quite daunting for many. They are also well qualified to help you when it comes to dealing with a range of complex issues such as how to optimize your affairs for tax purposes, provide for your children (and legislate for inheritance tax), or make use of your own company to make investments if you have one. A good financial adviser can deal with these and a raft of other issues that may crop up, which can save you a great deal of time and effort. In essence, they can be particularly helpful when it comes to *financial planning* as much as specifically how to invest. This can be particularly useful for anyone with significant wealth, particularly complicated affairs or, in particular, approaching retirement (when things get inherently more complicated).

That said, I would argue that once you have acquired the level of knowledge required to identify a top-quality financial adviser, it isn't that much of a leap to acquire the knowledge required to run your own financial affairs, particularly if you are some years from retirement. The point still remains that doing so will save you a great deal of money over the years, and will no doubt make you feel far more empowered and in control of your life.

To go back to my driving analogy, most of us learn how to drive, rather than employ a driver. I would repeat that if you were able to learn how to drive, you will be able to learn how to invest. It is no harder and will not take any longer. Whether you decide to employ a financial adviser or not is obviously entirely up to you, but you will be far better placed to make that decision by the time you have finished this book and understand better what you should pay for their services.

The eagle-eyed among you may have spotted a paradox in the above section. How can I complain that financial advisers haven't spent enough time studying and then say that you don't need to spend that much time learning about finance to do well? The answer is that those of you who don't want to spend much time learning about money can still do very well using a formulaic approach that we will look at later. It won't take you long to achieve this level of knowledge. However, to be fully up to speed on finance, so that you can give advice to people, should be a much longer road to travel. Hopefully this makes sense. It certainly should do by the time you've finished this book.

By learning a little about how to look after your own money, you can ensure that you give consideration to the full range of financial products available in the world today, benefit from the very best investment methods available, and maximize your chances of saving thousands of pounds or more in commission and fees. This leads us neatly on to the next reason why you will do a far better job than many professionals you might use.

2 Charges, fees and costs

As *MoneyWeek* magazine has put it: 'If the evidence is any guide at all, then there is one thing that all investors should watch out for before they put their money to work: costs.'

As with any other product or service, financial advice and financial products cost money. Oddly enough, they are also the only ones I'm aware of where a majority of people who are paying for them don't actually understand how or what they are being charged. If you have a pension or an ISA, do you have an accurate sense of what percentage of your money each year is being eaten up in fees? If you have used a financial adviser in the past, do you know exactly how much of your money is now their money?

If you answered 'no' to these questions, don't worry; almost everyone does – which is extremely odd when you think about it. You wouldn't buy anything else without knowing how much it costs, but here is our strange financial-literacy blind spot again.

The difference between paying the right amount and the wrong amount for getting your financial house in order will make a huge difference to your future wealth. We shall see why in detail when we look at compound interest in Chapter 3, but to give you a quick example: if you were to invest your maximum ISA allowance for 30 years and return 10 per cent, you would end up with just under £2.85 million. If you had achieved 8 per cent, this number would be around £1.875 million. If you had managed to consistently achieve 12 per cent, the number would be just over £4.4 million!

If you end up paying too much for your financial products, over a lifetime of investment the difference can quite literally amount to a seven-figure sum. As we shall see later, having a basic understanding of how the industry charges for financial advice and financial products will save you a great deal of money.

Better-value ways of investing have generally not been promoted very well by the financial services community. You are unlikely to hear about them from your high street bank, and many IFAs are still charging too much. This is another reason so many people have a dim view of investment; they automatically go to their high street bank for financial advice, which is almost always a bad idea. By the time you finish this book, you will have a firm grasp of what you are paying to invest and whether it is the right amount.

3 Career risk

The third reason why many professional money people suffer from an inherent tendency to perform poorly with your money is known as 'career risk'. Assuming you have gone to a financial adviser and purchased a fund on their recommendation, there is a good chance that even the best of those funds may not do as well as you will by making the sorts of informed decisions you will be able to make once you've finished this book.

Simply put, a fund manager who does what everyone else does tends to have a lower risk of getting fired. If that person owns big blue-chip stocks in a terrible year like 2008, for example, they will lose the same amount of money as everyone else who owns big blue-chip stocks. There is safety in the herd. With everyone having had a terrible year, 'the market' gets the blame and everyone keeps his or her job. This is good for the cautious fund manager but clearly no good to you if you have lost a large chunk of your money, as so many people did in 2008.

Nearly all professional investors are limited to certain investment categories. They might be in charge of a 'UK equity fund' or a 'global bond fund', for example. We will learn more about what these are in Chapter 7. For now, we need only understand that in a bad year for the UK, no matter how good a professional investor is in their own niche, you will very likely lose money if you are in a UK fund. This problem can be avoided by ensuring that your money is well spread around the world and across different asset classes. Again, we shall look at how important this is later and you will learn how to achieve this.

Example: Tony Dye and the career-risk problem

A good example of this career-risk problem is the case of Tony Dye, a top fund manager in the 1990s. During the dot-com boom of the late 1990s he was – quite rightly – highly critical of what he saw as a crazy increase in the share prices of technology and dot-com companies. As a result, he refused to buy any of these sorts of companies. Sadly for Mr Dye, this meant that he made significantly lower returns than his peers, who had jumped on the dot-com bandwagon. Even though he was correct in his analysis (that dot-com and technology shares were crazily overpriced), he lost his job in 2000 – ironically just a month before the market peaked and then crashed – demonstrating how right he had been. People who were invested in the funds that outperformed Dye's in the late 1990s lost a great deal of money when the market turned. 'Safety in the herd' thinking on the part of fund managers can mean a serious lack of safety for you and your money.

4 Liquidity, or the 'supertanker turning circle' problem

The fourth big reason why you have a very good chance at becoming a better investor than even a very successful professional concerns the amount of money you will be looking after in comparison. If

you have only a few thousand pounds – or even only a few million
(!) – to invest, you will mostly be able to buy and sell things without
causing the price of those things to move much, if at all.

If a major investor who is looking after billions of pounds decides
that they want to sell one of their investments, it may take them several weeks (or even longer for some investments) and push the price
down. You or I might be able to buy a 'cheeky' little biotechnology
or mining stock and benefit from a huge short-term move in the
price. The big-money professional can seldom buy and sell enough
of that sort of stock to make much of a difference to the return on
their fund as a whole, which means that neither can you if you are
invested in that fund.

5 Excessive specialization among finance professionals

> The most powerful tool an investor has working for him or her is
> diversification. True diversification allows you to build portfolios with
> higher returns for the same risk. Most investors ... are far less diversified
> than they should be. They're way overcommitted to ... stocks.
>
> Jack Meyer, *Smart Money*

Jack Meyer, manager of Harvard University's multibillion-dollar
investment funds, produced an average of 15.9 per cent annually for
15 years (a 910 per cent compounded return). His statement, quoted
above, is yet another important reason why you will be able to do a
better job than many professionals with your money.

People who work in financial services, even those in top investment banks who are making the large bonuses we constantly read
about, are almost always incredibly specialized from very early on in
their careers. This means that there are relatively few who are able, or
even inclined, to see the big picture – and it is truly the big picture
that you need for consistent investment success.

Many investment professionals are just like doctors who tell you
how bad drinking and smoking are and then nip to the pub for several drinks and a few cigarettes at the end of their day. Over the years,
I have lost count of the number of smart City folk I know who have

all their money in the one asset class they know about, with the result that they are heavily punished during any bad year for that asset class.

At the risk of being a little on the repetitive side, I must reiterate that one of the most successful investing strategies over many years is being properly diversified. This means that you should ensure you own a wide variety of assets rather than just shares or just property, for instance. To repeat an example but to make a subtly different point, you will recall that over the last 20 years or so gold has performed exceptionally well (even accounting for its weakness more recently). It is amazing, however, just how few investment professionals have owned gold.

Any detailed study of the best thing to do with your money will suggest that you should have at least some of your money in precious metals, but relatively few of the many investment professionals who work exclusively with other asset classes – such as equities (shares) or bonds – would even have thought about gold. I know this from first-hand experience. As a result, they have missed out on part of their portfolio rising by a few hundred per cent in the last 20 years.

6 The financial analysis war

Another major disadvantage of finance professionals becoming highly specialized is that almost all of them end up subscribing to one or other of the two main categories of financial analysis – *fundamental* and *technical* – and are rabidly and, to my mind, irrationally critical of the other. It is very often the case that finance professionals who see themselves as using what is called 'fundamental analysis' feel the same way about finance professionals who use 'technical analysis' as cats feel about dogs. This is a great shame for both groups. I have quite literally heard the former describe technical analysis as 'black magic', and heard technical enthusiasts say that fundamental analysis is 'totally pointless'. Both of these are actual quotes from serious and highly paid City professionals, and these sorts of views are the norm rather than the exception. It seems to be a manifestation of human nature that people tend to choose a 'church' at some stage of their career. They are then at risk of 'doing an ostrich' going forwards.

I will explain more about the two approaches in Chapter 11, but for now it is enough to make the point that many of the best investors in the world use *both* of these types of analysis together. A good example is Anthony Bolton, one of Britain's best-known fund managers. He has a very fundamental approach to picking shares but is on record as describing his use of technical analysis as his 'secret weapon'. Using a combination of the two techniques, he returned an average of 19.5 per cent per annum over 28 years – a 14,460 per cent compounded return (this would have turned an initial invest-ment of £10,000 into £1.46 million). That is not a typo, by the way. Consistently high investment returns can and do turn thousands into millions over time. Interestingly, for those of you who know that his subsequent track record running a China fund has been pretty awful, his recent lack of success is further evidence of the importance of geographical and asset diversification.

I think it is a great shame that most investment professionals tend to choose either fundamental analysis or technical analysis, to the total exclusion of the other, when a combination of the two is self-evidently more effective.

In summary

- Most non-professional investors are at risk of losing money and making bad investments because they really don't know what they are doing.
- Even professional investors can have the cards stacked against them.
- If you are a well-informed 'amateur', then you have a huge advantage over both of these groups. You are truly in the investing sweet spot.

This is extremely exciting news, and what is even more exciting is that learning how to get into that sweet spot is far easier than you think. To continue with my automotive analogy, I would argue that learning how to make a huge difference to your finances is no harder than learning how to drive safely. But because virtually no one does it, few people find this out.

People who do spend a little time learning about money often find that life gets a great deal easier and a great deal more fun. The day you make several thousand pounds from a phone call or mouse click is a truly wonderful one and it opens your eyes to a world of possibility...

3
Two amazing facts about finance

'Those who understand compound interest are destined to collect it.
Those who don't are doomed to pay it.'

Tom and David Gardner, founders of The Motley Fool
(www.fool.co.uk)

I believe there are two amazing facts about finance to focus on immediately. Once you understand these, you should very quickly start to see the incredible possibility that effective investment offers you.

Fact 1: Compound interest is 'the eighth wonder of the world'

One of the main objections I hear when I share with people my excitement about the wonderful world of investing is: 'But that won't work for me, I make too little to have enough left over to invest.'

Wrong! Wrong! Wrong!

Many people believe that they need a big lump sum or the ability to save a large amount of money every month to make investment worthwhile. People often believe that investment is 'for the rich' and not for them. This is absolutely not true. With money, as with so many things in life, it is the tortoise who generally wins the race, not the hare.

> Those who understand money and end up with lots of it tend to be those who understand that little and often is the road to success.

You are much more likely to save a small amount of money right now than you are to save a large amount of money at some time in the future. I'm sure you are familiar with this psychology – it is also true of going to the gym, revising for exams, doing housework, and so on. As you are about to see, time is one of your biggest allies in becoming wealthy, so you must take action now or as soon as possible. Start small but start now. If you do start small, no matter how small, you will enable yourself to benefit from the magic of compound interest immediately.

What is compound interest and why is it so important?

If you take nothing more away from this book than an understanding of the incredible power of compound interest, then you will have

44

joined a lucky (and generally wealthy) few. None other than Albert Einstein described compound interest as 'the eighth wonder of the world'. Compound interest is, quite literally, a form of free money ... and it is free money that grows like a weed over time.

But how can this be?

Well, imagine that you invested £1,000 today. Imagine, too, that whatever you invested it in went up by 10 per cent this year. In this scenario, you would have £1,100 one year later: your original sum, plus £100 of interest, or return on a share or other investment. Simple so far. Now comes the 'free money' part. Assume you invested that £1,100 for another year and achieved 10 per cent again. The following year you would have £1,210. This time you have made £110 of interest (1.1 x £1,100 = £1,210), but £10 of that interest is essentially *free money*. It is the *interest you have been paid on your interest* – or, to put it another way, the *return on your return*.

At first glance this may not seem particularly exciting, but over time the effect is incredibly powerful. Let's look more closely at some examples ...

The power of compounding

Say you've decided to have a go at this investment thing. For the sake of argument, you start with £5,000 and manage to invest £250 per month going forwards. These might seem like numbers too small to make you a millionaire, but are they?

Let us look at what happens to that money over the next few years if you are a straight 'saver' compared to what you might achieve as an investor with compound interest on your side.

The saver (or 'mattress stuffer') will put their £5,000 lump sum into a current account that, as is effectively the case today, is paying no interest whatsoever. They then add £250 a month into the same current account each month going forwards. After one year the saver would have £8,000 squirrelled away: the £5,000 he or she started with, plus 12 payments of £250 (totalling £3,000).

That is certainly 'better than a punch in the face', as a City trader might say, but now let us see how this compares with someone who decides to *invest* their money. For the purposes of illustration, we'll look at the difference assuming a few different rates of return:

- At 0 per cent the saver would have £8,000, as we have established.
- At 8 per cent the investor would have £8,584 at the end of the year.
- At 10 per cent they would have £8,737.
- At 12 per cent they would have £8,893.
- … and at 20 per cent the investor would be sitting on £9,544. (These numbers are all rounded to the nearest pound.)

We can immediately see a meaningful difference between what the investor has managed to achieve after a year versus the saver. Of far more interest, however, is what happens over a number of years. Table 3.1 illustrates the incredible power of compound interest.

TABLE 3.1 The power of compound interest

After x years	Saver 0% return	Investor 8% return	Investor 10% return	Investor 12% return	Investor 20% return
1	£8,000	£8,584	£8,737	£8,893	£9,544
5	£20,000	£25,991	£27,816	£29,796	£39,568
10	£35,000	£57,214	£65,286	£74,752	£132,538
15	£50,000	£103,731	£126,936	£156,423	£383,182
20	£65,000	£173,035	£228,370	£304,794	£1,058,910
30	£95,000	£430,117	£669,845	£1,064,024	£7,792,017
Assuming £5,000 lump to begin and £250 saved each month					

Source: Plain English Finance

So, if you start saving £250 a month at the age of 30, keep at it and pay it into top-performing assets, you would end up with nearly £8 million by the age of 60.

That is not a typo …

Time is key: £5,000 becomes nearly £1 million

As another example of how powerful this can be: if a grandparent or wealthy relative were to invest £5,000 the day a child is born, and that investment were to achieve 10 per cent per annum until the child retires, with no further investment at all, that initial sum would have grown to around £1 million by the time the child turned 55 (£945,000 if you calculate it as 10 per cent annually, or around £1.2 million if you compound monthly at 0.83 per cent – that is, 10/12).

This is why many of the top hedge funds in the world have a stated aim of trying to make 1 per cent per month, every month. Over time this seemingly modest ambition will yield significantly better results for their investors than for investors in racier funds who try and 'shoot the lights out' every year and are up 30 per cent one year and down 20 per cent the next. As we shall see in more detail later in the book, in investment, slow, steady and consistent wins the race and small numbers add up to very big numbers over time. Investment is one of the best real-world examples of the famous case of the tortoise beating the hare.

How can we have a pensions crisis when you can turn £5,000 into £1 million with such relatively modest returns?

Costs are key

Crucially, please note the huge differences that a small change in the percentage return can make over time. For example, over 20 years the difference between making 12 per cent and 10 per cent is nearly £76,500, and this is when using these reasonably small numbers. A change of just 2 per cent in your return will make a huge difference. Ten years later, the difference will be closer to £300,000. This is why, as noted in Chapter 2, it is very important to watch the costs of any financial product you are buying. It is fair to say that very few people even understand what the costs of their financial products really are, or how to find these costs out – let alone the impact they will have on their ability to make money. This is another key reason why so many people suffer poor performance when they invest.

Many of you will be looking at these numbers and thinking that these kinds of returns are impossible. There is no question that statistically it is hard to achieve a reliable 20, 12, 10 or even 8 per cent return on your money. That said, it is entirely possible to achieve them (the lower numbers at least) if you are prepared to look at the world in a certain way and learn a little. As we have already seen (in Chapter 2), just investing in gold over the last 20 years or so would have achieved these sorts of returns. Timing your entry and exit with a technique I will show you later could have achieved substantially higher than even 20 per cent (see Chapter 11 for how to use the RSI).

There are many investment professionals who have achieved these sorts of long-term returns. Table 3.2 gives just a few examples, but there are plenty more. For the sake of simplicity, the table gives you an illustration of the money you would have made investing a £10,000 lump sum with these folk at the start of their run. If you had been making regular contributions, you would have made significantly more than the number in the right-hand column. Hundreds of pounds would have turned into millions.

I made this table in 2012 at the time of writing the first edition of this book. I have kept it through both subsequent editions because the point it makes still stands.

In the years since, I could point to a number of similar examples. Terry Smith at Fundsmith has returned nearly 300 per cent in the last eight years, averaging 19.3 per cent per annum since launch. Similarly, Tom Slater and James Anderson at Baillie Gifford's Scottish Mortgage Investment Trust have increased the value of that fund by more than 220 per cent in the last five years. I mention these two specifically because, happily, I have been recommending both of them for some time.

It is also worth noting that these investors have achieved their incredible returns over many decades and in spite of the inherent disadvantages confronted by professional investors that I outlined in Chapter 2. You have none of these disadvantages.

So you can see that the difference between someone keeping their money in a savings account, or 'under the mattress', and someone who invests their money is completely life-changing, even if you are starting with relatively small amounts of money.

TABLE 3.2 Example return on investments

Investor	Company	Average return [&]	Time period	Return start/finish [%]	So £10,000 became:
Warren Buffett	Berkshire Hathaway	20.20%	1965–2010	394,000%	£39,400,100
Anthony Bolton	Fidelity London	19.50%	1979–2007	14,660%	£1,466,100
Joel Greenblatt	Gotham Capital	50.00%	1985–1995	5,766%	£576,700
Jim Rogers	Soros Quantum Fund	38.00%	1969–1980	3,456%	£345,700
David Swensen	Yale Endowment Fund	16.20%	1985–2008	3,160%	£316,100
Peter Lynch	Fidelity Boston	29.20%	1977–1990	2,795%	£279,600
Seth Klarman	Baupost Group	20.20%	1982–2012	2,076%	£207,700
David Einhorn	Greenlight Capital	21.60%	1996–2012	1,879%	£188,000
Benjamin Graham	Columbia University	14.70%	1936–1956	1,553%	£155,400
Jack Meyer	Harvard Endowment Fund	15.90%	1990–2005	915%	£91,600

Source: Plain English Finance

For what it is worth, let us look at what could be achieved if you were able to save your entire UK ISA allowance of £20,000 a year (£1,666.66 a month). Your ISA allowance is the amount you can invest each month in the UK without having to pay tax on any gains you might make. Table 3.3 illustrates this for you.

Ignore the averages

Please take a moment to look at all three tables in this chapter. It is very important that you get a really good sense of just how powerful an effect investment can have on your wealth. Very few people realize the enormous numbers you can generate over time.

Cynics will say that the above examples are misleading because most investors fall far short of these sorts of returns. All I am asking for you to do is acknowledge the *possibility* of making great returns on your money. There is plenty of research that says that, on average, you can't beat the market over the long run. To me that is like saying: 'Research shows that the average adult takes 35 seconds to run the 100 metres.'

I am not interested in averages. I am interested in doing my best to work out who the 'fastest runners' of the investment world are and, having done so, to invest in them, with them or like them. There are ways of consistently achieving the sort of returns highlighted above – you just need to find them.

Do not borrow money

Compounding works both ways, so do not borrow money if at all possible. It is very important to note that if you do borrow money, the power of compounding hits you in reverse – over time you end up paying more and more to whomever you are borrowing from. Luke Johnson, the entrepreneur behind Pizza Express and former chairman of Channel 4, refers to this as 'the gruesome mathematics of leverage in reverse'. This is why you must eliminate debt and make lifestyle changes to achieve this if needs be.

TABLE 3.3 Return on saving your full ISA allowance of £20,000 a year

After	Saver	Investor			
X years	0% return	8% return	10% return	12% return	20% return
1	£25,000	£26,339	£26,687	£27,039	£28,503
5	£105,000	£130,776	£138,432	£146,651	£186,127
10	£205,000	£318,114	£357,900	£403,897	£674,217
15	£305,000	£597,218	£718,993	£871,235	£1,990,092
20	£405,000	£1,013,040	£1,313,102	£1,720,247	£5,537,651
30	£505,000	£2,555,525	£3,898,874	£5,054,712	£40,886,331
Assuming £5,000 lump sum to begin and £1,666.66 saved each month...					

Source: Plain English Finance

We will see how to do this later in the book. Nearly all debt is expensive. It is challenging to make a 15 or 20 per cent return on your investments, but it is almost certain you will pay at least this on your debt. Another reason why so many people fail at the money game is that they use far too much debt in their life. Please note that I am talking about credit cards and unsecured loans here, rather than mortgage products or student loan debt. Mortgages and student loans are a special case, which we will think about in more detail later.

In summary

So we can see from the power of compound interest that if you can achieve a half-decent return on your money, even a relatively small amount can become a very large amount in time. This is arguably the most important thing you will ever learn about money.

Got it? Then let's move on to the second amazing fact about finance and see how you can very easily start making this free money from your hard-earned cash ...

Fact 2: You have access to financial products and information sources that are better than ever before

One of the paradoxes of the last few years is that people have been so focused on the 'global financial crisis' that they have generally missed some very interesting developments in the finance industry as a whole. It is only in the relatively recent past that the financial services industry has developed to the point that people from any background can invest in almost any asset class in almost any country and can do so easily, quickly, cheaply and, in the UK in particular, tax-efficiently too.

Let's say you thought that the price of oil was going to increase. (Don't worry for now about how you might have come to form this opinion.) Today you can own some oil with the click of a mouse, and with far lower fees than in the past. You can even make money betting that the price of oil will fall if that is what you believe will happen. Or perhaps you think that Brazilian farmland is going to increase in value, as the world's population grows from 7 to 9 billion and Brazilian crops enjoy increasing demand. You can benefit financially from this belief from the comfort of your home.

Not that long ago, these sorts of investments were very difficult or even impossible to make. If you wanted to benefit from growth somewhere like India, China or Singapore or to make money from gold, oil or Brazilian farms, you needed a large amount of money, a relationship with a private banker somewhere like Switzerland, and a willingness to pay high fees and deal with lawyers. In the last few years, thanks to the Internet and intense innovation from financial services companies around the world, these hurdles have pretty much disappeared. As a result, investing is far simpler for us than it was for our parents or grandparents.

These days, if you have a basic grasp of what you are doing, you can easily and cheaply become the owner of almost anything. You have never been in a better position to make money out of a good idea than you are today. Sadly, very few people have any idea how to do this.

The reason for this is that the vast majority of people fall into one of three categories:

1 Those who do not invest any money at all
2 Those who do invest but use their high street bank for financial advice
3 Those who do invest but go to a substandard financial adviser.

There are now almost as many financial products available in the world as there are wine producers. Sadly, the main high street banks – and many IFAs – are like a wine merchant who sells a very limited range of mediocre wines at high prices.

There is a wonderful world of investment opportunity available out there if you know where to go. The key is choosing the right things to own, knowing how and where to buy them, and paying the right price for them. This is certainly no walk in the park, but it isn't the Herculean task that many people who work in finance would have you believe. You are also better placed to solve the puzzle than many finance professionals, for the reasons presented in Chapter 2. With a little bit of knowledge, you can soon arrange your financial affairs so that you can benefit from the incredibly exciting diversity of investment opportunities available today. You can keep your costs low, minimize the tax you pay and, if you really know what you're doing, even make money when your investments fall in price – as well as when they rise.

Moving swiftly on

So now you are up to speed on the power of compound interest and the fact that it is easier than ever before to invest. Knowing these two facts alone gives you a huge advantage over most people.

Now we shall turn our attention to two incredibly important, big-picture investment themes …

4

Two crucial investment themes

'Barring the cataclysmic unforeseen, the outlook for business is good
and will become even better as time goes on.'

J. Paul Getty, *How to Be Rich*

This quote from the late J. Paul Getty, once the richest living American, illustrates his views on finance at the time of the Great Depression (c.1929–39), when many people felt as pessimistic about the state of the world and their own financial situation as they do today. Though it may not have seemed like it at the time to many people, how right he was given the record of history ever since ...

What you need to know about economic growth and inflation

This is where things get exciting. If you got your head around the two amazing facts in the previous chapter, and can get to grips with the two themes discussed here, then your knowledge of finance will quite literally be in the top tiny percentage of people in the world and you will be very well placed to make a superior return on your money as a result. Our two crucial themes are:

1 *The world economy keeps on growing.* Forget the 'financial crisis' or the 'recession' (or Trump, Brexit, Syria, aliens or killer bees). The fact is that the world as a whole continues to grow. If you are invested in this fact, you stand to benefit enormously. Warren Buffett identified a fundamental truth about investment when he said that 'there is always a bull market somewhere.'

2 *There is significant real inflation in the world.* I touched on this in the introduction, but we will look at it in more detail in this chapter. In recent years, governments all over the world have been inventing vast quantities of what I call 'fictional' money. I use the word 'inventing' rather than 'printing' because very little of this new money is actually printed as notes or minted as coins; it is simply 'invented' in computers. All this new money creates inflation.

It is vital to know that this is happening and understand what to do about it. This inflation is bad news for anyone who doesn't understand it, but it can be reasonably good news for the tiny minority of people who do, because they can choose investments that benefit from it. They can 'own' inflation.

As we saw in Chapter 2, gold has performed exceptionally well for many years – achieving high single-digit to low double-digit returns for the last two decades or so in all of the major currencies in the world. This performance is a direct result of what I am talking about. People who understand inflation tend to own gold and, as a result, have made more than 11 per cent average annual returns (in GBP) on that investment going back to the start of the millennium.

Now, let us look at each of these themes in more detail.

The world economy keeps on growing

The world is getting richer ...

The world is much richer today than it was ten years ago, and certainly much richer than it was 20, 50 or 100 years ago. In fact, the last decade has seen humanity produce something like 25 per cent of all economic output ever in the whole of human history. It seems rather incredible that at the same time that this cornucopia of wealth has been created, so many people in the developed world feel that the world is the worst it has ever been.

Humanity, in aggregate, is the richest it has ever been. And the world will continue to get significantly richer due, quite simply, to population growth and economic and technological development.

... But you are getting poorer

In recent years, people in many modern Western countries might be forgiven for having lost sight of the inherent truth that the world is getting richer. Many in the developed world are poorer today than they were previously, having suffered dot-com and property crashes, the 'financial crisis' of 2007–8, rising job insecurity and the significant 'stealth' inflation we are looking at.

In fact, most Westerners are quite right to feel as if things have been getting harder economically. As indicated in the introduction, if you take out the richest 1 per cent of the population, the other 99 per cent of people in countries like the UK and USA have been getting poorer in real terms for several decades. The inflation-adjusted wage of the average American has not increased since 1973, and the UK is no different. Why?

Because globalization has meant that billions of people elsewhere in the world have finally been able to compete for the Earth's inherently limited resources. These include oil, fresh water, agricultural products, timber, metals and so on. For centuries, markets for all of these things were completely dominated by people from developed countries. This is because developed countries were obviously the first to industrialize, and they used their technological and military superiority to build empires and take a great deal more than their 'fair share'.

However, technological and societal developments have meant that in the last few decades, roughly since the end of the Second World War, people in the developing world have increasingly been able to compete for jobs and capital with those in the West. This has increased the *real* cost of things. With China's decision to pursue economic development in the late 1970s, and the fall of the Berlin Wall a decade later, this process has accelerated.

This is a key part of the paradigm shift I referred to earlier in the book. Like it or not, those of us in 'rich' countries are losing our relative and absolute economic power to billions of hungry, aspirational and hard-working people elsewhere.

With the increased promotion of free trade after the end of the Second World War, international trade and the global shipping industry exploded. At first, developing countries were able to catch up with the West only in the relatively unskilled agricultural sector, as well as in extractive primary sectors such as mining. Increasingly, however, they have made great strides in many more lucrative manufacturing sectors too. Just think of post-war Japan, the Four Asian Tiger economies of Hong Kong, Taiwan, South Korea and Singapore after that, and the more recent wave of countries that includes places like Brazil, India, Vietnam and Turkey. We are all intuitively aware of how successful these countries have become – just think about where so many of the products in your home come from.

Today further technological developments, primarily in telecommunications and travel, mean that a tidal wave of people from scores of different countries are now competing with Westerners for highly paid jobs in a wide range of white-collar sectors: IT, engineering and business services such as finance and consultancy.

All of this has driven very strong economic growth in the developing world, most notably in the BRIC countries – Brazil, Russia, India and China – but in many others too: the MINT countries of Mexico, Indonesia, Nigeria and Turkey; Thailand, Singapore and many other parts of Asia; multiple South and Central American countries; several parts of the Middle East; and, more recently, some of the more stable African nations.

Countries that previously didn't have a middle class at all now have one that numbers in the tens, even hundreds, of millions. Statistics show that the growth in car ownership in countries like China and Brazil has been astonishing, as their populations have started to catch up with those in the developed world. Today Brazil's economy is not far off the size of the UK's (having actually been larger in the recent past). China buys more cars than America and has 8,000 miles of high-speed railway, more than anywhere else in the world. Twenty years ago it had no high-speed trains at all. This has happened incredibly quickly.

Let's see this in numbers*

To show this idea in numbers, the global gross domestic product, or GDP (a measure of the total amount of wealth generated by a country each year), the total of all economic activity in the world, increased from about $32 trillion (32,000 billion dollars) to $74 trillion between 2000 and 2010.

To put it another way, the world economy as a whole grew no less than 131.25 per cent (from $32 to $74 trillion) in ten years. If you had been able to simply 'own the world' then your wealth would have increased by at least 131.25 per cent (significantly more if compounded, that is to say if you re-invested any income you earned).

---

* I have left the numbers in this section unchanged from the last edition of the book. As you might imagine, calculating something as complicated as the economic output of the entire world is a difficult job and there are in any case various different methodologies for working it out. For this reason, I have left the numbers I used originally because I am strongly of the opinion that whether global GDP is $82 trillion or $85 trillion, this in no way diminishes the overall point I am making.

Furthermore, while you should never trust forecasts blindly, it seems highly likely that the trend for the world economy to grow will continue because of population growth and technological development. When I was writing the first edition of this book in 2010–11, the International Monetary Fund (IMF) estimated that global GDP would be $82 trillion by 2015. In fact, it had already reached almost $85 trillion by 2012.

As its title suggests, therefore, one of the key things this book will teach you is how you can 'own the world'. Given the improvement in financial products already highlighted, it has never been easier or cheaper to do so.

An environmental aside

For those of us who care about the environment, these global growth numbers might be seen as potentially bad news. After all, the more the world's population and economy grows, generally the more raw materials we use and the more pollution and waste we generate. This has been a serious personal concern of mine for a long time. As *The Economist* puts it: 'If China's consumption of raw materials and energy per person were to rise to rich countries' levels, the world simply would not have the resources to supply them.'

This is even more worrying when you add in India, Pakistan, Indonesia, Latin America, Turkey, Nigeria, Mexico, Africa and all of the other hugely populous and rapidly industrializing parts of the world. A full discussion of the ecological and environmental impact of global economic growth is beyond the scope of this book, but I would like to point out that it is possible for there to be economic growth that actually improves our environment, otherwise known as 'sustainable development'. An example of this would be the emergence of companies that facilitate fractional car usage.

Many readers will be familiar with Zipcar, which uses clever IT so that you can pick up a car, use it for a few hours and pay only for that time. When I wrote the last edition of this book, Zipcar was operating in over 50 cities in the UK, the USA and Canada, and had expanded into Europe. At the time of writing this new edition, they are in over 300 in countries as far afield as Turkey and Taiwan.

Zipcar estimates that each of their vehicles takes at least 20 personally owned vehicles off the road, and the research group Laffer Associates estimates that car sharing could halve the sale of cars in the USA
by 2020. As the Zipcar model is replicated across an increasingly urban-
ized world, growth in such companies will contribute to increasing
GDP numbers while benefiting the environment at the same time.

Advances in IT systems will hopefully facilitate the development of
these 'collaborative consumption' business models across a wide range
of human activities. There have certainly been plenty of compelling
recent examples of this phenomenon, perhaps the best known of which
are Uber and Airbnb, revolutionizing urban travel and the hotel industry respectively since I wrote the first edition of this book in 2012.

These sorts of developments give me more confidence than ever
that human ingenuity and scientific breakthroughs will enable the
whole world to grow economically without destroying our planet.
There are a number of books in the bibliography at the end of this
book that deal with these issues and provide an uplifting read. I would
highlight a few in particular:

- *The Rational Optimist: How Prosperity Evolves* by Matt Ridley
- *Abundance: The Future Is Better Than You Think* by Peter
  Diamandis and Steven Kotler
- *The Sixth Wave: How to Succeed in a Resource-limited World* by
  James Bradfield Moody and Bianca Nogrady
- *What's Mine is Yours: The Rise of Collaborative Consumption* by
  Rachel Botsman and Roo Rogers.

So what can I do?

Despite what many of us in the West feel, the world is still growing
and will likely continue to do so. People in the developing world
will quite likely get relatively richer and many people in developed
nations may continue to get relatively poorer.

Growing competition from the developing world is inevitable.
Sadly, over the last 20 years, individuals and governments in the
West have avoided the erosion of their living standards as a result of
increased global competition by 'doing an ostrich' and borrowing

vast sums of money, primarily from the developing world. This is one of the reasons we find ourselves in our current predicament.

Rather than over-borrowing, a far better option is to invest in the dynamism, ingenuity and hard work of these developing countries. Doing this is one of the main reasons the top 1 per cent of people in the West are richer today than ever before. This 1 per cent have been shareholders in the explosive growth of the emerging world.

> You need to own the world in order to make superior returns on your money.

We will look in more detail at how to do this in Chapter 10. For now, however, it is time to look at our second crucial theme.

There is significant *real* inflation in the world

I believe it is worth repeating the following John Maynard Keynes quote, given the importance of the point it makes:

> By a continuing process of inflation, governments can confiscate, secretly and unobserved, an important part of the wealth of their citizens …
> There is no subtler, no surer means of overturning the existing basis of society than to debauch the currency. The process engages all the hidden forces of economic law on the side of destruction, and does it in a manner which not one man in a million is able to diagnose.

Since the early 1970s central banks all over the world have been printing money at a faster and faster rate. Or, to put it more accurately, they have been inventing money rather than printing it. They don't physically print much of it these days but simply add some zeroes to accounts in a central computer.

The sheer scale of the acceleration in recent years is extraordinary. Just look at the steepness of the line in Figure 4.1, which shows the phenomenon in the USA. (The 'St Louis Adjusted Monetary Base' the graph refers to is simply because it is the St Louis branch of the Federal Reserve that publishes this data.)

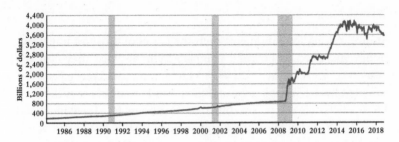

Figure 4.1 Accelerating increase in money supply (1984–2018)
Source: Federal Reserve Bank of St Louis

The situation in the UK is no different, as we can see from Figure 4.2:

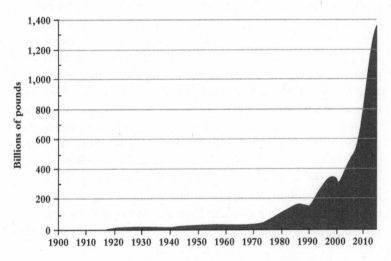

FIGURE 4.2 UK public net debt (1900–2015)
Source: www.ukpublicspending.co.uk/

This causes real inflation. While it is not really necessary to understand exactly why or how inflation has occurred, it is very important for your financial future that you understand that it is happening, very important indeed. To explain …

'When I was a lad ...'

Stop and think for a moment about the prices of the most important things you need to buy, and compare them to what they cost ten years ago, or even when you were a child. You should really get a feel for what has been happening and the point I am trying to make here. How much did your parents buy their first house for? How much did your house cost, if you are a homeowner? What is that house worth now? Does this increase mean that 'you can't go wrong with bricks and mortar', or is there something more complicated going on?

Now think about how much your first pair of jeans cost, or your first car, or the first you can remember buying of pretty much anything: chocolate bars, pints of milk, loaves of bread. Hopefully, you get the picture. If you really think about it, nearly everything you need to buy has gone up in price significantly. Pretty much the only exceptions to this trend have been consumer electronics products such as televisions and computers.

This is inflation at work. Many people think that they understand inflation. I would argue that the reality is that most people have only a vague idea of its existence, and they absolutely don't 'get' its sheer magnitude and what it means for their long-term financial situation.

This is extremely bad news for most people but relatively good news for the small minority who do understand. The value (purchasing power) of one pound or one dollar has fallen by around 90 per cent since 1971. Worse, this negative trend in the value of money is accelerating thanks to the actions of politicians and central banks all over the world as they continue to invent large amounts of new money out of thin air. In the UK and the USA, this is called quantitative easing (QE).

But what is inflation?

'But inflation is still really quite low – 2 per cent or something, isn't it?' I hear you say.

Yes, but what is 'inflation' as reported by governments? Here is a little story that may help explain why official government inflation numbers are of very little use to us. Understanding this is incredibly important for your financial future.

In the 1980s the British government changed the definition of 'unemployment' on numerous occasions. Each time it changed, the unemployment number 'fell'. It is not hard to argue that all that was going on here was that people we would most likely understand to be 'unemployed', such as adults who didn't have a job and wanted one, were no longer defined that way and so dropped out of the numbers.

Some were reclassified as 'disabled' (those earning disability benefits) – now a huge number in the UK – while others were said to be on a 'youth training scheme' or reclassified in any number of dubious ways to take them *off* the headline unemployment numbers discussed in the media.

At the time that I wrote the first edition of this book, the UK had about 2.7 million 'unemployed' (happily, this number has fallen a long way since then). But there continue to be another several million who do not have a job but are classified differently to keep them out of the headline unemployment numbers. On the other side of the Atlantic, the US authorities play similar games. Perhaps the best example of this is that anyone who has been out of work for longer than a year in the US drops out of the statistics entirely. Because they are no longer eligible for any state support, they are no longer 'unemployed', according to the definition the US government uses.

This leads to a ridiculous situation where the US government reports a 'fall' in unemployment and the stock market rallies (goes up), but the only reason the unemployment number has 'fallen' is that 300,000 people have been out of work for more than a year. They are still unemployed but are no longer counted in the statistics discussed in the press. In February 2012, 1.2 million more people 'fell out' of the numbers and the market didn't bat an eye. Those people still don't have jobs – but the official unemployment number fell yet again.

By about 2015 this meant that the US government was claiming that they had an unemployment rate of about 8 per cent. But if you actually worked out the percentage of working-age adults who don't have jobs and might like one, the real number was closer to 16 per cent (and north of 20 per cent if you use the methodology that was used until the early 1980s). You can see this in Figure 4.3.

Amazingly enough, the US authorities don't even try to hide the higher number. Instead, they refer to it as 'U6' unemployment. The 8 per cent is called 'U3'. I am consistently amazed that the media and politicians focus on U3 and ignore U6. By definition, U6 seems a far better

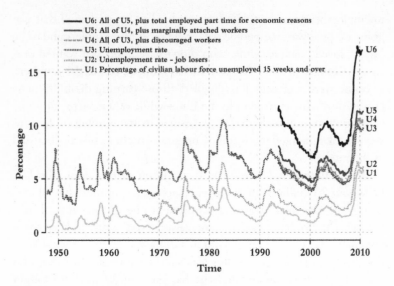

FIGURE 4.3 Measurements of unemployment in the USA (1950–2010)
Source: Courtesy of ShadowStats.com

representation of what unemployment actually is (people who don't have a job and might want one!). This is just another example of the press and much of the financial analyst community being asleep at the wheel. The only benefit is that you can use it to your investing advantage.

Figure 4.4 illustrates another way of looking at the same thing. Note the huge difference between today and past recessions in the USA. This difference is not captured if you look only at the 'official' U3 number.

Unemployment? I thought we were talking about inflation?

'Why is this relevant to inflation?' I hear you ask.

The answer is that governments all over the world have been playing the same trick – or worse – with their inflation calculations. The US authorities made the biggest change to the calculation in 1996 when President Clinton implemented adjustments recommended by something called the Boskin Commission. If the pre-1996 method was still being used, US and UK inflation today would be closer to 10 per cent, as you will see below.

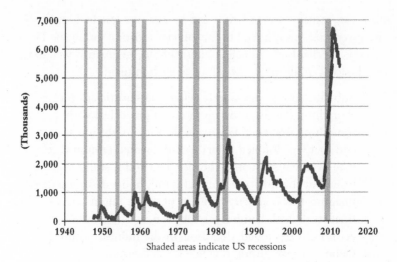

FIGURE 4.4 US civilians unemployed for 27 weeks and over (1940–2010)
Source: Courtesy of ShadowStats.com

I cannot stress enough how important it is to understand this reality. In my experience, almost no one does. Or, at the very least, they do not understand the scale of the problem. I have been constantly amazed by the complete ignorance of the facts among members of the general population and investment professionals alike. Few journalists seem to understand what is actually going on; nor do virtually any of the people I have worked with in the City, many of whom are analysts and economists at major investment firms. As a result, understanding why today's inflation numbers are essentially a fiction may give you an investing advantage.

Substitution, weighting and hedonics

'Trickery and treachery are the practices of fools that have not the wits enough to be honest.'

Benjamin Franklin

There are three particularly dubious ways in which governments ensure that inflation numbers end up always being lower than the true increase in your cost of living (so you think you are wealthier than you actually are and they get to pay out less in social security, given that this is linked to the 'official' inflation numbers). These dubious mechanisms are called 'substitution', 'geometric weighting' and 'hedonic adjustment'. Let's look at each in turn:

- **Substitution** is very simply when the statisticians replace something that is going up in cost a great deal with something that isn't. For example, they might replace cod that has doubled in price with farmed salmon that may even have become cheaper. The cod is still twice the price but the inflation number hasn't budged. As you can imagine, this is an easy game to play. You might replace fillet steak with hamburgers or even, as one gnarly old economist has joked, dog food, in the fullness of time.

- **Geometric weighting** is where the authorities include something that has gone up in price a lot as an inappropriately low percentage of the calculation. For example, the healthcare sector represents just over 17 per cent of the US economy but it makes up only 6 per cent of the US inflation calculation. Healthcare inflation has been notoriously high in recent years given the ageing population's demand for it (running in the double digits), but it hasn't had anything like the impact on inflation numbers it arguably should have done, as the authorities have just made it an inappropriately small percentage of the calculation.

- **Hedonic adjustment** is, in my opinion, even more gratuitous than the last two. This is when an item is reduced in price for the purposes of the inflation calculation because the authorities argue (subjectively) that you're getting more for your money and you are therefore *effectively* paying less. Let's say that last year a 50-inch television from Sony or Samsung cost £1,000. This year there is a new 50-inch television that has a slightly better screen and improved functionality and still costs £1,000. The statisticians will then say that the TV is, say, 20 per cent better than last year's TV and adjust its price in the inflation calculation from £1,000 down to £800. The TV actually still costs £1,000,

but they have included it in the calculation at £800. This
trick is used to adjust the price of nearly half of all the
products that go into the inflation calculation.

I am not making this up. This is not a conspiracy theory. This
information is all widely available online if you 'read the small print',
as it were – it's just that a significant majority of our journalists and
financial professionals don't.

John Williams, one of the leading commentators on this subject
since the late 1980s, has said: 'Inflation, as reported by the Consumer
Price Index (CPI), is understated by roughly 7% per year due to
redefinitions and flawed methodologies.'

You can see this reality in Figure 4.5.

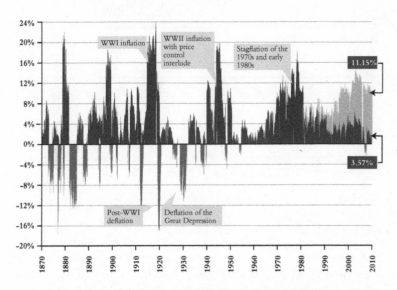

FIGURE 4.5 Monthly inflation (1872–2010): Official (BLS) annualized
inflation = 3.57%; ShadowStats = 11.15% The **dark grey areas** show
inflation based on the BLS Consumer Price Index (CPI). The method
for calculating inflation was slightly adjusted in the early 1980s and
more dramatically in the mid-1990s. The **light grey areas** show inflation
calculated consistently with the pre-1982 method.
Source: Courtesy of ShadowStats.com

Figure 4.6 is a more recent chart, in which the picture is even clearer. The lower, paler line is the 'official' number after the various arguably dubious mechanisms used to keep it artificially low, and the top line is the real number.

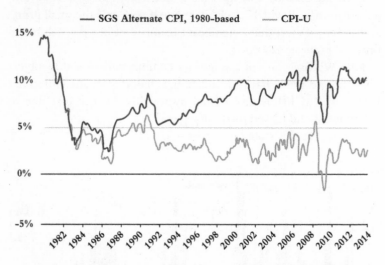

FIGURE 4.6 Annual consumer inflation – official versus SGS (Shadow Government Statistics) (1980-based) alternate inflation (year-to-year change, through October 2014 (Bureau of Labor Statistics [BLS], SGS))
Source: Courtesy of ShadowStats.com

Hidden inflation

There are other ways the official inflation numbers misrepresent the *actual* increase in your cost of living. Another source of the 'hidden inflation' that doesn't make it into the official numbers is sometimes called 'ghostflation' or 'shrinkflation'. This is where a company gives you less of a product for the same price 'on the sly', something that has been prevalent in the last few years.

Some readers may remember a major national pizza chain in the UK being accused in the press of making their pizzas smaller while keeping the price the same. Equally, although this may seem like a strange example, an American friend of mine recently pointed out that a standard packet of a famous brand of cookies currently contains 39 cookies. This compares to 45 only a year ago. This is a 13.3 per cent reduction in the amount you receive, with no change in price – effectively 13.3 per cent inflation.

In the UK market, you may be aware of precisely the same phenomenon with Cadbury Creme Eggs. Cadbury is using cheaper chocolate and offering only five eggs for the same price that previously bought six. Not that long ago, I also noticed that my packet of Walkers crisps contained 30g rather than the 35g that was sold not that long ago (not to mention the fact that a leading UK newspaper ran a story about these stated weights rarely being matched by the weight of the contents).

Based on the above, Cadbury eggs are 16.6 per cent more expensive than they were last year and Walkers crisps at least 14.3 per cent, but none of this appears in any inflation numbers. To be fair to the Office of National Statistics, it has produced written papers about how it tries to deal with this phenomenon, but my reading of that output is that it doesn't include a sufficient number of products for which this is relevant.

If you start paying attention to these sorts of things, you realize that examples can be found across a wide variety of products. Many companies are dealing with severe input-cost inflation, and one of the easiest ways for them to keep their historical profit margin is, quite simply, to give you less for the same money in the hope that you won't notice.

Inflation is 'zero' but so many things are at all-time highs

As I have already pointed out: if inflation is 'zero' or 'very low', then how is it that a London house can cost as much as five or ten times what it cost only a few years ago? (Much the same can be said for so many other residential property markets all over the world: Sydney, Singapore, Tokyo, New York, Vancouver and so on. The list is long.) How come my 'low-cost airline' flight this year has cost me the same as a British Airways business-class fare a decade ago? How is that a Picasso and a large ruby broke records at auction not long before I wrote the last edition and, in November 2017, only a few months before writing this edition, a Leonardo da Vinci painting, *Salvator Mundi*, sold for no less than $450.3 million at auction in New York? How is it that nearly all stock markets continue to hit all-time highs (despite people being bearish on them for at least five years)? The answer is because inflation numbers 'are cooked like a thanksgiving turkey', to quote award-winning US financial newsletter writer Byron King.

It is quite incredible that the points made above are understood by so few people, especially among journalists and senior finance professionals. Suffice to say, inflation and unemployment numbers regularly discussed in the media are essentially fictional.

And neither is there any real 'threat' of deflation. A multi-decade period of deflation in the Victorian era coincided with one of the biggest explosions of wealth creation and technological advancement in history. Deflation means that things are getting cheaper – in other words, that standards of living are increasing. The only people who should be afraid of deflation are governments or individuals who have borrowed vastly too much money, since deflation makes their debt more expensive in real terms.

All of this is important because, as we have already seen: 'By a continuing process of inflation, governments can confiscate, secretly and unobserved, an important part of the wealth of their citizens.' What John Maynard Keynes was describing is precisely what is happening today, and this confiscation of wealth is why governments on both sides of the Atlantic do such a great job of producing nonsensical numbers: so they can get away with it. 'But why don't financial analysts, economists and journalists call these numbers into question if this is the case?' you ask – and well you might.

The first thing to say is that many do. I am calling the numbers into question in this book, after all. A brief Internet search will rapidly unearth independent and extremely well-qualified analysts trying to put the right numbers into the public domain (shadowstats.com is a good example of this, but there are plenty of others).

With this sort of work widely available, it does consistently amaze me how nearly all mainstream analysts and journalists seem to be asleep at the wheel. I confess I find it vexing when I hear a politician talking about 8 per cent unemployment in the USA, or zero per cent inflation in the UK, and a journalist just taking these nonsense numbers at face value.

It is also worth noting that GDP numbers are 'inflation adjusted'. If you accept the premise that there are serious flaws in the inflation numbers, then, by extension, the GDP numbers are also inaccurate. If, for example, you use what I deem to be more accurate inflation numbers published by folks like ShadowStats, then many Western economies are actually going backwards in real terms (i.e. they are in recession) while their politicians claim they are growing.

One further point to highlight is that stock market indices also need to be inflation adjusted if you are to compare apples with apples. At the time of updating this book, much has been made of the fact that the FTSE 100 has just hit an 'all-time high', 'eclipsing' the last record high, which was set in 1999.

In 1999 the FTSE 100 Index peaked at 6,930. In February 2015 it hit 6,949 and at the time of writing this third edition in June 2018 it is at 7,555. But even using UK RPI inflation numbers, which I think have serious flaws, prices for UK consumers are up by over 50 per cent since 1999. This means that the FTSE 100 would have to be well north of 10,000 for it to be above its 1999 peak in *real terms*. Using more accurate inflation numbers and adjusting for the weakness in the pound, the index would have to be even higher than that. Hardly any of those writing the headlines in the UK press seem to understand this reality (as far as I can see, at least).

Every cloud has a silver lining, though, and the good news is that if you understand the real numbers, you have an information advantage over those who don't, and you can use this to make more *real* money from your investments.

How do they get away with it?

Many analysts and journalists have raw intelligence and a 'great education' but are too young or blinkered to see the big picture. They have learned about 'inflation' on the job, never stopping to look under the bonnet and attempting to understand how the numbers are actually calculated, or how this has changed over time. As Henry

Ford put it: 'Thinking is the hardest work there is, which is the probable reason why so few engage in it.' Or, as Voltaire would have it: 'Common sense is not so common.'

It is often easiest to work within the existing paradigm or follow the conventional wisdom rather than confront complexity and the disapproval of the 'mob' (or your boss) by rocking the boat. I know from first-hand experience that there is no upside for a young analyst at a major investment bank pointing out that, when it comes to published inflation and unemployment numbers, the emperor isn't wearing any clothes.

Furthermore, those in the know who 'get' the realities of inflation – senior staff at major investment banks, hedge fund managers, commodity traders, some politicians and central bankers – can turn it to their significant financial advantage. They have very little incentive to blow the whistle. It is similar to the situation at WorldCom or Enron a few years ago: some in senior management knew what was happening but it suited them to keep quiet as long as they could get away with it.

In summary

To conclude not only this chapter, but also the first part of the book, I want to note that the actions of many governments in recent years have led to a situation where we are in the throes of significant monetary inflation. And when there is significant inflation, the value of cash falls as the price of 'things' increases.

The smart investor benefits from this by making sure he or she owns the very things that are going up in price. As a basic rule of thumb, this includes many financial assets, shares, precious (monetary) metals, commodities and property. We don't need to understand in detail why stock markets, gold, oil, wheat, cotton, coffee, art, houses, jewellery and wine go up in price when there is inflation. It is enough just to be aware that this is the case, just as it has been for the last several years.

That said, it should hopefully seem logical to you that if you have a fixed supply of 'stuff' and the supply of money doubles, then the price of that 'stuff' will double, all other things being equal. In other words, if twice as much money is competing for the same number

of things (bread, milk, eggs, cars, houses, gold), then the person selling those things can put the price up. This is precisely what has been
happening in recent years.

Armed with this knowledge and an understanding that the global
economy continues to grow, we are now ready to do something
about it and start making some serious money.

So let us now look at exactly what to do to benefit from our two
facts about finance and our two crucial themes. But before we do, it
is perhaps worth summarizing what we have learned so far:

- It has never been more important to understand what
  is happening in finance, and to arrange your affairs
  appropriately.
- It isn't as hard to do this as you might think. You are only a
  few hours away from achieving it.
- You need to ensure you benefit from the incredible power
  of compound interest.
- Financial products today are better than ever – if you know
  where to go to find the best ones at the right price. But
  you won't find them at your high street bank.
- The world economy is still growing and will continue to
  do so. You need to 'own the world'.
- There is significant real inflation in the world. You need to
  'own inflation'.

PART 2

Down to basics: what do you need to know?

- What role does property play in creating financial surplus?
- What are your choices when it comes to pensions?
- What are the types of accounts and investment vehicles that you need to know about?

5
Creating financial surplus

'If you would be wealthy, think of saving as well as getting.'

Benjamin Franklin

It should be clear from what you have read so far that if you want to be wealthy, if you want to have real financial security and the finer things in life, there is a very simple formula that is well understood by the rich and has remained unchanged for the several thousand years since humans invented money:

> Live on less than you earn and invest the rest.

We have seen how powerful compound interest is. Even if you do not have much money to invest, do not let this put you off. Start saving something immediately and let compound interest and time work their magic.

If you want to win at the money game, it is absolutely imperative that you create financial surplus in your life and invest that surplus in a good variety of assets. If you have failed to do this in the past, a primary reason may have been that, even if you managed to save some of your income, you didn't know where to invest it and so you felt there was no point. Perhaps you didn't trust the financial services industry to give you good advice?

This is entirely fair enough, but read on and soon you will have a better idea than most of how to invest your money – and you will feel confident that you can do it.

As such, let us first turn our attention to how you are going to find some financial surplus.

The crucial role played by property in creating surplus

You are going to be best off saving and then investing a minimum of about 10 per cent of your monthly income. Many of you will read this, and be thinking that you can't create financial surplus. You might have three kids and be barely making ends meet at the moment. Saving 10 per cent of your monthly income seems completely unrealistic.

Without wanting to sound overly harsh, if this is what you are thinking then you are highly unlikely to become wealthy. You will have to hope that you win the lottery or a long-lost relative leaves you some money. Worse, you may end up having a fairly impoverished retirement or not being able to retire at all.

The truth, however, is that pretty much anyone should be able to arrange their personal affairs so they can live on 90 per cent or less of their income, almost no matter what they earn. If you think you can't, then (with relatively few exceptions) it is just that you are not prepared to take sufficiently radical action.

Don't despair, though! There are two tricks that can have you saving 10 per cent of your monthly income very quickly.

The first is a psychological one: you simply work out how you can best *spend* 90 per cent of your income each month, rather than how you can save 10 per cent of it. This is obviously a simple case of the 'glass half full versus glass half empty' scenario, but the weird thing is that it actually works. Psychologists refer to this kind of phenomenon as 'reframing' – a very powerful technique for change in any area of your life.

If you say to yourself, 'I am going to spend 90 per cent of my money on x, y and z', and then automate what happens with the remaining 10 per cent, you might find it easier than you thought to have 10 per cent of your income available for investment.

Obviously, the best way to do this is by making a detailed budget. Many people have a budget of one kind or another but I think it is fair to say that relatively few people make a sufficiently detailed one, which is why so many of us can spend so much time wondering where on earth all our money has gone!

To avoid this problem, I would highly recommend using one of the excellent budgeting tools available online, for example youneedabudget.com. This site works together with an app on your smartphone and, for most people, really is all that's needed in order to free up money for investment. If you don't believe me, just check out the reviews and testimonials online.

If you still can't find money for investment after a few weeks of using this kind of tool, then you might consider the second and slightly more radical of the two tricks: *move house!*

If you cannot save money given your current living arrangements, then change them. This will put you in a position to save money far more quickly than trying to buy fewer things, spend less in the pub or drink fewer cappuccinos every week. That said, 'self-storage' has been one of the fastest-growing industries in the last decade and the average Briton has more than a tonne of unwanted possessions. If you think about the amount of useless stuff you have purchased, it may surprise you how much you could have invested instead. Fans of the 1990s television show *Sex and the City* may remember an episode where the lead character, Carrie, can't afford the deposit on her apartment but realizes that she owns tens of thousands of dollars' worth of shoes. Please don't be that person.

So if you are renting: move, rent somewhere 10 per cent cheaper than your current home, and invest that difference. Although if you are making the change, why not even consider somewhere 20 per cent cheaper, invest 15 per cent and have 5 per cent more disposable income?

If you own a house, and your mortgage payments are eating up so much of your monthly income that you can't find 10 per cent of your money to invest, then sell the house and downsize. I appreciate this may seem like a fairly dramatic course of action, but it is the one action that can get you results in a reasonably short period of time, and, over time, this decision will set you up for life.

One of the primary causes of the financial crises in the USA and UK has been our unhealthy obsession with home ownership and the widespread failure of many people to understand how to value property over time, as against the other main assets you might put money into such as shares, bonds and commodities.

We have lived through at least 20 years of most people believing that 'you can't go wrong with bricks and mortar' or that 'rent is throwing money away by paying someone else's mortgage'.

These are simplistic statements that are often entirely incorrect. Like all assets, sometimes property is good value and worthy of investment, and at other times it is dangerously expensive. Many rich people understand this. Billionaire Jim Rogers, one of the best investors of all time, has twice sold all of his property on the eve of a crash (in 1987 and 2007). He regularly describes property as a fundamentally bad investment due to its illiquidity (how hard it is to buy and sell) and the large number of ongoing expenses associated with it. Bear in mind that this is a guy who made 4,200 per cent on his money in just over a decade. When it comes to all things financial, he knows his stuff. There are plenty of other examples of extremely wealthy and successful folk who share a similar view of property. This is perhaps surprising for many readers when you consider how unconventional such a negative stance is in polite British society (and that's putting it mildly).

Given the difference it can make to your finances, it is worth taking a closer look at property and how to value it. The decisions you make about property in particular will have a huge impact on your wealth over your lifetime – and the wrong decision can potentially damage your financial situation for life. As ever – the money game is a marathon, not a sprint. I would argue that this fact should be borne in mind when making a decision as big as buying a property.

Many people in the English-speaking world feel familiar with property as an asset class. There is a long tradition of owner occupancy in countries such as the UK, the USA and Australia, but this is less the case in many other countries in the world, including wealthy European nations such as Germany and France, where a high percentage of the population rent, often for their entire lives.

House prices are a national obsession in the UK and the USA, and regularly discussed in the press. Property tends to be an individual's biggest asset and there is also an inevitable emotional attachment to one's home, over and above the attachment one might have to a share or any other type of investment for obvious reasons: clearly, you can't live in a share certificate or a gold ingot.

The problem with this is that many people feel that they are 'experts' when it comes to property, and never more so than in the last two decades. There is nothing like a rampant bull market in an asset class to make everyone feel like a genius.

In reality, it is consistently amazing to me how many folk prognosticate on the housing market without understanding any of the key long-term measures of value or the impact of inflation and interest rates on the market. This is a very similar point to the one

I made earlier about how many people invest in shares without understanding how they are valued. Property is likely to be your biggest investment. It would make sense, therefore, to really understand how it is valued.

Many of the estate agents I have dealt with in London and New York who confidently held forth on the state of the property market have demonstrably failed to grasp much, if any, of what follows. This is entirely analogous to just how many financial advisers have an insufficiently broad understanding of financial markets.

The first thing to say is that over the long run – and I am talking about more than 300 years of data here – property is absolutely not the 'sure thing' most people have come to believe it is. 'You can't go wrong with bricks and mortar' can be a dangerous and entirely incorrect statement.

The trouble with anchoring

A facet of human behaviour long highlighted by psychologists, especially in the realm of finance, is that we tend to have relatively short memories and this leads to a phenomenon known as 'anchoring'.

Basically, what this means is that if something has been true in your personal experience (e.g. ever-rising house prices) you will tend to assume that this is the normal state of affairs. We tend to assume that something that has been true during our lifetime – or an even shorter period – will continue to be true. Our current obsession with property is a good example, and perhaps understandable given that we have witnessed a relatively long and very strong bull market.

A more extreme and potentially more illustrative example of anchoring and the trouble it can get us into would be the dot-com boom of the late 1990s. Amazingly, it took only two to three years before a very large proportion of people – even in the supposedly professional investment community – had become dangerously 'anchored', thinking: 'Technology stocks always go up and are not subject to the traditional rules of stock market valuation. It is different this time.' We are all aware of how this ended for many of the participants in that market. Lots of people lost a great deal of money. The same phenomenon seems to be happening in the world of bitcoin and cryptocurrency (more on that subject later). It is best to be aware of anchoring and other similar behavioural traits each and every time we consider a market. To get a truer picture of things, smart investors will do their best to look at a much longer time frame, difficult though this may sometimes be.

If we do this, we will see that, as with any asset class, over the long run property performs well at certain times and poorly at others. Given the experience of the last 20 or so years, it may come as a surprise to many readers that UK property basically did not appreciate in value at all from 1900 to 1960. That is no less than 60 years.

In his 1965 book *The Economics of Housing*, Lionel Needleman wrote:

> There are considerable risks attached to investing in housing. The housing market is both unstable and unorganized. House prices can fluctuate violently and yet houses are much less negotiable than most forms of investment.

How different this stance is from the conventional wisdom of today. People living in the 1960s would have thought you were completely crazy if you had suggested you were thinking of borrowing 110 per cent of the value of a house with a view to renting it out, or were planning to use a few property investments to fund your retirement (or, even worse, use your primary residence as your 'pension').

I do not claim to have a magic formula to predict exactly when property will do well or badly, but there are certain metrics and methods for giving us a fighting chance of figuring out whether we are closer to a strong period for housing or a weak one, just as there are for every other type of investment we will look at.

Given how significant an investment property is, and how your choices in this area will affect your monthly cash flow and your ability to invest in anything else, it would seem like a good idea to get to grips with these measures of value before making any investment decisions. Strangely, relatively few people do this, including many estate agents. This is one of the reasons we have experienced property bubbles and financial crises on both sides of the Atlantic and no doubt will again in future.

The key metrics

So let us look at key metrics we might use to understand real value in the property market. Like everything else you will find in this book, these really aren't that complicated. The tools used by smart professional investors are simple enough, and I would again argue that we should all have learned about them at school. However, in my experience they tend to be poorly understood by many people.

Inflation

First of all, I want to revisit the relevance of inflation. We have already discussed just how important inflation is when talking about wealth generally. It is especially important when considering the performance of a property asset given how much of an impact inflation has over the long term and given that property investments tend to be held for the long term.

Economists and behavioural psychologists describe a phenomenon known as 'money illusion'. This basically means that the majority of people do not take inflation into account either sufficiently or at all when thinking about changes in the value of something. This is particularly the case with property.

You will hopefully recall from the section on inflation earlier in the book that the values of the pound and the dollar have fallen in real terms by more than 90 per cent since 1971. This is one of the reasons why prices from the early 1970s seem so incredibly 'cheap'. In 1973, the year my parents bought their first house, you could buy a decent-sized home in London for £10,000. That same house would in all probability cost upwards of £500,000 today.

Does this mean that the 'lucky' person who purchased a house in 1973 has increased their wealth by a factor of 50? If you do not take inflation into account, then you might conclude that they have. The price today is exactly 50 times what it was in 1973. Surely, they have made fifty times their money?

The difference between wealth and money

Here we must look at one of the most important concepts in this book: the difference between wealth and money (particularly paper money). In the example above, if the individual concerned sold their house they would take away 50 times the amount of paper money (pounds, in this example) that they started with. They have grown their money by a factor of 50. Great news – at first glance, at least.

But what has happened to their real wealth? The key thing here is to look at how much the price of everything else has gone up by. The first and most obvious thing to look at is how much the price of other houses has increased. What I am about to say might seem blindingly obvious to the point of being ridiculous, but please bear with me as it is crucial to illustrating a key point.

Let us say the owner of this house wanted to sell it, cash in their 'gains' and buy another house in the same area. Have they increased their wealth in terms of houses in the area?

The answer should obviously be 'no'. If you sell and then buy in the same market then, all other things being equal, the prices in that market will have gone up just as much as the price of your property. Even though this person has 50 times the amount of pounds sterling that they had before, they can still only buy one relatively nice house in the same part of London; another similar house in the same area will cost exactly the same as the one they are selling – their wealth in terms of number of houses in the same area has not increased at all.

Now, it is quite possible that this person has always wanted to move to rural Scotland when they retire, and prices there are only 25 times what they were in 1973. If this is the case, our lucky seller has increased their wealth in terms of houses in rural Scotland by a factor of two. Thanks to the appreciation in value of their London house being double the appreciation of a house in rural Scotland, they can now buy twice as much house in rural Scotland than they could have done originally. Their wealth in terms of Scottish houses has in fact doubled. This is obviously good news (assuming they want to move to rural Scotland, of course) and shows that we should always be thinking about *relative wealth* when working out if we are doing the right thing with our money.

To expand on the example, let us say the price of a decent meal out for two in London was £10 in 1973 and today it is £100, which is probably about fair. We can see that the owner of the house is better off in terms of meals out given that these increased in price by a factor of ten times in pound terms versus their house which has gone up by fifty times.

Similarly, a flight to New York in 1973 cost about £85. To keep the arithmetic simple, let us say that the price today is £850. Our home-owner is also therefore five times richer in terms of flights to New York than they were in 1973 (their house is up by 50 times; flights are up by ten times). Again, there has been far greater inflation in house prices than in flights to New York (for lots of structural reasons).

The point here is that if you want to build wealth you must always be thinking about comparative value and purchasing power. A simple number of pounds actually tells you relatively little about whether you are truly getting richer or not. But perhaps the above examples seem a little esoteric. A more recent example over a shorter time frame might help solidify the point …

Is a £1 million house still a £1 million house when it's worth £1 million?

I happen to know a number of people who purchased a house in central London for around £1,000,000 in 2006 and 2007. They consider their house to be as valuable today as it was then. Even despite the 'terrible' economic news we have heard much of since late 2008, they can at least feel reassured that their property has not fallen in value, can't they?

Again, what follows may be a little hard to grasp but it is important that we do grasp it. Let us say that someone purchased a house in London in 2007 for £1,000,000. Here is a very important consideration that the large majority of people don't make: at that time £1 was worth about $2, so they had purchased a house worth $2,000,000. This much is easy to follow.

Today a nice estate agent assures our property owner that, due to all the same good solid reasons trotted out for the last 20 years (constrained supply, foreign buyers galore), their house is now worth £1,250,000 – for the sake of argument. Fantastic. The only problem is that in the meantime the pound has dropped to a value of around $1.32 (as I write). Of the 16 biggest trading currencies in the world, the pound has been the worst-performing currency against the US dollar for the last several years. This means that our friend's London property is now worth $1,650,000. Even though the value in pounds has increased by a quarter of a million, in dollars it has fallen in value by no less a sum than $350,000.

'Who cares?' you may well ask. 'This person lives in London, shops in London, sends their kids to school in London. Why is the dollar relevant?'

The answer is that this assessment of dollar value is actually extremely relevant to this person's true wealth, the main reason being that many of the important things this person may want to buy are priced in dollars (for now at least): oil, gas, rice, wheat, cotton, copper, timber, shipping – the list goes on and on.

Few people really, truly notice it, but when the pound weakens against other currencies, many of the things we need to spend money on become more expensive, usually after a small time lag. This is perhaps most obvious at the petrol pump, but you can see it in your utility bills and, if you're really paying attention, your grocery bills too (and when you go on holiday abroad, of course). The fact is that the pound sterling price of your property is a poor indicator of what is happening to your real wealth.

If your property is 'worth' the same in pounds today as it was several years ago but nearly everything you need to buy in your life (petrol, bread, eggs, milk, cars, electricity, train fares, insurance, healthcare) has gone up in price by between 20 and 30 per cent, then in real terms you are actually 20–30 per cent poorer than you were five years ago.

So we can see just how important inflation is when considering the true value of property. There are two other key valuation metrics that we must be aware of to give us the best chance of working out where we are in a property cycle: rental yield and the ratio of property prices to salaries.

Rental yield

One of the most useful ways of trying to work out if a property is funda-mentally (i.e. inherently) cheap or expensive is the return it would gener-ate for you if you were to rent it out. Working out rental yield is a simple calculation but one that surprisingly few people make when considering the purchase of a property, including many of the estate agents I have dealt with in London and New York. (In fact, a number of those I encountered in New York had never even heard of rental yield. To me that is like a doc-tor never having heard of a heart. Is it any wonder that, with 'professionals' like this, the USA suffered a massive bubble in property prices?)

Quite simply, rental yield is the number you get if you divide the assumed annual rental income from a property by the assumed value of that property. It is a number that you can then use to compare the returns on property to any other asset you might be thinking about, including shares, commodities, bonds or alternative properties.

Let us assume you owned the £500,000 London home discussed earlier. Let us also assume that you are able to rent it out for £1,500 a month. This means that you will make £18,000 per year. This is the 'gross' rental income. Expressed as a 'yield' we would say that this property is generating 3.6 per cent of *gross rental yield* for its owner (£18,000 / £500,000 = 3.6%).

Bear in mind, however, that as a landlord you will usually have to spend a certain amount each year on the maintenance of a property and on fixtures and fittings. There is also a chance that your property will lie void (empty) from time to time if you can't immediately find a tenant to replace one who has left. Both of these issues will obvi-ously have a negative impact on your rental income.

As such, you might prudently assume that a rental property will be void one month a year on average over time and that annual expenditure on maintenance, fixtures and fittings will approximately total another 10 per cent of the gross rental income. Continuing with the example above, this means that the 'net' rental income from the property is £14,700 – you take the gross income (£18,000), and subtract 10 per cent for wear and tear (£1,800) as well as a month's rent for potential void periods (£1,500).

This gives you a net or 'real' rental income of 2.94 per cent. This number is very useful as you can now compare it to the interest you might get on a current account, the return you might make on a share, or the return on a different property.

Capital growth

The rental yield is not the whole story. When we consider how good an investment a given property might be, we should obviously also consider potential capital growth. Let's take the above example again. Imagine that, as has been the case for some years in London, the price of the property increases. Let us assume it does so by 5 per cent, going from £500,000 to £525,000 in one year.

So, in this example, the return from the property is 2.94 per cent from rental income and 5 per cent from capital gain. We can say that the total return is 7.94 per cent. Not bad. Except that those of you who have been paying close attention should realize that there is one more piece of the puzzle to include in our calculation before we can be confident that we have the right number ...

Have you guessed what it is? Hopefully many of you will have realized that we must account for inflation. If we do not, then we are suffering from *money illusion*, as mentioned above.

The UK inflation number at the time I originally wrote this section was 5.2 per cent. You will recall from the section on inflation in Chapter 4 that there are strong arguments to suggest that even this relatively high number was a serious underestimation of the real inflation number at the time.

Nevertheless, just to keep things simple and because using that official number will still enable us to understand the point, if we now use all three components of the return you would make on a property, let us see what number we get in our example.

A simple calculation of the *real* return you make on your property is: net rental yield + capital gain − inflation.

In this example, this gives us: 2.94% + 5% − 5.2% = 2.74%.

Without wanting to complicate things too much, also bear in mind that inflation will affect the value of your rental income throughout the year. With inflation at 5 per cent, the £1,500 you receive in rent in January is worth £75 less at the end of the year. Your real return is, therefore, even lower than the 2.74 per cent stated above.

Tax

Many of you may already have thought of yet another consideration: tax. In the UK any increase in value (capital gain) on the property you live in (if it is considered your 'primary residence') is free of capital gains tax – the tax on your profit on that property when you sell it.

However, when considering property purely as an investment (i.e. if you are looking at a buy-to-let opportunity), capital gains tax will be due on the property when it is sold. The tax paid will depend on your financial situation at the time the property is sold. I will not further complicate this by going into any more detail. The only point I wish to make is that if you are considering the merits of a buy-to-let investment compared to any other investment, you will have to account for the tax you will have to pay if you sell the property, and this makes your real return even lower.

And, finally, the cost of money

Of course, if you are borrowing money from the bank to enable you to own the property this is yet another consideration when working out what your asset is doing for you – and a key one at that! Even though interest rates are at a 300-year low at the moment, you will still realistically be paying a percentage point or two today and, very likely, more than that in future, to borrow the money required to own your property if you don't own it outright. This rate will then have to be subtracted from the percentage return we calculated above. In this example, this would imply that this property asset is actually making a negative real return after you have accounted for inflation, borrowing costs and tax – even with London house prices increasing by 5 per cent a year, as in our example.

I would note at this point that the real return on much of the property market in the UK *has* been a great deal higher than in this example for several years, which is why it has been a great investment for so many people. It is also worth pointing out that property will still perform a great deal better than cash held in a current account, even in the above example, given that rental yield plus capital gain is significantly more than the real interest rate (after inflation) you will earn on money sitting in a bank.

Crucially, you will now understand how to work out the real return on your investment if you buy a property asset. This is extremely useful because it enables you to compare apples with apples if you want to work out the big picture of where it might be best to invest your money at any given time. Let us say that you did some calculations at the beginning of this year. If you thought that a property investment would generate a real return of 2.5 per cent before the cost of borrowing money (for the sake of argument), then you might consider this a pretty poor investment against a share that pays a 5 per cent dividend and has a strong chance of going up 10 per cent or more this year (giving a total return of 15 per cent) or against gold, which increased by more than 10 per cent per annum in sterling terms between 1999 and the present, as we saw earlier in the book.

When I lived in New York, I worked out that I was paying my landlord a 1.6 per cent gross rental yield based on the asking price of my apartment (and not including any assumption for maintenance, fixtures and fittings or void periods). I confess I was amazed by the estate agent in the sales office in my building, who kept telling me what a great investment it would be if I purchased the apartment from my landlord. In the time I lived there, my gold and silver investments went up over 40 per cent, and all I had to do to own them was click my mouse a few times. Compare this to the large amount of administration and complexity I would have had to worry about if I had bought that apartment (not to mention the tiny return I would have made on it).

Property is illiquid and comes with a heavy administrative burden

There is another key point to bear in mind here:

> Property generates a great deal more work than nearly all other investments.

It is very illiquid and costly to buy and sell. Transactions take a long time, with large numbers of payments due to lawyers, surveyors, real estate agents and the government. In addition, the government has a habit of moving the goal posts reasonably frequently to make matters even more complicated.

All of this having been said, compare the examples above to the situation in the 1990s. A good friend of mine's father has always run a small property company. In the early 1990s, after a significant property crash, he was able to acquire properties in and around London that enabled him to achieve 12 per cent rental yields. Given that there had just been a property crash, he obviously had a higher probability of making significant capital gains in the years ahead. He could realistically target real returns on the investments he made at that time to a total of 20 per cent or more. Contrast this with the examples above, which are more in line with today's reality, where the real return is around 2.5 per cent (or even less in New York). It should be obvious that investing in property had a much higher probability of making you serious money in the early 1990s than it does today.

Of course, none of us has a crystal ball but you can hopefully see that, by using the simple calculations outlined above, it is possible to significantly increase your chances of making better big-asset allocation decisions. We will see later on how it is also possible to make reasonably good assumptions about the total return you might make on other asset classes such as shares, bonds and commodities. Please don't think for a moment that you can ever get the timing 100 per cent right, but you can materially increase your chances of getting the timing roughly right, and this fact alone will have a huge impact on your ability to become properly wealthy over the course of your lifetime.

Now let's turn to our other useful measure of intrinsic long-term value in the property market.

Ratio of house prices to salaries

Another key metric worth considering when looking at property is the ratio of house prices to salaries. This is an important measure of affordability and, again, will help you to work out whether property is fundamentally cheap or expensive at any given time. If the average person in Britain is earning £30,000 and the average house costs £180,000, then this ratio is obviously 6:1. Clearly if the average salary is £30,000 and the average house costs £60,000 the ratio is 2:1. Before you laugh, this apparently crazily low ratio has existed in the past. The fact that you are probably imagining that a house couldn't possibly ever only cost only two times your annual salary is a result of anchoring, discussed above.

Another very important idea in finance generally is that of mean reversion. As you may well know, the 'mean' is a type of average. 'Mean reversion' is essentially the fact that anything measured will tend to go back to its average price over the medium to long term. It is worth knowing that the average ratio of UK house prices to salaries over the last several decades is actually between 3:1 and 4:1 depending on which data you look at. This tells us that when the ratio is 6:1, house prices are arguably fundamentally expensive and may well fall; when it is 2:1, house prices are fundamentally cheap and more likely to rise, all other things being equal.

I have included some charts (Figures 5.1–5.3) to illustrate this reality. Some of the charts I used in the previous (second) edition of the book, but I have also added new ones to reinforce the point.

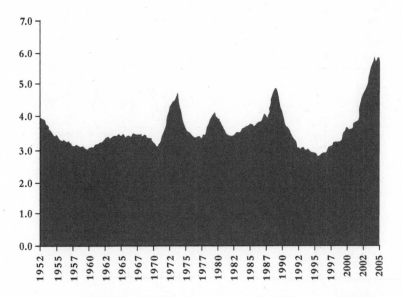

FIGURE 5.1 Ratio of average house prices to average earnings (1952–2005)

As you can see from the far-right-hand side of Figure 5.1, house prices went up a great deal from about 1993 to 2007. Salaries, however, did not keep pace with that increase in price. The result is that in that time frame, for the average person in the UK, houses became twice as expensive using the ratio we are currently considering – from around three times salaries to around six times.

If you were contemplating buying a house in 2006 and had looked at this chart, it should hopefully have been obvious that there was a higher probability that you were buying into the market at a high (expensive) level than at a low (cheap) level, no matter what your estate agent was telling you.

Considering how significant an investment property is, you might have decided to invest your money elsewhere and carry on renting for a while until the ratio came back down from such a high. You could argue that this is what the smart money would have done.

So what happened to prices? As Figure 5.1 implied, prices were too expensive compared to the long run. Figure 5.2 shows what happened next.

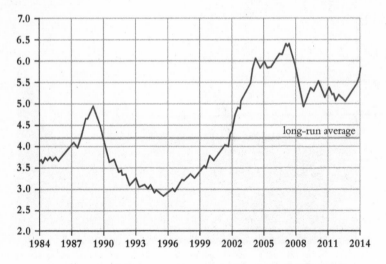

FIGURE 5.2 UK house price to earnings ratio (1984–2014)

As you can see – and you probably know already – 2008 was a difficult year for UK property. Bear in mind that the above chart does not account for either the substantial weakening of the pound in that time or true inflation, so the real story is even worse than it suggests.

I would reiterate that many people who look at the pound value of their property today and compare that to the pound value of the same property several years ago have a high risk of suffering from money illusion. If you compare the price of something in pounds from a few years ago to the price in pounds today, you must take account of real inflation. The fact that their property is 'worth' the same number of pounds does not tell the true story of that asset's actual value. We saw a powerful example of this phenomenon in the last chapter when I made the point that the FTSE 100 would have to be well north of 10,000 to be at *real* (inflation-adjusted) all-time highs versus around 7,500, which is where it actually sits. If you compare the FTSE's *nominal* level today to the same nominal level of a few years ago, you are not comparing apples with apples and precisely the same is true of properties.

This is even more the case in an era where the value of the pound against other major currencies has fallen so significantly. Against the dollar, the pound has fallen from around $2 to the pound to about $1.3 in ten years – that is, by no less than 35 per cent. It is crucial that you understand these other considerations when making vitally important decisions such as whether or not to buy a property. I would repeat that becoming wealthy over your lifetime is a marathon, not a sprint.

Again, I do not claim the ability to predict perfectly when it is time to buy and sell property but you should hopefully feel, intuitively, that understanding what you've just read is of significant value when considering the property market and whether it is a good time to buy that lovely house or flat you're looking at or not.

Of course, there are multiple factors that affect the property market. A big part of what drove the enormous increases between 1993 and 2007 were many commentators' claim that 'It's different this time' – just like they did during the dot-com bubble, and we all know how that turned out.

In truth, there *have* been many reasons for the historically unprecedented strength of British property during the last 20 years or so, especially with regard to London property. The ratio of London house prices to London salaries had powered on to a ratio against income of 8:1 at the time of writing the last edition of this book in 2015 and it now stands at anywhere between 10:1 (according to Nationwide) and 13:1 (according to the Office for National Statistics – ONS) depending on which statistics you look at.

Much has been made in recent years about a lack of supply driving the huge price increases we have seen. There is no question that this has been a factor (although there are actually 1.4 million more properties in the UK than households according to a 2017 ONS study*). Social changes such as large-scale immigration from relatively new EU countries such as Poland, higher divorce rates, and more young people wanting to move out of their parents' homes to live alone have created a higher demand for many types of property.

'Prime' central London property has also been particularly strong for a very long time for many reasons. There has been an explosion in the London financial services industry since the 'big bang' in the late 1980s. In addition, vast numbers of the world's wealthiest individuals see London as an excellent long-term investment (and dare I say money-laundering facility, given how annoyingly weak our controls on such things have been), due to its strong legal system, favourable tax treatment of foreign nationals, and perfect geographical placement for international business, as well as generally loving the quality of life the UK capital affords them and their families.

I would also note in this third edition of my book the significant effect that this multi-decade strength in the London market has had on much of the rest of the UK property market. This has been due to what I would call a 'cascade effect' that has been particularly powerful – something I confess I missed until relatively recently, at least the sheer quantum of it.

At the risk of veering into pastiche here, perhaps a little vignette might explain this point. Imagine that a thoroughly price-insensitive

---

* www.telegraph.co.uk/news/2017/02/03/number-empty-homes-hits-highest-rate-20-years-calling-question/

Russian oligarch, Nigerian oil baron or Chinese property mogul purchases a property in one of the most expensive parts of London, such as Chelsea, Knightsbridge, Holland Park or Mayfair. Imagine, too, that they acquire this property from an elderly British couple who have owned that property since the early 1980s. The elderly couple might have purchased the property for £750,000 then and are now selling it for no less a sum than £15 million (if you think these are nonsense numbers, they are not - I have an actual property in my head as I write this and any central London estate agent will tell you that I'm not making this up).

The key thing here is that the elderly couple have three adult children in their late thirties. Since this couple are already set for life financially, upon receipt of £15 million for the sale of the house, they pass on £5 million to each of their children. Their children then take the entirely understandable decision to look for a much nicer and bigger house for themselves and their families. They can't afford a family home in their parents' neighbourhood, given that there are Russian oligarchs and Nigerian oil barons willing to pay tens of millions, so they look further afield: Fulham, Wimbledon, Richmond, perhaps Battersea, Wandsworth or Clapham (sorry if this is a bit London-centric but I'm trying to make a point that is of relevance to the whole UK market and indeed property markets all over the world – this phenomenon has happened to a greater or lesser extent across the globe).

These three lucky children with £5 million of inheritance money each go looking for houses in these other neighbourhoods and are also reasonably price-insensitive for obvious reasons. They are happy to buy a property in the above-mentioned neighbourhoods that might have even cost less than £500,000 20 years ago for more like £2.5–£3 million.

You then have thousands of lucky homeowners from the outer boroughs of London who have made a seven-figure cash profit. These folk – retired middle managers, school teachers, black cab drivers – you name it – have all dreamed of moving somewhere pretty and rural or even foreign for their retirement. Upon receipt of their £2 million, they then go shopping as cash buyers in places like Kent, Surrey, Hampshire, Devon, rural Scotland (as per my earlier example) or even Thailand, Spain, Portugal, Cyprus or Croatia.

This cascade effect has been enormous, and you could argue may have made the ratio of property prices to salaries less analytically useful than in the past – after all, if a meaningful percentage of the market are cash buyers, their earnings are irrelevant. To illustrate this another way, those three lucky adult children inheriting £5 million each from our example above could all be on minimum wage working for a charity or in a bar for all we know, yet that would have no effect at all on their ability to buy a £3 million house. While it is difficult to quantify how large this cascade effect has been, I would argue that it has certainly been very significant. I think it goes some way towards explaining why the UK property market has disconnected somewhat from the long-run average ratio of property prices to salary and why first-time buyers in London are now willing to pay around ten times salaries, as you can see in Figure 5.3.

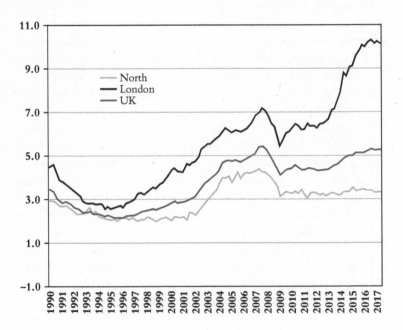

FIGURE 5.3 First-time buyers' house price to earnings ratio
Source: Nationwide

That said, I would argue that this cascade effect is something of a one-off – even if a long and durable one. It is what economists refer to as an 'exogenous shock' and may have run its course to a certain extent – certainly if the anecdotal evidence of what is happening in prime London as I write is anything to go by. When my father purchased a house in south-west London in 1984, Russia and China were communist regimes. There were basically no Russian or Chinese buyers of London property other than embassy staff – a drop in the ocean in the London market. In the last 20 years wealthy Russians, Chinese and plenty of extremely wealthy buyers from elsewhere have pumped untold billions into London property (and UK property by extension as I have explained above) but the supply of such wealthy buyers is finite by definition. We shall see how this plays out in the near future.

My fundamental point here, however, is that there is *some* analytical usefulness in looking at the ratio of house prices to salaries even if such ratios can get pushed to the sorts of extreme deviation from the mean we are seeing today as a result of other factors/exogenous shocks. Mean reversion is extremely powerful. Perhaps London's ratio of earnings to house prices should now be structurally higher than in the past: after all, there were 4 billion people in the world in 1984 versus more than 7 billion today – many of whom are wealthy and many of whom would like to buy a house in London.

That said, any chart you look at tells us we are a very long way north of long-run averages. The evidence of many decades is that this tends not to be sustainable. I would also argue that, outside of unique prestige markets such as London, New York, Sydney, Singapore and Vancouver, the ratio of house prices to salaries is a strong indicator of whether a market is expensive or not and certainly something you should consider when shopping for property.

Interest rates

Perhaps even more important than these factors, however, is the price and supply of money. The price of money, otherwise known as the interest rate, has been held extremely low for a long time by the

policies of central banks on both sides of the Atlantic. This fact, combined with financial deregulation and developments in the global
debt markets, means that there has been an unprecedented amount of
'cheap money' available to anyone who has wanted to buy property
in the last several years.

This more than anything is why the price of housing has been
going up for such a long time and by so much. When considering
where house prices might go from here, it is perhaps most instructive
for us to think about whether there will continue to be a vast supply
of money at low interest rates. To do so, we must understand how
interest rates are set and this means we need to have a basic understanding of bond markets.

If we consider interest rates first, we should be aware that governments have only a certain amount of power when it comes to setting
interest rates. Governments raise money partially from tax but also by
selling bonds. If no one wants to buy a country's bonds when they
are issued, then they are forced to offer them more cheaply. Cheaper
bonds mean higher interest rates because the lower the price of a
bond, the higher the implied interest rate. We will explain this in
more detail in Chapter 7.

At the time of writing the first edition of this book, this is exactly
what was happening across Europe. Interest rates in Greece, Italy,
Spain and even France had been significantly pushed up by a bond
market that refused to pay as much for these countries' debt as before
(and at the time of writing this third edition, Argentina has had to
raise its interest rates as high as 40 per cent in an attempt to prevent
money from flowing out of the country!). The only way for a country to combat this reality is by inventing money to buy their own
bonds. This is essentially what 'quantitative easing' (QE) is. As we have
seen, throughout history the policy of inventing money out of thin
air causes significant real inflation. Higher real inflation means lower
real returns on assets priced in the currency that is deflating. In those
countries that decided to combat this by printing money (particularly the UK and the USA), property markets are caught between the
'rock' of rising interest rates and the 'hard place' of rising inflation.

We must also consider the supply of money (as well as its price).
With many banks in Europe and the USA technically insolvent, these

banks need to keep hold of as much of their cash as possible. This means that even though the UK and US governments, in particular, are doing their level best to keep interest rates low by inventing lots of new money, actual bank lending fell through the floor during the last financial crisis as banks made people jump ever-higher hurdles before qualifying for a loan.

Figure 5.4 captures this point. Total bank lending in the UK for mortgages fell off a cliff.

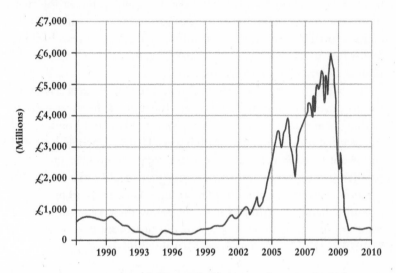

FIGURE 5.4   Gross advances for house purchases in the UK
Source: Nationwide

If there is less money available in any market, then the price of that asset class will fall, all other things being equal. This is a fundamental rule of economics and finance. (I would note that bank lending has since recovered in the UK and the USA – part of why the long-run ratio of prices to salaries is at an abnormal high; it remains to be seen whether this is a good thing.)

At this point, I would like to stress that it is not my intention in this discussion simply to outline a negative case for UK property. One very important feature of the property market is that it is the one asset that most private individuals can borrow meaningful sums of money to buy. We will say more about this shortly. I do, however, want to ensure that having read this section you are better equipped to evaluate the potential of property as an investment over the long run. You must always be thinking about the relative merits of an investment at any given time in your life.

I believe it is not controversial to state that much of the UK property market is currently suffering from historically low rental yields and high capital values (as demonstrated by a high multiple of income ratio). Property investors today must also confront the twin headwinds of the likelihood of increasing interest rates (and inflation) and potentially, again in the near future, a financially weak banking sector that is reluctant to lend money (e.g. to someone who might ultimately buy your property from you).

It is worth noting that many of these issues are largely irrelevant for the prime London market. This is a function of the sheer volume of the global rich who seek to own property in central London, and the fact that most of them are cash buyers. That said, people have said this about London before, and it hasn't stopped a number of crashes occurring throughout history. It seems that in 2018 the market in London is finally coming off quite strongly. I am aware of properties changing hands at 25 to 30 per cent below their asking price, and even the headline numbers are showing significant percentage falls (3.1 per cent in London in April 2018 alone (Halifax)).

The endowment effect

Something else to consider when looking at property prices is another well-documented facet of human psychology: the endowment effect.

Put simply, the endowment effect is when an individual believes that the current price or value of something they own must be the same or more than what they paid for it – or, frequently, what their highest perceived value of it was. Human beings are inherently reluctant to acknowledge when they have made a loss. We are hardwired this way. This is why many people doggedly hold on to shares that are worth much less than they bought them for, instead watching them fall further and further. Professional traders, by contrast, are often explicitly aware of the endowment effect and ruthlessly cut their losses as a result.

What happens in property markets time and time again is that, when the fundamentals turn bearish (negative), there is quite a long lag before prices fall. This is often due, in part, to the endowment effect: in more difficult economic conditions, the number and wealth of potential buyers falls, for all the reasons mentioned above (less bank lending, fewer people with high-paying jobs, fewer employees making bonuses, etc.). Someone who owns a property that was relatively recently valued at, say, £1 million will find that no one is actually willing to buy the property at that level. They will then refuse to accept that the property is now worth, say, £900,000 (the best bid they have actually received). Rather than admit that their property has fallen in value, these sellers will be inclined to hold out for the number they perceive their property to be worth. While this is happening, it should be obvious that the overall number of transactions falls off a cliff.

This is exactly what we have seen in much of the UK market for the last few years: the number of housing transactions has been at a record low in many parts of the country for some time. There is a 'Mexican stand-off' as sellers refuse to accept that their property might be worth less than the high valuations their estate agents have given them in the past, while, for their part, potential buyers simply cannot afford to pay that price.

This stalemate is broken in one of two ways: either economic and lending conditions improve and buyers are willing and able to pay the asking price, or economic conditions deteriorate and an increasing number of sellers are forced to accept the lower prices due to personal circumstances such as losing their job (or dying – increasing death rates are bearish for property as they often imply that more property will be put up for sale. With our ageing population, this will be another key factor in the next few decades.)

You can see that in the second scenario prices may often fall significantly in a short space of time, as waves of sellers finally cave in to lower prices. This is why we have property crashes, as neatly illustrated in Figure 5.2 a few pages back.

Can you really afford to buy?

At this point, I would like to highlight an interesting feature of the French mortgage market. The French have a very different approach to mortgage lending than those of us in the Anglo-American world. In France, with few exceptions, the basic approach is that the total of an individual's monthly mortgage and other debt payments should not exceed one-third of the buyer's gross monthly income.

This approach stands in startling contrast to where the UK and US markets got to in the last two decades, and it goes some way to explaining why the French property market has not suffered the same level of extreme boom and bust. When thinking about the US and UK markets, it is perhaps instructive to realize that until the 1980s they were not dissimilar to the current French market. I would argue that what then changed became a catalyst for the explosion in property prices on both sides of the Atlantic and set the stage for the horrendous property crash that was one of the primary drivers of the financial crisis in the USA – and which we may yet see in the UK in the years ahead.

How financial deregulation made borrowing too easy

Historically, getting a mortgage in both the UK and the USA had always been reasonably hard. An applicant needed a decent deposit, a reasonable track record in their personal finances and often had to demonstrate a grasp of the metrics we have just discussed face to face with a human being. They would have to provide all this to a bank manager (with whom they most likely had some previous relationship) before they were able to borrow money. Most mortgages were also interest and capital repayment products.

This all changed in the 1980s, when both Reagan and Thatcher deregulated the financial services industry. Deregulation meant that it became much simpler for individuals to secure a mortgage. As a result of structural changes in the banking sector, mortgage approvals were increasingly a centralized form-filling exercise, with borrowers no longer having any sort of personal relationship with their bank manager. In addition, many young bank managers and mortgage brokers didn't understand much of what we have discussed in this chapter, let alone this whole book.

As more people were able to secure funding, property prices inevitably increased. Very quickly, a self-fulfilling upward spiral in property markets developed: prices went up, which meant banks relaxed their lending criteria on the assumption that they would always be able to take back an asset that would be worth more in the future than now, thus underwriting the loan. This was only possible because so many bank staff were relatively inexperienced and had only ever seen a rising property market (anchoring at work again), as had the people buying properties. The US and UK property markets became a big game of musical chairs.

Bankers, CEOs and mortgage brokers got paid progressively more as the volume of business, on which their bonuses were made, flourished, giving them little incentive to question what was happening. House prices kept increasing and, thanks to a heady cocktail of money illusion and the endowment effect, people felt wealthier. In turn, politicians were happy, as there is no happier electorate than one that feels wealthy. In the 'noughties', particularly after 9/11, the stage was set for an even more frenzied bull market when Alan Greenspan, chairman of the Federal Reserve, cut real interest rates to less than zero and held them there for years. The real interest rate is the interest rate minus inflation, hence how it can be less than zero. All over the UK and the USA, people were effectively being paid to borrow money to buy property. It was hardly surprising that prices kept going up.

It is not controversial to suggest that, on both sides of the Atlantic, vast numbers of people who would never previously have been able to borrow enough money to buy a house were able to do so. A significant proportion of them had no understanding of basic finance, let alone the financial metrics discussed in this section. I would argue that several million bad decisions were taken across the English-speaking world as a result, without which we could never have had such a huge bull market in property.

Many of the best-informed market commentators saw what was happening and had started highlighting the likelihood of a crash some years ago. As often happens, many of these folk ended up looking foolish as they called the top time and again and then saw the market carry on going up. As John Maynard Keynes said: 'The market can remain irrational longer than you can remain solvent.' Put another way, this is a classic example of 'greater fool theory'. As long as there was a 'greater fool' and an equally foolish (or cynical) bank willing to fund them, the market carried on going up, even though people were making quite ridiculous decisions about the 'value' of the property they were buying.

The Northern Rock situation in the UK was a direct result of this. In the USA the whole edifice began crashing down in 2007, as an increasing number of people were unable to fund their mortgage payments. We have seen how this has played out in the USA: the most overheated markets, such as Miami and Los Angeles, saw prices fall as much as 70 per cent before they started to recover. To give an example of how bad things can get, one project in Seattle was originally trying to sell land for $300,000 a plot. Those plots were eventually sold for just $1,500. I suspect there will be more examples like this in future.

I will repeat that I do not claim to know whether the UK market will suffer as badly as many of the US markets have. There are plenty of arguments to suggest that London in particular will continue to be resilient, the basic reason being that nearly every wealthy foreigner in the world wants to own a place in London (particularly those who are able to get their money out of any country confronting political instability: in the last few years there has been wave after wave of buyers from places like Syria, Greece, the Ukraine, Libya, and various other nations in the Middle East and Africa in particular). The exceptional growth in the developing world I have discussed above has created thousands of new millionaires and a large number of new billionaires, and many of them see London as a great place for their money, especially with the pound cheaper against a basket of foreign currencies than it was a few years ago.

Although at the time of writing, anecdotal as this is, I am aware of one Russian oligarch who – after paying £65 million for a property in London not that long ago – would now accept £25 million and has yet to find a buyer. A significant crash in global financial markets will rob many of these global rich of a significant chunk of their wealth, resulting in less money competing for London property assets. Equally, any legislation aimed at reducing the amount of foreign money that is parked in empty London properties will have an interesting impact on pricing (and would be a most welcome development for those of us who live in London and who have had to endure property prices unquestionably heavily impacted by vast quantities of money from less than savoury sources). We can see the mood changing here at the time of writing, with the treatment of Roman Abramovich who has recently withdrawn his application for a UK visa. This is a very different stance from the UK government as compared to the past.

In addition, the potential loss of many thousands of jobs in London's financial services industry (and the non-payment of bonuses to its workers) implies a significant fall in the amount of money chasing London property assets. We shall see how this plays out in the near future. In the rest of the UK, what happens to property prices will, as ever, depend on supply and demand in each individual market and on how rental yields, total returns and multiples of income compare to the long-run average. They will also continue to be influenced by interest rates, inflation and available bank lending.

I hope that this section has been useful in outlining the key ways of looking at property and how to value it. Armed with these methods, you have a far better chance of making the right decision about when to buy a home and at what price. I fully understand that there is an emotional angle to buying a home that should be taken into account. Property is the only asset where this factor should have an impact on our decision-making process. That said, I still maintain that if you want to maximize your chances of building wealth throughout your lifetime, you should not be afraid to be patient and rent if the metrics and considerations we have looked at in this section suggest that the asset you are looking at is historically expensive. If you find yourself looking for houses and the only ones you like are priced at six times the combined income of you and your partner or spouse, then you should almost certainly consider renting for the time being.

But renting is just 'throwing money away', isn't it?

It is perhaps worth quickly addressing another fallacious belief – that renting is just 'throwing money away' or 'paying someone else's mortgage'. Is it really? Take the example from the beginning of this section: a £500,000 flat being rented for £18,000 a year. Let us imagine that this property loses only 10 per cent of its value in the year ahead (5 per cent because of the market and 5 per cent due to inflation). Our property is now worth roughly £450,000 in real terms.

This £50,000 decrease equates to 2.78 years' worth of rent (£50,000 divided by £18,000). In this scenario, it would be better to be the renter than the owner over the next three years. And this is a fairly conservative example. In the early 1990s many British properties fell by 20 per cent or more (signs are that these sorts of falls are happening right now in many parts of London and the south-east). A 20 per cent fall would mean the renter in my example could rent for five and a half years and still come out ahead of someone who had decided to buy such a property rather than rent it. If you buy a property at a historically high price, then you will almost certainly have been better off renting. Recent changes to stamp duty in the UK have reinforced this reality.

How much *should* you spend on putting a roof over your head?

As we have seen above, the French mortgage market will rarely give anyone a mortgage where the repayments of interest and capital exceed one-third of their monthly income. This might seem crazily conservative to many people in the UK right now but it is actually fair to say that it is crazy that this seems crazy (if you get my drift). Any long-run assessment of roughly what people should spend to put a roof over their head will come up with the number of 'about a third of income'.

This is a good rule of thumb. If your mortgage payments are costing you more than one-third of your monthly income, then, compared to long-run averages, you are likely to be paying more than you should for your home. This is especially true given where interest rates are at the moment.

> Interest rates are the lowest they have been in 300 years, and mean reversion tells us that there is a high probability that they will be higher in the future.

If you are paying a large percentage of your salary on your mortgage with interest rates at this incredible historical low, then you risk having to pay an even higher percentage of your salary in the future. It is only because the UK has seen such an unprecedented bull market in property that so many people have been willing to spend much larger percentages of their salary on their mortgage than they have done in the past.

Of course, moving home is a wrench, especially if you have children, but the alternative is surely worse. If you have arranged your affairs so that your home is a financial millstone around your neck, please try to inspire yourself by imagining the freedom you will feel if you remove that millstone.

If you have to live in a smaller property or a less fashionable neighbourhood, so what? Life is a marathon, not a sprint. The sooner you arrange your affairs so that you can create some savings to invest in assets other than property, the sooner your wealth will start growing meaningfully. If your home is only costing you one-third of your monthly income then it really shouldn't be that difficult to find 10 per cent of that income to invest in other assets.

If you do things properly, in the long term you will be able to have a lovely home, spare cash and the peace of mind that you can afford it. This is surely a far less stressful way of living your life than 'keeping up with the Joneses' and being anxious all the time. It is also more likely to make you properly wealthy in the medium to long term. If the only investment you have in your life is property, then you are missing out on substantial opportunities to grow your money – and your financial situation is fundamentally imbalanced.

Negative equity

I do appreciate that some people reading this may be suffering from negative equity. For those who don't know the term, this means that if you were to sell your house you would end up with less than you need to pay your mortgage back. I can imagine that this is a horribly stressful situation to be in. If you are in negative equity, it may not be immediately obvious that you can benefit from moving home. What you decide to do will be an intensely personal decision, based on your own specific circumstances.

Being completely honest, however, if I found myself in that position today I would be very worried about two things:

1 The very real risk that interest rates are likely to increase in the years ahead. Remember, they are at a 300-year low and this is not sustainable.
2 Obviously linked to this, the risk that the value of my property will fall further, for all the reasons discussed.

There is a chance that, if you hang on, things might get better and the value of your property might bounce, depending on where you are. But the future is unknown, and what if it doesn't? There is an equal chance that your property will fall further in value at the same time as your mortgage payments rise along with interest rates. Given the state of the UK and global economies, I am strongly of the opinion that there is a much higher chance of the latter scenario. Confronted with this reality, wouldn't it be better to bite the bullet, downsize as much as possible – and as soon as possible – and use the money you free up to pay back the rest of that loan?

Other debts you may have

For those of you who have outstanding loans or credit card debts, you will want to pay these off before you start investing. This is because the interest rate you are being charged on any debt is highly likely to exceed the return you will be able to make on investing your money.

Free up as much of your income as you can, then use it to make any repayments as quickly as possible. See your new extra 10 per cent (or more) of cash as a debt-destroying laser beam. And whatever you do, don't despair. Whatever financial situation you are in now, if you take these steps and keep at it, time will fly by and one day you will wake up and find yourself in a much better situation than you ever dreamed was possible. As Bill Gates has said: 'Most people overestimate what they can do in a year and underestimate what they can do in ten years.' (I believe this is a great way of thinking about any area of significant change in our lives: money, health and fitness, relationships ... pretty much anything.) Be bold and make the changes as soon as you can. You will feel great as soon as you do.

Take action now

It is fair to say that a key feature of human nature is inertia. We read things, nod in agreement, realize that we should take some sort of action and then switch the television on. We are all guilty of this.

Remember that if you want to have an income of about £30,000 a year when you retire you need to build a pension pot of around £750,000 at current annuity rates of around 4 per cent. You need to take action so that you can succeed in achieving this. I would strongly recommend that, whatever your situation, you take some action now, even if you have to start small.

If you are already able to save and invest 10 per cent of your income, then please carry on reading. If you are not able to save and invest that proportion of your income right now, then stop reading, grab a pen and paper, and think about how you are going to change your situation so that you can. If you need to move house, then get online right now and start trying to find somewhere 10 per cent cheaper. Alternatively, you could downgrade your car as most people spend far more on cars than is sensible. Where there's a will, there's a way. Set yourself the target of being able to save 10 per cent of your salary within the next three months. Come back to this part of the book once you have succeeded. Good luck.

To conclude

Whatever your current living arrangements, I would hope that you can see that changing them in order to free up extra money each month (if required) is actually quite an exciting proposition, and is surely preferable to carrying on with a large debt burden and the resultant stress.

6

Types of account and the importance of an ISA

'Start by doing what is necessary.'

St Francis of Assisi

So you have managed to free up some money each month. Now you need to optimize your financial services providers. Many people are quite understandably bewildered by the complexity of the financial services industry. Much of the industry likes to keep it that way so they can charge you high fees for bad products.

If you are going to flourish financially, you need to have a much better than average grasp of the type of accounts available to you and the best ones among them. To optimize your finances, you will need to make the best arrangements with your current account and pension, and, most importantly, ensure you have an excellent ISA account. These are easy wins.

Your current account

You would arguably have to be living in a cave not to know what a current account is. The majority of people have one. It is, however, fair to say that most UK current accounts leave a great deal to be desired. First, they offer appalling interest rates; I confess I actually laughed out loud not that long ago when I was queuing at a major high street bank and saw an enormous poster proudly advertising an account that paid 1.8 per cent gross interest.

This was for an account that had a monthly charge 'from £7.95'. Assume, for simplicity, that you are a basic-rate taxpayer and that you are 'lucky' enough to be paying 'only' £7.95 a month for this account. Your net interest rate with this bank would be 1.44 per cent. On this basis, you would have to keep more than £6,625 in that account just for the interest you earned to pay off the monthly charges. I'm amazed a bank would even advertise such a terrible product but there it was plastered on the wall of this branch. Why do we let them get away with it?

You will probably be aware that the big UK banks have been caught mis-selling products, time and time again. In 2012 one of the major UK banks was fined several million pounds for mis-selling a product to pensioners. We need only look, too, at the payment protection insurance (PPI) scandal and the long-standing consumer campaign against unfair overdraft charges.

Importantly, the major banks' other financial products tend to be nowhere near as good as those offered by less well-known players in the market. Their ISA accounts, for example, tend to offer a tiny fraction of the flexibility and choice you can find elsewhere, yet they often charge higher fees. The only reason they can get away with this is because they have such a captive client base. Many people have no idea that they can (and should) go somewhere else. We will discuss this further in the section on ISAs later in this chapter.

Despite all the above, I do not advocate changing your current account. In my experience, it is virtually impossible to get away from these issues, no matter which bank you use in the UK. What is key is that you optimize how you use your current account. I would hope that, having read this far, you would never accept a return of 1.8 per cent gross on your money. My advice with regard to your main bank is simply to keep as little money with it as possible.

Work out what you need to live on each month, add a margin of error, and then ensure that any surplus is *automatically* paid every month into accounts that will enable you to make real money.

For most people in the UK, the most important of these will be your ISA account, but we must also consider your pension situation, so let us look at that first.

Your pension

I would be surprised if anyone reading this has not heard the word 'pension'. Nevertheless, I hope you will forgive me if I suggest that the vast majority of people have, at best, only a basic understanding of what a pension is, what can be done with it, and what issues they need to be aware of in the years ahead. A lack of knowledge about pensions is yet another opportunity for much of the financial services industry to sell you bad products with high costs.

There are two main types of pension:

1 One provided by the government or state
2 Private or occupational pensions built up by an individual, often with the help of their employer.

Government/state pensions

Earlier in the book, I made the point that state pension systems all over the world are essentially bankrupt – they are really just a great big confidence trick or pyramid scheme that is at risk of collapsing at some point in the future. To many people, this seems like a controversial statement. I think it is worth briefly demonstrating why it is not.

The state pension is unquestionably doomed due to a combination of enormous demographic change and the complete failure by more than one generation of politicians to address the implications of that change. In 1909 the UK government started to provide a small pension to people over the age of 70. If you think about it, this wasn't actually that much of a financial commitment. Life expectancy in 1909 was far shorter than it is today, and relatively few people survived into their seventies. The ratio of workers to old-age pensioners was very high – that is to say, a high percentage of the population were working and paying tax, and a very small percentage indeed were retired and drawing a pension.

In the hundred-plus years since then, this situation has been turned completely on its head. There is perhaps nowhere more illustrative of this change than Japan. When the Japanese launched their generous welfare state after the Second World War there were around 45 workers for every pensioner. This ratio is forecast to be 2:1 by 2020. Arguably, it is this more than anything that accounts for the fact that Japan's stock market is still trading far below its 1989 peak and the country's economy has been struggling for decades. The Japanese Nikkei index peaked at over 39,000 in 1989. Today, nearly 30 years later, it is trading at around 22,500. There is a huge and inescapable black cloud on the Japanese economy's horizon: more old people than the rest of their society can afford.

Sadly, this is happening all over the developed world. Modern countries are burdened with social security systems that were put in place when the entire structure of their societies was completely different from today's.

Faced with this demographic reality, what governments all over the Western world needed to do in the last few decades was to ensure that, more than ever before, we all saved and invested. Sadly, most of them did the exact opposite. Rather than running budget surpluses, and saving and investing to provide sorely needed capital for our futures, governments all over the developed world have consistently spent far more than they have earned in tax receipts. They have then made up the difference by borrowing on global bond markets and, more recently, simply 'inventing' money out of thin air (quantitative easing).

They have also done a terrible job at ensuring that people make the effort to sort out their own financial affairs, primarily because finance is such an unpopular subject. You don't win elections telling people they need to spend less and save and invest more – or at least no politician in recent decades has been brave enough to articulate this point. Australia and Norway are wonderful exceptions. From the mid-1980s Australians have had an extraordinarily good national pension system, which has forced most people to save for their retirement, and Norway has done a fantastic job investing the proceeds of its oil industry. (I would contend that Australia's world record-breaking 26 years (!) without a recession might have something to do with this policy but this debate is very likely outside the scope of this book.)

In the USA, however, matters have been quite differently handled: Figure 6.1 shows the sheer scale of what successive administrations have done/are doing in terms of borrowing.

This graph is pretty extraordinary, especially when you look at the incredible acceleration in borrowing over the last few years, but even this fails to tell the full story. If you add up the *unfunded liabilities* of the US government – that is to say, the money they are committed to spending on pensions, healthcare and so on in the future – the number is well over $200 trillion. This is why Niall Ferguson, Professor of History at Harvard University, describes government accounts as 'essentially fraudulent'.

To put this in perspective: the US economy generates about $18.5 trillion of economic output each year. If we use the $200 trillion number, this implies that the USA owes *11* times what it makes. This is like you earning £30,000 a year and having £330,000 of credit card debt. The interest alone would cost you most, if not all, of your annual income (and that is with interest rates at a 300-year low, remember).

Many analysts think the situation is even worse, and the $200 trillion could prove to be a conservative estimate in the long run. But

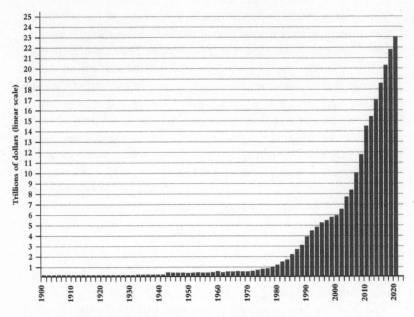

FIGURE 6.1 US national debt (1900–2020)
Source: www.usgovernmentdebt.us

even using the official numbers, we can see just what a mess American finance is in and, most importantly, how the politicians are totally failing to deal with it:

US tax revenue:	$2,170,000,000,000
Federal budget:	$3,820,000,000,000
New debt:	$1,650,000,000,000
Official national debt:	$14,271,000,000,000
Recent budget cuts:	$38,500,000,000

Thirty-eight-and-a-half billion dollars of budget cuts might sound like a good effort from Washington, but take away eight zeros and pretend this is a normal household budget and things become much clearer. The numbers above are basically the same as those in the following list.

Annual family income:	$21,700
Money the family spent:	$38,200
New debt on credit card:	$16,500
Outstanding balance on credit card:	$142,710
Total budget cuts:	$385

These figures come from 2010/11 – the numbers are actually far worse today. As you can see in Figure 6.1, national debt in the USA is now more like $21 trillion, up from the $14.3 trillion quoted above. US debt is highly likely to get even worse under President Trump. The point I'm making here is that, year after year, these problems get worse but there is no political will to take the necessary steps to solve them. The situation in the UK is no different. I find the debate about 'austerity' quite maddening given that UK government expenditure as a percentage of GDP is still around the 40 per cent mark. On both sides of the Atlantic the only way out of this situation, in the eyes of the politicians at least, seems to be by printing (inventing) vast sums of money.

As we have seen, inventing money devalues that money through inflation. This has happened time and time again throughout history.

You will not get a pension you can live on from the government. As a result, Western governments have basically two choices when it comes to pensions:

1 Own up to the fact that they can't afford to pay people a pension any more.
2 Print vast amounts of 'fictional' money with which to pay people a 'pension', thus creating rampant inflation.

The result for you will be the same: either you don't get a pension, or you get a pension paid in money that can't buy much of anything any more. To a certain extent this has already happened.

So far, governments on both sides of the Atlantic have taken the money-printing option, and it is extremely likely this will continue, for the simple reason that they can get away with it because so few people understand what is going on (remember the John Maynard Keynes quote about only 'one man in a million' understanding inflation).

For obvious reasons, a politician who stands up and says, 'Sorry, you can't have a pension, we just can't afford it any more', has a much shorter lifespan than one who says, 'We are taking positive steps to solve the financial crisis with a £100 billion package of quantitative easing (QE).'

Both statements have essentially the same result but only a small minority of people understand this. No matter what your political inclinations, no matter how you view the role of government, the simple fact is that we can't afford to pay for society's pension and healthcare requirements the way we have for the last few decades. There are just too many retired and retiring people compared to productive workers. If you are below the age of about 50 and want to have enough wealth to live on in the future, then you will have to make your own provision for that future. Let us, therefore, turn our attention to private pensions.

Private/company pensions

The state pension, then, is very small and highly unlikely to exist in any shape or form by the time you retire, at least if you are any younger than about 50 today. As far as I'm concerned, it is therefore of limited relevance to your financial future. We must look instead at the various kinds of personal or private pensions that exist.

Final salary or defined benefit pensions

The first of these worth mentioning is called a final salary or defined benefit pension. These 'do what they say on the tin' in that you are guaranteed a certain level of income in retirement. This kind of pension is relatively rare these days other than in the public sector. The reason for this is that they are basically too expensive for any private company to be able to afford to provide. Only the government, which is able to invent money out of thin air, can even think about guaranteeing a certain level of income to people for decades after they retire.

All you need to know about final salary pensions is that, if you are lucky enough to have one, be very grateful and don't tamper with it. That said, you should be aware that many of these schemes are currently in the red. If you have a final salary pension, you should call the provider and establish where you stand in terms of what you might expect to get back at retirement age. If the news isn't good, then you will want to ensure you are taking steps to make up for any shortfall. We will look more at the specifics of how you might do this later in the book.

That having been said, you might also be interested in finding out what the transfer value of the scheme might be if you do have a defined benefit or final salary pension, given that it could be a surprisingly large number.

To explain: back in the 1980s when interest rates were, say, 10 per cent, if you had a defined benefit (final salary) pension that was paying you, say, £10,000 a year (to keep the maths easy), this implied that the theoretical 'pot' that was there to pay you that return was £100,000. Your employer (or the state) had a notional £100,000 of pension pot earmarked for the purposes of paying you an annual income. With the interest rate at 10 per cent they could therefore pay you £10,000 a year of income without touching the pot.

Now imagine what happens with 5 per cent interest rates (again – to keep the maths simple). You should see that the implied pot required to pay you that £10,000 a year with interest rates at 5 per cent is now £200,000. All other things being equal, the 'value' of an income stream (your guaranteed £10,000 per annum of defined benefit/final salary pension) today is about two times what it was when interest rates were two times higher (£200,000 x 5% = £10,000 as opposed to £100,000 x 10% = £10,000).

This means – broadly – that the current transfer value of a defined benefit pension (i.e. swapping your guaranteed £10,000 per annum of income for the implied pension pot that supports it) is about the highest it has ever been because, quite simply, interest rates are the lowest they have ever been and the two are inversely related.

What this means is that if you felt you could return more than 5 per cent, say, on the pot, you might be better off transferring your

defined benefit pension into a self-managed pension before interest rates go back up again. It is important to stress that it is utterly
crucial that you would only do this after careful consideration and
taking professional advice. First, you must ensure that you don't end
up making 1 per cent on your pot if you transfer out (thus making
yourself worse off).

Secondly, you must ensure you are confident you are not at risk
of becoming a 'Lamborghini pensioner' – that is, taking your big six-
figure transfer value to spend on said sports car, rather than investing
prudently for your retirement.

Defined contribution pensions

Leaving aside the state pension and the increasingly rare animal that is
a final salary pension, we should now turn our attention to the broad
category of pension most people have: a private pension of some
kind. Even in the days before the state pension was at risk of disap-
pearing entirely, it wasn't very much money anyway. Many people
aspired to retire on a much higher income than what they would get
from the state. As a result, the government realized that it would be
a good idea to encourage anyone who wanted to save and invest to
provide for his or her own future. For several decades now, governments have permitted individuals to make their own private pension
arrangements, often organized through their employer.

As a result, if you work for a big company, you are likely to have a
pension provided by your employer. This is usually known as a 'work-
place', 'occupational' or 'company' pension. If you are self-employed
or work for a smaller company, you may have your own private pension that will invariably have been arranged for you by a financial
adviser. This is likely to be a self-invested personal pension, or SIPP. If
you have your own company, you may have something similar called
a small self-administered scheme (SSAS), which will probably also
have been set up by a financial adviser.

A SIPP or SSAS is simply a pension account that gives you the
same tax benefits as an occupational pension, but also allows you to
invest in a wide variety of assets and make your own decisions about
what to invest in.

Although it is by no means always true, few occupational schemes are as good a vehicle for pension investment as a SIPP or SSAS. This is simply because SIPP and SSAS accounts are so flexible, and likely to be far more so than the pension scheme your company runs. Large companies tend to outsource their pension schemes to one pension provider. The result is that employees in a company scheme will often have only quite a narrow range of options to invest their pension in.

Those of you who have an occupational pension with your employer may find you have little freedom to invest your money how you like. Your company will very possibly offer a limited product with fairly tight parameters on the type of funds you can choose. If this is the case, don't worry too much. There will still be a way to optimize what you do have in that scheme. We will get to this when we look more specifically at how to invest and what to invest in. Your approach will be broadly the same for your pension and ISA money.

Crucially, for those of you who do have one of these pensions, do you know what it is invested in? British shares? American bonds? Cocoa futures? If you are anything like most people, you will either have no idea at all or only a relatively vague idea. You will almost certainly also have no idea what fees you are paying for these funds and these may be higher than they need to be.

Above all, don't worry about your lack of knowledge. Out of several hundred people I have asked in the last few years, only one person could tell me about their pension arrangements in detail. Amusingly, those I asked (and who *couldn't* tell me) included nearly everyone I know who has a high-powered job in finance. As for me, for the first several years of my career I certainly couldn't have told you much about my pension arrangements, that's for sure.

This pension situation, therefore, is one of the first things you should sort out. It won't take long. You simply need to ensure that you are doing the best you can with your pension money. If you don't know what your pension is invested in or what costs you are paying, it is unlikely that any pension you are building up is working anywhere near as hard for you as it could be. Over time, this could have a six- or even seven-figure impact on your life.

Whether you are employed or self-employed, any pension you have will almost certainly be a *defined contribution* pension – that is to say one where you put in a certain amount, and what you get back at the end is a function of both how much you have invested over the years and, far more importantly, your investment performance. The main differences between saving your money in a pension fund compared to elsewhere is the tax treatment and access to your money. Money saved in a pension account is not taxed when it goes in. This is obviously good news. The quid pro quo, however, is that you are not able to touch that money until you retire – which could be many years from now depending on your age. This is less good news, as we shall see.

Controversial advice

Now, I am going to make what might seem to be quite a controversial suggestion: if you don't *already* have a pension and if, like most people, you have less than £1,666 a month to save and invest (the current annual ISA allowance divided by 12), you might actually consider not organizing a pension at all.

The reason for this is simple: although you get a tax break on any money you put into a pension, you are essentially not able to access it until your retirement – when you are 55, at the earliest. This may be many years from now. Given the uncertainty we are currently dealing with and the parlous state of government finances, I see a high risk that future generations of politicians will find your pension pot simply too hard to resist as a source of funding. If you are in your twenties, thirties or even forties, I think it is a substantial gamble to assume that the UK pension system will exist in anything like its present form by the time you retire. Remember that the government is essentially bankrupt. To me, there is too much uncertainty about what may or may not happen to any money you commit to a pension account and I would much rather you have immediate access to your money.

There are many examples throughout history of governments passing laws that permit them to take control of pension assets. If you think this is something that hasn't happened for decades, think again. One relatively recent example was in late 2008, when the

Argentinian government passed a law to nationalize $30 billion of private pension money. Thousands of middle-class Argentinians who were saving diligently lost control of their own money. Using Argentina as an example might seem like a crazy comparison but it really isn't. By some measures, Argentina in 2008 was actually in a better position financially than the UK is in today.

Few people remember that former Labour Prime Minister Gordon Brown changed the tax treatment of dividends in pension accounts in 1997. This resulted in £5 billion less per year for holders of pension accounts. Even more recently, in March 2015, the then Conservative Chancellor, George Osborne, reduced the lifetime pension allowance in his budget speech, moving an estimated £600 million from pensioners to the public coffers. This 'lifetime allowance' has been reduced from £1.8 million in 2012 to £1 million in 2016, having come down via £1.5 million and £1.25 million. Each time the threshold is reduced, the government is effectively taking money from people who have the self-discipline to save and invest wisely.

I would stress that I have no political axe to grind here: in the same month that George Osborne reduced the allowance again, former Labour leader Ed Miliband announced his intention to use pension assets to fund a reduction in student fees and underwrite his 'compulsory jobs guarantee' policy. Tom McPhail, who heads up pensions research at leading UK financial services company Hargreaves Lansdown, reacted to this news at the time by saying: 'We need our politicians to take a long-term view rather than raid the pensions piggy bank to pay for other policies.'

This is why it may be a better plan for you to focus on building your wealth in an ISA than in a pension. Some might argue that ISA accounts are no safer than pension accounts in this respect, in that any future government may raid ISA assets as well as pensions. I would suggest that ISA funds are less likely to suffer this fate for one main reason: the aggregate sum invested in ISA accounts is a fraction of what is held in pension funds.

If a future government is going to undertake the significant administrative burden of getting new legislation through Parliament to get their hands on our savings in one form or another, it would be far more worthwhile to do this vis-à-vis pensions than ISAs.

A cynic might also argue that ISAs tend to be owned, in the main, by Britain's elite – including those who would be legislating any such changes in the future.

This is why you must think about your own personal circumstances when deciding how to allocate your hard-earned readies to regulated accounts such as pensions and ISAs. So let's look in a bit more detail at a few different scenarios to see what the best course of action might be depending on those circumstances.

Your pension is matched by your employer

First, I would like to stress that, despite the points I made above, if you work for a big company that will *match* any contributions you make to your occupational pension account, then it is probably a good idea that you maximize your contributions to this account. That is to say that, for you, your pension should almost always be prioritized over an ISA.

Investment is all about risk versus reward. It seems highly likely that the fact that you are getting an automatic 100 per cent return (reward) from your employer (in matching your contributions) will more than make up for the risk from future governments moving the pension goalposts. If you have a defined contribution occupational pension and a generous employer, then by all means max out your pension contributions to max out their matched contribution. Just make sure that all that money is going into a group of assets that are diverse in terms of type and geography – that is, that you 'own the world'. We look at how to do this specifically later in the book.

The only scenario I foresee in which those of you with this kind of generous employer should *not* follow this advice is if you intend to leave conventional employment any time soon – for example to start your own company. As I have mentioned, another negative aspect of pensions generally is that you are basically not able to touch any money that goes into it until you reach the age of 55 at the earliest.

If you are considering the entrepreneurial route, you may want to have as much cash available to you as possible when you start your business. It probably goes without saying, therefore, that you will want to ensure you keep the maximum amount of your savings immediately accessible rather than locked up, even if your employer is willing to double your contributions for you.

So, unless you foresee a need to get your hands on as much cash as possible in the near future for these sorts of personal reasons, those of you with a generous employer should max out any pension contributions which will be matched by said employer. You constitute an exception to my 'ISA over pension' rule.

You have a large income

There is another type of person who might also consider making pension arrangements: someone who enjoys a very significant income versus the UK average. Why? Well, in the tax year 2018/19, each individual is able to invest £20,000 in an ISA account, which equates to £1,666 a month. They are also able to make £11,700 a year of capital gain without paying any tax. This implies that someone on a high salary could put £1,666 a month into an ISA account (or twice that for a married couple). They could then put a sizeable additional sum to work in other investments, such as the stock market, in a very tax-efficient way. If they invested, for example, £100,000 and made an 11 per cent return, they would still not be subject to any tax (given their £11,700 capital gains allowance). In fact, a couple could invest £100,000 each on that basis and, as financial transfers between spouses remain untaxed, this money could come from either party. Only then might they consider using the tax benefits of a pension account.

An investment account running order

This is precisely why many people might actually think about investment in this order:

1 Maximizing contributions to a good-quality ISA account.
2 Buying precious metals. We look at this later in the book.
3 For those who still have any money left, investing in other financial investments *outside* of an ISA account (often in something called a general investment account, or GIA)

and/or using spread betting, given that this is yet another potential source of tax-free profit.

4 For anyone able to max out their ISA, buy precious metals, max their capital gains allowance and allocate a sensible amount to spread betting but who still has money left over – they could then consider putting additional funds to work in a pension account.

The combination of successful ISA investment, buying bullion regularly, maximizing annual capital gains allowance and the educated use of a spread betting account thereafter will be more than enough for the vast majority of people to achieve suitably ambitious financial goals without troubling the tax authorities and do so without locking their money up for decades too! This is yet another investment advantage we have today and in the UK in particular, which too few people know about and make use of.

Inheritance tax and auto-enrolment

Before we move on to look at ISAs, precious metals and so on in more detail, there are two final points on pensions that I would like to address. First, recent changes to the tax rules made by George Osborne mean that you can now pass on assets in your pension account to your children without paying inheritance tax. For someone wealthy, whose total assets exceed the current inheritance tax threshold of £325,000 (£650,000 per married couple), this could be helpful and some might argue I have failed to recognize this advantage of a pension over an ISA.

But I would argue this is actually not that relevant. Remember that anything you pass on to your children seven or more years before you die is free of inheritance tax anyway. If you are organized about it, then I think the advantages of flexibility and access to your money (by using the accounts we are talking about here) outweigh this inheritance tax advantage. That said, the key here is to be organized. If you get to your fifties and you've built a good deal of wealth using non-pension accounts, then you might consider making some large payments into a pension account for several years at that point to gain the tax benefits (assuming they still exist – which I think is far from a safe assumption).

The other issue I need to at least mention, and which you may have already read about, is something called 'auto-enrolment'. Most workers in the UK are in the process of being automatically enrolled in a pension scheme by their employer. Between 1 and 3 per cent of a worker's salary will be paid into a pension fund that will then be matched by between 1 and 4 per cent by their employer.

You are permitted to opt out of this but I think this will almost certainly be more hassle than it is worth, given how relatively small the sums involved are. I would advise permitting your employer to sort out this pension for you, making sure this money is going into the best investments allowable (more on this shortly), and then just ensuring that you are *also* making payments into an ISA (and other vehicles if you can afford it).

The three categories of pension arrangements

To summarize, then, you will fall into one of the following three categories regarding your pension arrangements.

Category one

You have a pension with your employer, who makes contributions, and/or can only invest in products offered by your employer's pension scheme.

Action to consider: Ensure you own the best funds available to you under your employer's existing scheme. You will understand better how to do this once you have read the sections on investment that follow. If you are paying a reasonable chunk of your salary into the pension scheme but your employer does not match these payments, and assuming you have the option to take that money as cash, you may want to consider paying it into an ISA account instead. Whether you decide to do this or not will depend on what you think of your company's pension arrangements, what your past performance has been, and what the costs of the pension product are as compared to your ISA account. You will understand how to evaluate these factors once you have read the rest of this book.

Category two

You are self-employed or working for a company that does not provide you with a pension but you have a pension pot built up from previous employment.

Action to consider: Do not make any further contributions to that pension unless you can afford to save more than your ISA allowance of £1,666 a month. With your existing pension pot, ensure you own the best funds available to you within your scheme. Again, after reading the rest of this book you will have a better idea of how to do this.

You may also consider opening a SIPP (personal pension) account and transferring across what you have saved so far. If you choose the right provider, this should give you enormous freedom in terms of what you can invest those funds in and will quite possibly cut down the fees you are paying, thus improving your performance.

Category three

You do not currently have any pension arrangements.

Action to consider: If you do not have a pension at the moment and have less than £1,666 a month to save and invest, which describes the vast majority of people, it may not be worth you opening a pension account. Focus instead on your ISA arrangements. If you are lucky enough to be able to save and invest more than £1,666 a month in the future then you can come back to this question and think about saving the surplus in a pension vehicle of some kind. As we have seen above, you may also consider making stock market investments outside of an ISA account, even before making payments to a pension, as you will be able to make £11,700 of capital gain per annum before you have to pay any capital gains tax, over and above the tax benefit you get from an ISA. (Please be aware that these numbers are correct at the time of writing but may change in future.)

To conclude on pensions

It is fair to say that the whole issue of what to do about your pension arrangements is probably the most complicated topic we look at in this book. If you are still confused about your best course of action, particularly if your existing pension arrangements are complex, then it is probably appropriate for you see a good financial adviser. This is particularly the case if you are already at or very near retirement age. Many people's financial affairs as they hit retirement are relatively complicated – especially given how many changes have been made to the pension rules in recent years.

The 'set and forget' investment strategy for building wealth we will look at in this book is intended to be as simple to follow as possible and very much aimed at *growing* your money. You can use it no matter how complex your various pension arrangements are *up to* retirement but, once *at* or near retirement, you are likely best served seeking some professional advice.

On retirement, you will need to think about switching your investments from 'accumulation' to 'income' (more on this later), about whether you might take a lump sum out of your pot, about how much of your money to draw down going forwards, and all sorts of other considerations such as what to do with any property you own. If you are at or near retirement, then I would strongly urge you to consider seeing a financial adviser. You should just make sure that they know what they are doing and do not charge too much for their services – something we will look at later in the book.

For everyone else, however, let us now turn our attention to what, for most people in the UK, is arguably the most important vehicle for you to build wealth – your ISA account.

Your (N)ISA

Even if you set aside my thoughts about pensions, if you really want to make giant strides in terms of your financial situation then you need to start saving some money from your income each month anyway. No matter what your view of the UK pension system, you basically can't touch pension money until you are 55 at the earliest.

If you plan on building fun-money sooner than it takes for you to go grey, then you will need to save and invest cash separately from any pension arrangements you have. When you see how much you can make doing this you will want to do it. Start as soon as possible.

As you will have read above, if at all possible you should aim for at least 10 per cent of your salary after tax being *automatically* paid into your investment pot every month. Once you have set this up, you will very quickly adjust to your new financial reality. After you get used to it and you start seeing your pot grow, you might even consider upping the percentage to 12, 15 or even 20 per cent of your income. The more you invest, the faster you will become truly wealthy.

Whatever you manage to save, the upside of doing so is life-changing and, due to the fundamental mathematical laws of compound interest, highly likely to make you a serious amount of money over time, as long as you are doing the right thing with your money in the right kind of accounts.

As long as you are saving less than the £1,666 per month we mentioned above, you will be able to invest all of this money using an Individual Savings Account (ISA). Obviously, this applies to the majority of people. Please note that, since the first edition of this book was published in 2012, the ISA has been replaced by what some firms call the 'NISA' or 'New ISA'. This new product is even better than what came before, as it gives you more flexibility with what you can do with the account.

What is an ISA?

An ISA is simply a type of investment account in which the government lets you invest a certain amount of money each year. Crucially, any gains you make on the money in that account are not subject to tax. We are very lucky in the UK to enjoy the existence of such a product. You can open an ISA account with a number of different companies in the UK, from the main high street banks to a number of more specialist organizations, such as stockbroking firms. To open an ISA account all you need to do is fill in a form or two and transfer some money into the account, either as a lump sum or a monthly payment.

Most ISA providers will let you open an account with as little as £100 to begin with or with a minimum of £25 a month of regular payments, for example by direct debit or standing order.

Cash versus stocks and shares

This is a very important distinction that far too few people understand. Until 2014 there were two broad categories of ISA account: the 'cash ISA' and the 'stocks and shares ISA'. A cash ISA was not that different from a current account. You opened an account and deposited cash. The only difference was that you got a slightly higher interest rate, depending on who you opened your ISA with, and you didn't have to pay tax on any interest you made (the main point of ISA accounts generally). By now it should be clear that I would take a dim view of holding cash in your ISA account. With real inflation at the sort of level it is at today, you will most certainly be losing *real* wealth on any money you hold as cash, as the interest rate you are likely to receive will be lower than real inflation.

A stocks and shares ISA was a slight misnomer in that it simply enabled you to invest any money held in that ISA account in a wide variety of assets (if you had an account with one of the better providers). That is to say that you could buy products such as bonds and commodities, as well as just 'stocks and shares'. Today's NISA (new ISA) is really just an amalgamation of the two types, meaning that you can choose to have up to £20,000 a year (at the time of writing) in any combination of cash or investments, at your discretion.

It is shocking how many educated people have been unaware of the existence of stocks and shares ISAs, believing that you could only ever achieve the pathetically low returns offered by cash ISAs, and who therefore ignored the ISA as a financial product altogether. Such individuals (if married) have missed out on the opportunity to shelter significant amounts of money from tax for many years. For some, this may have resulted in a seven-figure administrative failure. The fact that so many people fall into this category, including the editor of the first edition of this book, whom I employed on the basis that they had expertise in financial services (!), is a massive black mark against the mainstream financial services industry.

If you are to have any chance of making a *real* return on your money, you need to invest in things that have a chance of outperforming inflation. We will look in more detail at how you might do this, and at the sorts of investments you might put in your ISA, in the next few chapters. For now, it is enough for us to focus on ensuring that you do open an ISA account – and that you do so with one of the best providers in the UK market so that you get the flexibility you need to succeed, at the lowest possible cost.

Finding the best ISA providers

As you might imagine, over the years I have spent a great deal of time looking at various different ISA providers in the UK market and have personally had accounts with no fewer than eight of them. I will not name my favourite ISA providers here since this book is, by its very nature, a static information source. I am well aware of who I think the best ISA providers are at the time of writing but financial services companies are constantly launching new accounts and improved products. As such, you can find specific information about the firms I believe to be the best in the UK market on our website (plainenglishfinance.co.uk/).

Avoid the high street banks

It can be argued that the high street banks are a bad place to have an ISA. As we have seen, the ideal ISA account will enable you to buy a massive range of shares or funds and will ensure that you can do so at low cost. If you open an ISA with many of the main high street banks, you will generally only be able to choose from a restricted range of in-house ISA funds. These tend to be limiting in terms of what assets you can end up owning in your ISA.

This is another key reason why so many people have a negative view of investing – if the only ISA (or other investment account) you have ever owned is a high-cost, low-performance product or cash ISA from a high street bank, you are extremely likely to have seen very little happen to your money over the years and you will have a pretty dim view of investment generally, and ISAs in particular.

Tax-free profits

The key thing about having an ISA is that you will not have to pay tax on the profits you make from any investments you make within that account. This is hugely beneficial to growing your money more quickly. To give an example from my own experience, I invested my 2010–11 ISA in silver. I was lucky enough to sell my position for a 163 per cent profit about eight months after my original purchase. This meant that I had turned my original ISA allowance of £10,200 for that year into about £27,000. If I had done this outside of an ISA account, I would have owed the government nearly £5,000 worth of tax. Thanks to the ISA, I owed them no tax on those profits whatsoever. Of course, this was an exceptionally good 'trade'. In no way am I suggesting that you will regularly make these sorts of returns – but it does show that they are possible.

As a reminder: if you are in the happy position of having more than £1,666 a month (or £20,000 a year) to invest, you will be able to make up to a further £11,700 of tax-free profit per year on investments outside your ISA account. This is the size of your annual personal capital gains allowance. You should simply ensure you have a non-ISA/'normal' stocks and shares dealing account with the company that keeps your ISA money (sometimes called a General Investment Account, or GIA). Do your best to make just under £11,700 a year in profit in that account, and ensure you crystallize that profit each tax year.

For the vast majority of people, therefore, it is possible to make life-changing profit from stock market investments without having to pay any tax. I would repeat that far too few people understand this reality – a real failure of our education system in my view.

The Lifetime ISA

Before we continue to the next section, I should just take a moment to mention something called the Lifetime ISA, or LISA.

The government introduced this new type of ISA in April 2017. It is only of relevance to people over the age of 18 and under the age of 40. If you are over the age of 40, you are not permitted to have one.

The main point of a Lifetime ISA is that the government will add 25 per cent on top of whatever you invest in the account, up to a maximum of £1,000 per year. If you are under 40 years old and put £4,000 into a Lifetime ISA account, the government will then top it up with another £1,000.

At first glance, this looks great – but stops being so, in my view, when you read the small print and realize what a fiddle it all is. To explain: you can only *keep* the 25 per cent bonus money when you withdraw money from the ISA:

1 To buy your first home using a mortgage plus a conveyancer or a solicitor (as they will have to administrate the LISA for you to keep your bonus money) and where that home costs less than £450,000

2 If you are over 60 (i.e. 20 or more years away from now)

3 If you are terminally ill.

If you want to withdraw the money in any other scenario, you will have to pay back the government bonus.

My view, therefore, is that you should think quite seriously about whether or not you are going to buy a property worth less than £450,000 any time soon and whether all the faffing about having a separate LISA account and doing all that extra paperwork when you buy a house is worth it for the sake of £2,000–3.000. It may well be, but it may also be a total waste of time, for example if you're going to want to buy a more expensive property or if you're not going to buy a property for some years, by which time the government of the day may have changed the rules anyway.

This is clearly a matter of personal choice, but I think that there is every chance a future government will change the Lifetime ISA terms or get rid of it all together. I personally think that using one is a whole load of extra hassle and administration for a pretty marginal gain, and would rather simply have a normal ISA account and do my best to maximize contributions to it every year.

The spread betting account

Before we finish this section on the various different types of financial account you might consider, we should very briefly cover something called 'spread betting'. Many people have not heard of spread betting but, for an individual who is prepared to put the time in, it can be a powerful way to make money from investing. If you do spend the time to learn how it works, it is one of the most powerful tools for making money available today, and we are lucky that we have access to it in the UK, as there are relatively few countries in the world with a developed spread betting industry. It is illegal in the USA, for example, which is a great shame for Americans. So what is spread betting, and how does it work? The first thing to say is that it is, without doubt, a method of investing that is worth using only if you are prepared to put in a decent amount of work. It is fairly complicated, and if you don't know what you are doing it is possible to lose a large amount of money very quickly.

If you have a spread betting account you are, quite simply, able to bet on the movement of a massive range of assets. Rather than betting on horses, dogs or the cricket score, you are able to bet on a vast range of shares, bonds, stock market indices, commodities and other investments. You do this by betting a certain monetary value 'per point' on whatever asset you have a view on. Let us say you thought the gold price was going to go up. You would 'go long' (i.e. buy gold), and decide how many pounds per point to bet.

At the time of writing, gold is trading at around $1,300. If you wanted to go long, you would have to decide how many pounds to bet per point. If you bet £1, you would end up theoretically owning £1,300 worth of gold. This would mean that if gold went back up to $1,800 you would make £500 (£1800 − £1300 × 1). If you had bet £10 a point you would have made £5,000, and so on.

Two great aspects of spread betting are:

1 You can end up with a theoretical exposure to whatever you are betting on that is worth far more than you have in your trading account. If you wanted to own £1,300 worth of gold, as per the example above, by actually buying some gold you would need to buy £1,300's worth. If, instead, you make a bet through your spread betting account, you would need only a fraction of £1,300 and you would end up with the same theoretical exposure. It sounds rather complicated (to be fair, it probably is), but if you understand what you are doing this can be extremely powerful. You can end up effectively 'owning' thousands (or even millions) of pounds' worth of an asset using a much smaller deposit.

2 You can bet on things going down as well as up. If that thing falls in price, you make money. This is called 'shorting', which we will be looking at in more detail in Chapter 7.

To repeat a key point about spread betting: you must ensure you learn enough about it before you start. Depending on who you ask, between 80 and 90 per cent of people who spread bet lose money. If you are going to use this kind of account, it is crucial that you learn enough to put yourself in that top percentage of people who don't.

In summary

So now we have looked at the various different financial accounts you can (and should) use to build wealth, let us look in more detail at the different kinds of financial vehicle available to you. Remember that one of the best things about investment these days is that you are able to invest in a truly extraordinary range of things very cheaply and easily. This is poorly understood by most people, but having even a basic grasp is a serious string to your bow.

7

The types of investment vehicle you will need

'Personal finance isn't that hard.'

Ramit Sethi, best-selling author and founder of personal
finance blog iwillteachyoutoberich.com

In the previous chapter, we dealt with the array of financial *accounts* there are to choose from; now we need to deal with the seemingly bewildering array of financial *products* that exist. Once you have money in your (N)ISA and/or pension accounts, you are ready to put that money to work by buying the right selection of financial products within those accounts. In order to do this, you need to understand a bit about what products are available and their relative merits.

Asset classes

There are several main categories of financial product, otherwise known as 'asset classes' or 'investment vehicles', with which you can store (and hopefully build) wealth. Some of them are relatively well understood by the general population, but I think it is fair to say that most of them are not. If you have never really known what a 'bond' is, or exactly what a 'share' is, you have come to the right place.

The main types of individual investment vehicle we are interested in are:

- Cash
- Property (or real estate)
- Bonds
- Shares (otherwise known as stocks or equities)
- Commodities
- Funds
- Insurance products.

To a lesser extent, there are two further categories that are of interest to the more expert investor:

- Foreign exchange (often called forex or FX)
- Derivatives.

...and many readers will be aware of a tenth asset class or investment vehicle that has garnered a great deal of attention in the recent past: crypto assets such as bitcoin and ethereum and related blockchain investments. Given how much press these have received since the publication of the last edition of this book, I will include them as our tenth kind of financial product:

- Crypto assets/blockchain.

The importance of funds

It is probably worth noting at this point that, for the majority of private investors, *funds* are arguably the most relevant of these investment vehicles. This is quite simply because a fund allows you to own a large basket of any of the other products on the list, or even a mix of them from several categories.

As an investor in a single fund you can end up owning hundreds of shares, for example. In certain types of fund, you might even end up owning a mixture of shares, bonds, property and commodities within the one fund. This is very important for a number of reasons, which we will look at in more detail shortly.

As ever, do not worry that there is too much to learn. The above list might look quite daunting, with no fewer than ten categories of investment product to understand. Don't worry. It is true that you could read several hundred books on each and every single one of the categories above; however, you will also be able to arrange your financial affairs successfully without having to gain an in-depth grasp of any of them. You really don't need to know what a share or bond is, or how commodities trade in any great detail, in order to make a huge positive difference to your financial affairs. That said, it is key to have a *basic* understanding of what they are, if only so that you can better understand the suggestions that follow later in this book.

Asset allocation

As we have seen briefly already, what is also of great importance is having an idea of what proportion of your wealth you should have in each of these categories. Dividing your resources among the different investment vehicles is what is known as 'asset allocation'. Asset allocation is actually one of the most important things to be aware of when investing, and it is something that far too few people understand or even think about. It is also something that changes as you get older.

When you are young, you want to be looking to grow your money. As you age, however, you will want to ensure that you are investing more and more safely to preserve the pot you have made and be able to earn a decent income from it. At the simplest level, this means that the older you are, the more of your wealth you should hold in bonds and cash – and the younger you are, the more in shares (equities).

Another key thing to understand is that there has been a huge obsession with property in recent years.

> Many people in the UK and USA have almost all their wealth in property and cash – and in the long run this is inadvisable.

As we shall see, over time it is actually best to own a mixture of all the above types of financial vehicle. If you only have property, there is a risk you will fail to become wealthy in your lifetime. To give yourself the best chance of becoming truly wealthy, you need to ensure that you are aware of, and are exposed to, the other asset classes – particularly shares, bonds and commodities.

General considerations common to all asset classes

Each of the above types of investment vehicle has certain individual characteristics, but the two most important considerations when we look at any of them are:

- How safe your money is when invested in that asset class
- What sort of percentage return you might expect to make.

Put another way, when we consider the relative merits of an invest-ment vehicle or financial product, we are concerned with both the return *of* our money and the return *on* our money. As I have already said, it is not necessary for you to have an in-depth understanding of each of the types of financial product listed above. All you need is to understand a little about what they are, how safe they are and what sort of return they might give you.

So, with this in mind, let us look very quickly at each in turn.

Cash

First, let us just be clear that, for the purposes of this discussion, 'cash' means money on deposit at a financial institution such as a bank or building society. 'Cash' is also quite obviously the word we use to describe what you have in your pocket, wallet or purse, but we are looking at the merits of cash as an investment vehicle here and you don't get paid interest on what you carry around with you (sadly).

Obviously, the great thing about cash in a bank account is that it is basically secure. Barring a financial crisis, massive natural disaster or revolution, you should always have access to any money you have in a bank account, and the amount of money you have in that account will not suddenly be less one day than it was the day before because the 'market has crashed'.

As cash is seen as safe, the percentage return you can make on it (i.e. the interest rate) tends to be low as a result. When you are a saver and have money on deposit at a bank or building society, they are paying you an interest rate as a thank you for providing them with money they can then lend out to borrowers. They will then charge those borrowers a higher interest rate than they pay you, which is how banks make their money – or at least how they used to.

As always, we must not forget inflation ...

That is pretty much all we need to know about cash as an investible asset: it's all about the interest rate. But before we move on to the next section, there is one other key factor we need to be aware of when thinking about cash: inflation.

When considering how safe your money on deposit at a bank or building society actually is, you must understand the difference between the interest rate your bank is paying you (the 'nominal rate') and the interest rate your money is actually earning (the 'real rate'). The difference is inflation.

In a previous chapter, I mentioned a current account at a major high street bank paying 1.8 per cent interest, and how this equates to 1.44 per cent for a basic-rate taxpayer. We have already seen how even official government inflation numbers in the UK have been at about 4–5 per cent in the not too distant past, but that real inflation (based on more honest methods of calculation) is quite possibly higher than that. If your money on deposit is earning 1.44 per cent when inflation is running at around 5 per cent, then you are losing more than 3.5 per cent of your wealth every year in real terms. It is for this reason that believing 'cash is king' can be a dangerous way of looking at the world.

Losing 3.5 per cent of your wealth in a year does not sound very safe to me. When inflation is high and interest rates are low, real interest rates are negative. The calculation is very simple: *real* interest (return on cash) equals *nominal* interest (what your bank is paying you) minus inflation.

It is important for your long-term financial success to keep as much of your wealth as possible in assets that have a positive real return. When real interest rates are negative, as they are now, you should look to have only as much cash as you need in order to pay for things in the short term. (Some of you may be aware that the actual accurate method of calculating real return is a tiny bit more complicated, but the simple method above makes the same point.) It is perhaps easiest to think about the 'short term' as less than one year. So work out what you need to live on each month, add any other purchases or expenses you think will crop up this year (holiday, car, university tuition), add a margin of error for safety and invest everything else in assets other than cash. With that, let us turn to those other assets.

Property

We looked at property in some detail in Chapter 5, when we discussed the creation of financial surplus. When we consider the return *of* our money, property is obviously one of the better asset classes. A house or flat will always have some value, given that there is always demand for places to live, and it is almost certainly never going to be worth nothing at all (as can happen with a share).

That said, as with so many investments it is important to understand how to value property to give yourself a fighting chance of buying it at a good level over time. We looked at the ideas of rental yield, capital gain and property prices as a multiple of salary in Chapter 5, so there is no point in going over those again, but it *is* worth remembering that these metrics enable you to compare property as an investment to all the others.

There are a couple of additional points that it is probably worth making. As we have said, many people in the UK and the USA have a very high percentage of their net worth, or in many cases all of it, tied up in their primary property. However, one of the most important things you need to bear in mind if you wish to grow your wealth in the safest way possible is asset allocation. If you already have a huge percentage of your net worth tied up in property, you should probably focus on investing in other asset classes before you consider another property investment (such as a buy-to-let flat, for example). However, this will obviously depend on the returns you think you can achieve after inflation when you compare the various different options, as we have already discussed.

There are, however, two other categories of property investment to think about over and above where you live: commercial property, and foreign or overseas property (and overseas commercial property, for that matter). It is often the case that there will be interesting opportunities in either or both of these categories, and these are worth considering even if you already have a large percentage of your wealth in UK residential property via your primary residence. One of the ways of getting exposure to overseas and/or commercial property is through owning a fund. We shall look in more detail at funds shortly.

Property and borrowing money: a key point

I would like to make one final important point about property as an asset class: unlike any of the other main asset classes, private individuals have traditionally been able to borrow reasonably large sums of money in order to invest in property. To a great extent, this is a unique feature of the property market. Most individuals are not able to borrow money to invest in shares or commodities, for example, although there are exceptions – usually wealthy individuals with a track record and a private banking relationship, or those who know how to use spread betting effectively.

Mortgages enable individuals to control an asset with a value significantly more than the deposit they have saved. In a strong market this is obviously great news for the investor; at various points in the last couple of decades, it was common practice to be able to buy a property with a deposit of only 5–10 per cent. Lenders such as Northern Rock were even offering 110 per cent mortgages ahead of the financial crisis of 2007/8, effectively lending buyers their deposit.

In a strong market, this is good news for property investors. If you can put down £25,000 (or even less) to control a £250,000 property, for example, and that asset then increases in value sufficiently fast, you can build real wealth very quickly. However, using debt (otherwise known as leverage or gearing) to buy any asset is a double-edged sword. In a bull market, you are able to use other people's money to grow your wealth. This has benefited many people in the English-speaking world over the last few decades – or at least the ones who ensure they take profits and sell those properties before the market corrects.

If you have borrowed to purchase an asset and that asset then falls in value, you end up with nothing to repay your loan. We discussed this briefly when we looked at negative equity. It can be a very painful situation, which is one of the reasons that people can go very wrong with property investment.

As a general rule, the fact that you can borrow money in order to buy a property means there are opportunities for the smart investor to make great money doing so. It is crucial, however, to make sensible assumptions about what might happen to the value of what you buy and to the cost of the money you borrow. The subprime crisis in the USA came about primarily because many thousands of people assumed US property would always appreciate in value and only thought about their monthly payment today, rather than considering what might happen to that monthly payment in the years ahead. I would hope that the points made earlier in the book will help to ensure you don't make the same mistake.

Bonds

Many of us are familiar with the idea of a loan. To put it simply, a bank will lend you a certain amount of money. After a given amount of time you will pay them the money back, plus an agreed amount of interest to compensate them for being without the money for that time. This is why it is helpful to understand interest rates as the 'cost' or 'price' of money. Arguably, fewer people are familiar with what a bond is but it is simply this: *a loan divided into many pieces so that it can be made by lots of people.*

To explain: imagine a big oil company plans to build a new refinery and needs £1 billion to do so. They might go to a big bank and ask for a £1 billion loan. If the bank were particularly relaxed about the strength of that oil company, they might well simply lend them the money and ask for an appropriate interest rate as compensation. More likely, however, they would feel that £1 billion was too large a sum to be owed to them by one company and that the deal was too risky for them to do by themselves. This being the case, they might do one of two things.

The first approach would be to ask other banks if they would be interested in lending some of the £1 billion. Let us say that they actually do find nine other banks who are happy to lend £100 million each, or four banks who are each happy to lend £200 million. This would then be known as a 'syndicated loan' – a group (or syndicate) of banks has clubbed together to reduce their exposure (known as 'credit risk') but ensure that the deal still gets done. In this scenario, not only would the original bank receive interest on its loan, but it would also charge a fee for organizing the syndicate. This is one of the things an investment bank does.

The second option would be to print many pieces of paper, each one of which would represent a small fraction of the value of the £1 billion loan, and to offer those pieces of paper for sale to anyone who was interested in providing that small fraction of the loan and receiving interest as compensation. This is essentially exactly the same process as with the syndicated loan, except that the pieces of paper are called 'bonds' and their existence means that the loan can be syndicated to hundreds, or even thousands, of investors all over the world – rather than to just a small group of banks.

For this example, let's say the bank prints one million bonds, each of which is worth £1,000, and the oil company is committed to paying 5 per cent interest on those bonds. When the bank offers these bonds for sale, potential investors can buy as many or as few of them as they like. For each one that they buy, the oil company will owe them £1,000 plus 5 per cent interest. The interest paid by a bond is referred to as its 'coupon'. This is because in the past, when a bond was literally a piece of paper, it had a detachable coupon for every interest payment the owner was entitled to receive.

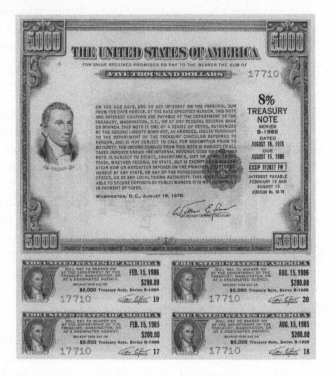

FIGURE 7.1 Example of a bond with coupons

If you bought a bond that was to be redeemed in three years and which paid 5 per cent interest by paying the holder 2.5 per cent twice a year, there would have been six coupons. When bonds were originally invented, the bondholder would literally have taken those coupons to a bank every six months and exchanged them for the cheque or cash equivalent of 2.5 per cent of the face value of the bond. Today these payments tend to be automated (unless they are what are called 'bearer bonds', which fans of 1980s movies and Bruce Willis may recall were what the criminals were after in the film *Die Hard*).

I should clarify another feature of bonds, which concerns how long the buyer is lending the seller money for. A bond may entitle its owner to 5 per cent a year and their original money back in three years or five years, or even longer. Some government bonds last as long as 50 years. As you can imagine, a bond which promises to pay you 5 per cent a year for ten years will tend to cost more than one which pays you 5 per cent a year for two years, all other things being equal.

The secondary market for bonds

A further crucial aspect of bonds is the existence of a secondary market. Say you purchased £10,000 worth of the oil company bonds in the example above, but a month later you read that the oil company is in financial trouble (or perhaps you just need your money back suddenly). You might decide you would rather have your money back than hold on to the bonds and collect your interest payments. Luckily for you, it is very likely that somewhere out there in the world is someone who still thinks the oil company is a good bet and would like to own your bonds and collect the interest. As a result, you will be able to sell your bonds to that person via an intermediary such as an investment bank.

One important thing to bear in mind at this point is that it is pretty unusual for a private or 'retail' investor (i.e. you) to buy bonds directly. Most bonds, whether issued by a company or a government, trade in amounts that are generally too big for the average private investor (but small enough for someone very rich, which is another advantage for the wealthy). Because of this, you would usually look to get exposure to bonds by owning a bond *fund*, which we will look at in more detail shortly.

Government bonds

The next important thing to say about bonds and the bond market is that they are a government's main source of money other than taxation. It is vital that we understand something of this in order to fully appreciate what is happening today and further strengthen our understanding of what to do about it.

Governments all over the world have essentially only two ways of raising money to pay for the vast array of things they want to fund. The first is taxation. This is reasonably well understood by most of us. We all pay tax in a wide variety of obvious and not so obvious ways, and the companies we work for and from whom we buy products and services do too.

However, since taxes were created thousands of years ago, very few governments have been able to survive on less than what they have taken in tax. Historically, the primary reason for this failure of political elites to survive on tax revenues was the cost of waging war. In times of war, the costs borne by governments skyrocket. Ships must be built; soldiers must be paid and supplied. And these costs are what led to the creation of the bond market.

For the last several centuries, in times of emergency or war, governments have been forced to spend significantly more than they have earned in taxation. They have made up the difference by selling bonds to their population and, more recently, to foreign investors including other governments. This is the second of the two ways in which governments are able to raise money.

There is basically no other way for a government to raise money other than from taxation or from selling bonds to investors. A rare exception to this would be where a government sells assets such as land, gold reserves or foreign embassy buildings or military bases, for example. These sales are obviously not a recurring income stream and tend, as a result, only to be used in emergencies or when those in power feel markets are at a particularly advantageous level. Governments can be pretty bad at this, as we saw when Gordon Brown sold a large proportion of the UK's gold reserves close to a record low.

Sadly, even though most countries have enjoyed unprecedented peace since the end of the Second World War, nearly all Western governments still make a regular habit of spending far more than they are able to raise from taxation. (We have already seen this in the graphs of US and UK government debt in Chapter 4. The only real exceptions are small economies with a huge natural resource endowment per capita and decent political leadership, such as Norway.) Nearly all governments in the world have made up the shortfall by selling bonds – that is to say, by raising debt. (Remember that a bond is just a loan divided into lots of little pieces after all.)

You might be surprised to learn that for a long time this policy was entirely sustainable. Banks offering mortgages, loans and credit cards are obviously comfortable offering such debt products to wealthy individuals who enjoy high annual earnings. There is a very good chance that those individuals will pay back their debt. In the same way, investors all over the world were comfortable lending money to the governments of countries with high and usually rising annual 'earnings' by buying their bonds. Translated into the language of the bond market: investors were happy to buy the government bonds of countries with a high and growing gross domestic product (GDP).

'Risk free'

Financial theory assumed, until very recently, that lending money to the government of a modern country such as the USA, the UK or France was 'risk free'. If you were to buy $10,000 of bonds from the US government for your pension, for example, you assumed there was no chance at all that you would not get your money back plus the interest promised. After all, the US government was deemed to be so big and rich that no one even considered for a moment the idea that they wouldn't be getting their money back. Even if some incredible catastrophe were to occur, the US government would still be able to print as many dollars as it liked.

In fact, printing money is precisely what they are doing today. They can no longer afford to pay bond investors the interest and principal on their bonds without inventing new money to do so. The trouble with inventing lots of new money (i.e. quantitative easing, or QE) is that it devalues that money, as we discussed in the sections on inflation earlier. As a reminder – if you double the supply of pounds, dollars, yen or euros but the supply of 'stuff' remains fixed, you will not create any more wealth but will, rather, simply double the price of everything, all other things being equal. This is why any policy of handing money out to people is counter-productive and doesn't make anyone wealthier in real terms in the medium to long run.

While investors all over the world continued to believe the bonds of wealthy nations were essentially risk free, it should be intuitively obvious that they were prepared to earn pretty low returns on those bonds. Given a choice of places to invest your money, you may be willing to accept a lower return on 'risk-free' money, which you feel you are guaranteed to get back, than you are on a riskier investment where you worry you may not. Part of the whole crisis of the last few years is that, increasingly, investors all over the world no longer see the bonds of many developed countries as 'risk free'. This is a very important change, as it has an impact on interest rates and inflation. Let us look quickly at why this is.

Government bond prices and interest rates

At this stage, I would like to briefly explain the relationship between bond prices and interest rates. Imagine that the US government is selling a one-year bond worth $100 and offering to pay $5 of interest. This means that, if you buy the bond, you are entitled to $100 of capital and $5 of interest at the end of the year.

If you pay $100 for this bond, your return on that investment will be 5 per cent. This should hopefully be easy to understand. You pay $100 and after a year you get $105 back. A simple percentage return calculation shows us that this is 5 per cent.

However, in the 'secondary market' that we talked about earlier, bond prices constantly move up and down depending on what investors all over the world feel about the country or company that issued the bonds. As such, you can end up paying more or less than $100 for $100's 'worth' of bonds. In the above example, if you were to pay $101 for the bond, your return would end up being about 3.95 per cent. This is because you are now losing 1 per cent of your capital (you paid more than $100 for the bond but only get $100 of capital back at the end of the year), and your percentage return on the $5 of interest is a tiny bit lower than before (5/101 instead of 5/100).

If you were to pay $99 for it, your return would be about 6.05 per cent. This time you are making a tiny bit more than 1 per cent on your capital (you paid \$99 but receive \$100 back at the end of the year), and your \$5 of interest represents a slightly higher fraction of \$99 than it does of \$100.

> Lower bond prices mean higher interest rates and vice versa.
> They are two sides of the same coin.

This is important to understand. Governments that need to raise money to pay for all the things their tax revenue can't cover must sell bonds to investors at home and abroad to make up the difference. If those investors are less confident about the financial strength of that government, they will be prepared to pay less for that country's bonds. This will mean that the price of the bonds falls, and lower bond prices mean higher interest rates. More accurately, lower bond prices *are* higher interest rates.

How the bond market drives interest rates

In 2012 investors from all over the world were becoming significantly less willing to buy the bonds of countries in Europe such as Greece, Italy, Spain, France, Portugal and Ireland. As a result, these nations were only able to sell their bonds at increasingly low prices. This pushed interest rates in these countries up by some margin and showed us that the massive global bond market (thousands of investors from all over the world with trillions of dollars, pounds, euros, yen, etc.) is more powerful than pretty much every single country in the world when it comes to setting interest rates. Even the US government has far less power to set interest rates than you might think.

In fact, the only difference between the troubled European countries and the USA and the UK is that both the USA and the UK can invent new money out of thin air to buy their own bonds (QE) as they have control of their own currencies (rather than the euro, which is controlled by a group of nations – meaning that no single nation can print more of it unilaterally). QE keeps bond prices up (and therefore interest rates down) but it also creates inflation (devaluing the dollar and the pound), so I would argue that the effect is still negative in the longer term.

As you might imagine, falling bond prices are also something of a vicious spiral: as interest rates rise, the government needs to pay more to borrow money, making investors even less willing to invest in that country's bonds.

You may already be aware that rising interest rates put the brakes on an economy for the following reasons:

- People are less inclined to take out a mortgage or other loan or form of credit. This depresses the housing market and the retail sector.
- Those who have a variable rate mortgage see their monthly payments go up and have less to spend as a result, which means the rest of the economy suffers. If interest rates increase too much, people may even end up being forced to sell their home – something we are likely to see a great deal of in the next few decades, sadly.
- Companies are less likely to hire people or acquire a new factory or piece of equipment. If their cost of capital has increased and they have to pay more to borrow money to invest, then they will make fewer investments.

Any government that has mismanaged its financial affairs will find itself having to drop the prices of its bonds in order to sell them. This results in the extremely unpopular and economically damaging reality of higher interest rates, as the alternative is not being able to raise money on the bond markets at all.

Given that neither of these options is a vote winner, plenty of governments throughout history have gone with the other option we have just mentioned: inventing money out of thin air to buy their own bonds. This is what the UK and the USA have been doing for the last few years, and it's what the Europeans were having an argument about in 2012. The Italians, Irish, Spanish, Portuguese, Greeks and so on need to invent money out of thin air to deal with their enormous debts. German politicians, however, are reluctant to let them do this, given their more prudent approach to economics. Germany suffered brutal hyperinflation in the 1920s as a result of printing lots of new money, and fear of inflation is very much ingrained in the national psyche as a result.

Inventing money has been attempted dozens of times throughout history and been described in various different ways (debasing coins, printing money, QE). It has almost always resulted in economic disaster for the country or society involved (ancient Rome, Weimar Germany in the 1920s, Argentina and many other Latin American countries in the 1980s and 2000s, and more recently Zimbabwe – home of the $100 trillion note as recently as 2009 – and Venezuela as I write).

FIGURE 7.2 The Zimbabwean $100 trillion note

For most of history, neither the UK nor the USA played this game. They were strong enough that they could pay back their debts with real money and could keep bond market investors happy buying their bonds at low interest rates. Sadly, this is no longer the case. In the last several years, both the USA and the UK have had to resort to inventing money to buy their own bonds in order to keep interest rates artificially low.

Some of you may have noticed that this is a third option, yet I previously stated that there are only two ways for a government to raise money. I stick to my original statement because this third option is not a way of raising *real* money at all. Let me explain ...

In a nutshell, QE is when the government simply invents some 'money' in a computer and uses it to buy the bonds that it couldn't sell at the more expensive lower-yielding level because normal, professional investors wouldn't pay that price. In recent years, the US Federal Reserve has bought up to 80 per cent of all new bond issuance in the USA, and the UK authorities as much as 50 per cent of all new UK bonds. That is to say, they are buying between 50 and 80 per cent of their own bonds. This is an extraordinary case of 'robbing Peter to pay Paul'.

As we have already seen, if you invent money the effect is inflationary. I have made the point before but will make it again here: if you have basically the same amount of 'stuff' in an economy and the quantity of paper money doubles, the price of that stuff will double (generally after a certain time lag). This is because inventing money does not cause any more stuff to be created – more oil to be found or wheat to be grown, for example – and therefore the supply of stuff remains the same, but the amount of money everyone has to pay for that stuff increases eventually. (There is a school of economic thought that would argue that inventing money can, in fact, cause more 'stuff' to be made. If there is more money sloshing around in an economy, then people are more likely to take out loans or build a factory and so on. This is one of the reasons why central banks have played this game. I would argue that the evidence of history is that every time this has been tried, the amount of new money created exceeds the quantity of new real economic activity and, as a result, the effect is ultimately inflationary and not wealth generative.)

If the government doubles the amount of money in existence in order to buy its own bonds and avoid dealing with the consequences of its previous actions, you will need your employer to double your salary just to stand still financially, all other things being equal. Do you anticipate this being a possibility? I didn't think so.

We have already seen the following John Maynard Keynes quote a few times, but it bears repeating yet again to really make the point now we have a better understanding of what he means: 'By a continuing process of inflation, governments can confiscate, secretly and unobserved, an important part of the wealth of their citizens.'

This is exactly what is happening. If you think that the idea of a government doubling the money supply is far-fetched, then think again. We have already seen that the US money supply has more than tripled in the last few years. As best-selling economic writer and pundit Bill Bonner notes: 'It took 95 years to get the Fed's holdings to $600 billion. In the space of three years it has added $1.4 trillion more.'

The situation today is even worse. It is worth noting that this is the growth using the official numbers. There are many smart analysts out there whose numbers suggest that the real situation is far worse. At the same time that the US and UK governments are doubling and tripling their money supplies (or worse), by manipulating the inflation numbers, they are also keeping a lid on people's understanding of how bad this is for their wealth.

Many politicians really don't understand this stuff

Perhaps even more worrying than this endless money printing and misleading inflation numbers, however, is the fact that many of our lawmakers (and journalists for that matter) simply do not understand these issues. This means the situation is highly unlikely to be resolved any time soon. I was reading a story not that long ago about a US congressman who was sitting on a key finance committee, listening to arguments from academics and finance professionals. After an hour or so he put his hand up and asked: 'Sorry, but what is this "QE" you keep talking about?'

The fact that an elected politician, sitting in the US government and partly responsible for making US financial policy (a policy that affects you!), asked this question is absolutely shocking and goes some way to helping us understand why we are in the state we are in. We saw a similar performance from the US Senate at the time of writing this third edition when Mark Zuckerberg, CEO of Facebook, was interviewed in Congress. It seems that a good proportion of US policymakers don't understand finance or the Internet either. Less than ideal! As crazy as it sounds, large numbers of the people in charge on both sides of the Atlantic have no idea what they are doing, financially speaking. They just don't understand the economics.

This is abundantly obvious to me day in day out as I listen to journalists and politicians being interviewed on the radio. I narrowly avoid throwing things around my kitchen in rage on a regular basis as a result. Once you have finished reading this book you will, without exaggeration, quite possibly understand more about economics than many US and UK politicians and generalist journalists.

While a US congressman or British MP working on economic policy should not be forgiven for being unfamiliar with the term 'QE', I think it is entirely fair that you might not have fully understood what it was before reading this book. As ever, understanding this concept is another string to your bow in terms of being able to improve your financial situation. To paraphrase an earlier quote: those who understand QE are destined to make money from it, and those who don't are destined to suffer.

Bond default

One final aspect of bonds which is important to understand is that unless the company or country issuing the bonds goes bankrupt they are legally obliged to pay the bondholder their interest and their money back. If a company or government cannot pay this money back due to bankruptcy, this is known as 'default'. Default in the government bond market has been relatively rare (it is more common with corporate bonds, i.e. those issued by companies – for obvious reasons).

Given the relative rarity of government default, bonds have traditionally been viewed as the safest financial investment you can make – similar to keeping your money in a deposit account. You are almost certain to get back your original money plus the agreed interest. The downside is that the return you make is small. You might be paid just 2–3 per cent on your holdings in bonds. And don't forget that you need to account for inflation when considering what your *real* return is. If inflation is running at 5 per cent or more, for example, then you will be losing *real* wealth if you own bonds that yield less than 5 per cent. For bigger returns, you will have to look elsewhere. One of the first places to go looking for higher returns is stocks and shares, otherwise known as 'equities'.

Shares/equities/stocks

Many people are aware of the existence of 'stocks and shares' but in my experience few really understand what they are, including a large number of the folk who invest in them. This is clearly bad news for them and is another reason why people think investment is risky. Perhaps the best way for us to grasp them at a fundamental level is to have a quick look at how they developed.

Along with the debt market and bonds, shares were an extremely important development in human history. It is not an exaggeration to say that without their invention, the Industrial Revolution and the enormous technological and social developments of the last few centuries, which have made us all substantially better off, would have been impossible.

But why?

Because their creation enabled large groups of people to pool resources and spread risk like never before. The 'joint-stock company' was brought into existence in the Netherlands and Britain in the early seventeenth century largely in order to fund the exploration and exploitation of the East Indies.

People in Europe had acquired a taste for all things Eastern, but getting there and back was extremely dangerous. A sea voyage could take years and there was always the risk that an entire fleet of ships might be lost on the way. It quickly became clear that even the aristocrats and royal families of Europe could not afford to fund such voyages by themselves. Fleets of ships were incredibly expensive as a percentage of the gross national product, or GNP (the nation's total economic output/wealth).

The solution was the creation of a 'company' and the selling of 'shares' in that company to anyone who was interested in investing. Essentially this meant that an investor who contributed, say, 1 per cent of the costs associated with a voyage would be given a piece of paper that recorded their entitlement to a share of 1 per cent of any profits made.

The difference between this and a bond was that the share investor had no guarantee of a return. Someone buying a bond was essentially guaranteed to get his or her money back (plus the agreed interest) unless the bond issuer went bankrupt (defaulted). Someone buying a *share* would only be entitled to that percentage of any profits made. If the voyage lost a minimal number of ships and came back to Amsterdam or London with lucrative cargo, the shareholder would have made their fortune. If, on the other hand, the fleet was decimated by storms or piracy, the investor might find they had lost all of their original investment.

Not much has changed, except that you can now buy yourself shares in far more things than a risky voyage to the East Indies. Today you can own shares in a fantastic diversity of human activity, from all over the world. Some of these activities, like the seventeenth-century voyages of the Dutch and British, carry with them a high degree of risk and potential reward. Others are inherently much safer.

I believe it is important to note at this point that had it not been for the creation of the stock market and the funding it provided, there would be few large commercial buildings, no aviation and no automotive industry or roads; no extraordinary improvement in medicine and healthcare; few if any of the small daily luxuries that we take for granted (toothpaste, toilet roll, running water, inexpensive clothing, newspapers, televisions); no film and entertainment industry; and no opportunity to assemble a meal comprising ingredients from every corner of the earth from your local supermarket (Italian olive oil, Argentinian wine, Scottish steak – you name it).

There would, however, very likely have been significantly more war. Since global capital markets enmesh different nation-states together – in a way that means that the costs of war, in the main, massively outweigh the benefits – stock market capitalism has had the added benefit of making the world far more peaceful as it has grown and spread. (This is why the USA will almost certainly never again go to war with Japan, for example. Nowadays the two nations are just far too economically entwined.)

As such, the stock market has quite demonstrably been one of the greatest inventions in human history. It has lifted billions out of poverty, saved them from malnutrition and increased short lifespans; it has increased our comfort and given us more leisure time and travel, and has been largely responsible for making the world a fundamentally more peaceful, interesting and healthy place.

Stock markets facilitate the sharing of risk between thousands of individuals and/or organizations, and allow the concentration of a sufficient amount of capital to be focused on one extremely complex task in order to get that task done. No single individual could afford to invest enough or accumulate all the skills needed to provide any of the things I've listed above, or create the microchip, fibre optics or the smartphone.

I genuinely don't wish to be overly political here, and I am very happy to concede that an unattractive feature of stock market capitalism can be significant wealth inequality (more on this later), but I would ask any self-proclaimed anti-capitalist of the likes of UK comedian Russell Brand (who wrote in his book *Revolution* that stock markets are 'bollocks' after admitting on the very same page that he knows nothing about them!) to think deeply about what has had to happen in the forests and paper mills of Finland, and in the shipping and trucking industries of Europe and about what has been spent on building a massive network of convenient retail outlets in this country just to get toilet paper into his home! Workers' cooperatives simply cannot provide any of the above – which is why people in communist Russia had a complete dearth of all the things we take for granted in modern Western democracies and were grindingly poor and invariably hungry. A failure to understand this reality is genuinely dangerous for everyone's future standard of living, whether you are rich or poor, and for human progress as a whole.

Rather than rail against stock markets, a far better course of action for individuals and for society as a whole is to take a little time to understand them and to get involved. Happily, when you buy a share in a company – otherwise known as a 'stock' or an 'equity' – you quite literally become a part-owner of that company. This means that you are then entitled to your proportional share in the company's profits. If you think about it, this is a very exciting invention. By owning a share in a business, you can benefit from the work of everyone involved in it, and you can start to do this with very little money. Stock market investment is not the preserve of the wealthy – or certainly should not be; it is available to anyone who is willing to find out about it and get involved. It is this involvement that will give them a much better chance of becoming wealthy themselves.

I would argue, in other words, that the causality runs the opposite way to what many people think. Too many people incorrectly think 'the stock market is only for rich people', when what they should be thinking is 'if I learn about and use the stock market, I have a reasonable probability of being a rich person' – or comfortably off at the very least. As we have seen, over time small numbers can become big numbers. I would argue that the richest 1 per cent of people in the world – the developed world at least – are generally quite simply the most economically and financially literate 1 per cent of people. This is truer today than at any other time in history, primarily because it has never been easier to become an owner of businesses – both administratively and in terms of the small sums needed to get started.

In 1989, when the *Sunday Times* first published their 'Rich List' of the wealthiest 1,000 people in the UK, a very significant percentage of the list had inherited their wealth. In 2018, by contrast, 94 per cent of the people on the list had created their own. This has largely been a function of what I'm talking about here. I'm not suggesting that everyone can become a multi-millionaire, but what I am saying is that if you can't beat them, why not join them by becoming an investor in companies just as they are, even if on a smaller scale?

When considering buying shares in a company, you should always remember that you are becoming a part-owner of that business. As such, you should think about two key things:

1 Is this a good business (preferably a very good business)?
2 Am I paying the correct amount for my slice of this business?

When I speak to people about investing in shares, they often tell me with great enthusiasm about the great companies they have invested in, but they do not stop for a minute to consider what price they paid for those companies in *real* terms. It might not be particularly controversial to say that Tesco, Marks & Spencer and Shell are three excellent companies – or Microsoft, Intel and Coca-Cola in the USA, for that matter. But finding a great company is only the first job. Working out what to pay for that company is the next task – and it's the fundamentally more important one.

Let us take Tesco as an example. At any one time in the last ten years, you could have bought Tesco shares for as little as 160p or as much as 485p. At the time of writing the first edition of this book in 2012 they were about 328p. At all three of these prices Tesco has basically been the same excellent retail company (despite the recent accounting scandals the company has suffered) but you can see that the people who purchased their shares at or close to 160p may well be on their way to a happy early retirement, while those who bought theirs at 485p have lost a significant chunk of their money.

How to value a share

So how can an investor work out when a price is good or bad? 'Hindsight is 20/20', as they say, but how might we have known that 160p was a good price for Tesco and 485p a bad one at the time? As ever, the books written in a bid to answer such a question could fill an entire warehouse, but I will do my best to outline the key ideas here in plain English.

It all goes back to the point that when you buy a share you become a part-owner of the business. This means that you are entitled to a share in any profits the business makes, just like the seventeenth-century investors from London and Amsterdam who were entitled to the fruits of a successful expedition to the East Indies. What you need to work out is how much you should be paying for your share. Annoyingly enough, and as counter-intuitive as this sounds, the share price alone does not give you this information.

To work out how much you are paying for a share in *real* terms, you must think about how much profit a given company is making now (and is likely to make in the future), and compare how much you might have to pay for your share of that profit to how much you might pay for the same share of another company's profits. This is actually much simpler than it sounds. Let us look at a quick example.

The P/E ratio

Imagine you are thinking of investing in one of two companies that do basically the same thing. As we were using Tesco earlier, let us use Tesco and Sainsbury's for this example. Now imagine that both companies are going to make £100 million of profit this year (these numbers bear no relation at all to the real world but will make things easier to understand). Imagine, too, that there are 100 million shares in existence for each company.

Remember that in essence a share entitles you to a percentage of the profits in a company. If you own 5 per cent of a company, you effectively own 5 per cent of that company's profits (and its assets). Hopefully you can see that each Tesco or Sainsbury's share 'owns' £1 of profit. We call this number 'earnings per share' (EPS). Both of these companies are set to make £100 million of profit this year and there are 100 million shares of each. Therefore, each share 'owns' £1 of profit. If you owned 1,000 shares, you would 'own' £1,000 worth of profit. Simple enough.

Now here comes the part where you will realize that you are perfectly capable of understanding shares – or the basics at least. Imagine that Tesco shares currently cost £10 each and Sainsbury's shares cost £8. Can you see that if you buy a Tesco share, you pay £10 to own £1 of profit, but if you buy a Sainsbury's share you are paying only £8 to own £1 of profit?

The price of a Tesco share is ten times the earnings per share and the price of a Sainsbury's share is eight times the earnings per share. This is a ratio that we call the 'price to earnings ratio' ('P/E' for short). All other things being equal, you can see that Sainsbury's shares are 'cheaper' than Tesco shares. A lower P/E ratio means that you are paying less for the same entitlement to profit. Crucially, simply looking at the share price does not give you the same information (without thinking about earnings). Now, let us introduce a third company into the equation to clarify this point.

Imagine that Morrisons is also going to make £100 million of profit this year but there are *200* million Morrisons shares in existence, rather than 100 million. We can see immediately that for each Morrisons share you own, you are entitled to only 50p of profit, rather than the £1 your Tesco or Sainsbury's share would get you, since there are twice as many shares with claims on the same amount of profit.

Now, let us say that Morrisons shares cost £6 at the moment. Are they 'cheaper' or 'more expensive' than Tesco and Sainsbury's shares, which are trading at £10 and £8 respectively? Hopefully you can see that even though the Morrisons share price is less than the other two, for every £1 you spend on a Morrisons share, you only get 50p of earnings (profit) rather than £1, because there are twice as many shares to split those profits between. In this example, Morrisons shares have a P/E ratio of *12* times the earnings per share (£6 divided by 50p). Therefore, the Morrisons shares are actually 'more expensive' than both the Tesco and Sainsbury's shares.

Here is a quick summary table:

TABLE 7.1 A comparison of Tesco, Sainsbury's and Morrisons share values

Company	Profit	No. of shares	Price (£)	Earnings per share (£)	P/E multiple
Tesco	£100,000,000	100,000,000	10	1	10
Sainsbury's	£100,000,000	100,000,000	8	1	8
Morrisons	£100,000,000	200,000,000	6	0.5	12

Source: Plain English Finance

The P/E ratio is arguably the single most important thing you will ever learn about shares. It is frightening just how many people think that a share costing £5 is always 'cheaper' than a share that costs £10. The share price tells you nothing about how fundamentally expensive or cheap a share is – unless you are also looking at the multiple of profits that each share costs. If you are now incredibly confused, please go back and read through the example again. As soon as you understand this concept, you will know more about shares than the majority of people and you will have taken your first step towards being able to invest in them successfully.

So, to establish whether a share is truly cheap or expensive, you have to work out what you are paying for the profits you will be entitled to and for any other value in the business. If a share that costs £5 is entitled to profits that equal half those of a share which costs £10, the two shares actually 'cost' exactly the same (all other things being equal). The P/E multiple is widely available online and in the financial press; it is your first step to understanding whether a share is expensive or cheap.

Earnings yield

The next thing to think about is what we call 'earnings yield'. If you think about Tesco in the example above, you would be paying £10 for the right to £1 of profit this year. This means that you are making a 10 per cent annual return on your £10. Assume that you invest £10 today and Tesco continues to make £100 million of profit every year for the next ten years. You will make £1 of profit for each of your shares every year. You have paid £10 and you get £1 back each year, that is, 10 per cent. This is the earnings yield and it is easily calculated by simply dividing 1 by the P/E ratio and multiplying it by 100 to get the percentage. In the above example, Sainsbury's has an earnings yield of 12.5 per cent (1 divided by 8) and Morrisons of 8.3 per cent (1/12).

Why different shares have different P/E ratios and earnings yields

The next thing to think about is why one share might have a higher P/E ratio (and lower earnings yield) than another share. In the above example, Sainsbury's and Tesco shares should theoretically be the same price – and Morrisons shares should actually trade at exactly half that price – since they are all making £100 million of profit (but Morrisons has twice the number of shares to split that same amount of profit with).

So why do the Tesco shares cost more than Sainsbury's shares? Again, thousands of books have been written on the subject, but broadly speaking there are two reasons for share prices to differ:

1 Expectations of future profits
2 Value in the business other than profit.

One reason why you might be willing to pay more for one share than another is if you expect that company's profit to be higher in the future than the other company's profit will be. Let us say that we expect Tesco to make £120 million next year but Sainsbury's to make only £90 million. If this is the case, we would be willing to pay more for Tesco shares than Sainsbury's shares.

The other basic reason why we might be willing to pay more for Tesco than Sainsbury's could be that there is more value in Tesco than in Sainsbury's for reasons other than the profits they might make. You might have already worked this out, but imagine that Tesco owns £1 billion worth of property and Sainsbury's only owns £500 million worth. In this example, imagine they both make the same profit this year and are very likely to make the same profit next year. All other things being equal, Tesco might then be a better investment than Sainsbury's. This introduces us to another idea known as 'book value'.

Book value

The book value is simply the value of all the assets a business owns, as added up by their accountants, and it is yet another way we can compare the value of one share to another.

Imagine that a company has lots of property and lots of cash in the bank. If you own a share in that company, you effectively own a share in those assets – as well as a share of any profits. The book value can be divided by the number of shares to give an idea of the value of existing assets that each share is entitled to. This ratio is called 'price to book'.

A fascinating thing to be aware of is that it is entirely possible for some shares to be trading at less than book value. That is to say that if you bought that share and the company was then wound up (i.e. closed down), you would be entitled to more money back than you spent on your shares. When a company is in this situation you can feel fairly secure that you are investing when the company is cheap. It might be cheap for a reason, such as falling profits, but you could quite possibly be paying 80p to own 100p worth of 'intrinsic' value, for example.

The whole point here is that if you have a basic grasp of some of these valuation metrics then you are giving yourself a decent chance of buying a share when it is good value. If you buy a share when it is good value, you vastly increase your chances of making a decent return. In my experience, many people investing in shares do not have even a basic grasp of these 'valuation metrics', which is one of the main reasons they risk losing money.

Dividends and dividend yield

Dividends are another very important aspect of shares to be aware of. We have already dealt with the idea of earnings yield (basically the amount of profit you are entitled to each year, expressed as a percentage of the price you paid for your shares). As you might imagine, however, most companies do not pay all of their profit out to their shareholders each year. A company will usually have lots of interesting things to spend those profits on if it wishes to continue growing. As such, the management of a company will decide each year how much of the profit to keep (this is called 'retained earnings') and how much to pay out to shareholders.

What gets paid out to shareholders is the dividend. Just as with earnings yield. The dividend yield is simply the percentage return on your investment calculated by dividing the value of your dividend by the value of your shareholding. When you look at a company, it is important to look at how much that company has traditionally paid out in dividends and what analysts think it might pay out in the future.

Looking at the whole market

We have looked very briefly at some of the fundamental ways of understanding the value of a share and I hope that, as with most of this book, it has made you feel as if you are perfectly capable of understanding these things. The key things you need to learn about finance just aren't that difficult.

Before we move on, I want to make one final point about shares, which is that all of the above metrics can be applied to the stock market as a whole. This means that at any given time we can consider the P/E ratio, book value or dividend yield of the entire stock market and compare it to other stock markets (e.g. compare the UK to the USA or Japan) or to the same market in other points in history. If we know that the P/E ratio or book value of a market is historically low, we have a much higher chance of making a great return on our money in the next few years than we would if those ratios were historically high.

Obviously, things are more complicated in the real world than in our examples. One of the issues you will confront when trying to use these metrics to analyse the market is whether the numbers are reliable. Another is that a cheap market can get even cheaper – meaning that if you buy it, you could lose money for a while – and an expensive one can get even more expensive, meaning that if you decided not to buy it you would miss out on the continued upside. Nevertheless, just as we said when considering property in Chapter 5, if you are aware of these sorts of key valuation metrics when considering any market for investment, you stand a far better chance of buying and selling at sensible levels in the long run than the vast majority of the population, who are investing without this knowledge.

We will look at equities in a little more detail in Chapter 10 for those of you who are interested, but for now we shall move on to our next asset class.

Commodities

Many people are well aware of what a commodity is, but it is perhaps still worth clarifying precisely. Wikipedia describes a 'commodity' as: 'A good for which there is demand but which is supplied without qualitative differentiation across a market.' That is to say that oil is basically the same whether it is supplied by Nigeria, Russia or Venezuela, and wheat is basically the same whether it comes from Russia, Germany or Canada (within reason). Compare this to something like a car, the value and price of which will be based on a large number of differentiating variables such as brand, top speed, engine size and finish quality.

Commodities have been used as a store of value throughout human history, and many commodities have also been used as money. The word 'salary' comes from the fact that Roman soldiers were originally paid in salt (*sal*), for example. Everything that follows is relevant to all commodities but it is worth noting that it is useful to think of the precious or monetary metals (gold and silver) as a separate category from all other commodities, given their accepted role as money (a role that hasn't really been shared by any other commodities for several hundred years). We will discuss this important differentiation in more detail, as understanding it will be one of the things that helps to grow your wealth in the years ahead.

As a general comment, I would stress that we should be particularly interested in commodities today. One of the world's best investors, Jim Rogers, starts his excellent book *Hot Commodities* by saying:

> Too many so-called smart investors consider themselves diversified
> if they have money in stocks, bonds, real estate and maybe, for the
> sophisticates, some currencies or timber. But commodities rarely, if ever,
> hit the radar screen.

A key part of the message of his book is that you must not fall into this trap. It is absolutely essential that you think about and have exposure to commodities if you want to grow your wealth in the next few decades.

Why you should think about commodities

There are a number of reasons why you should consider commodities as an investment today. Let us now look at three of them.

1 THERE IS A HUGE GROWTH IN THE DEMAND FOR COMMODITIES

Given the media coverage this particular piece of news received, many people will be aware that the 7 billionth human was born in October 2011. We have already discussed the world's rising population when we looked at global growth but it is perhaps worth repeating: the world's population is currently growing by more than 80 million people per year – more than 200,000 per day – and this will likely continue to accelerate over the next few years.

Just as important as this incredible growth in population is the fact that an increasing number of these people are getting wealthier. In China 20 years ago, hardly anyone had a car, and there were no high-speed trains and hardly any skyscrapers. Today the Chinese buy more cars per year than the Americans, have more miles of high-speed train track than anywhere else in the world, and have hundreds of skyscrapers and many more planned or in construction. This has obviously had a huge impact on the market for all commodities, particularly those used in the automotive, rail and construction sectors.

Until very recently, most people in the developing world also survived on very simple diets and could afford very little meat. Now millions more Chinese, Brazilians, Indians and so on consume chicken, fish, pork and beef than ever before. This ongoing trend has very serious implications for global agriculture and water supplies. We must not underestimate that, as millions of new consumers grow up and become richer all over the world, the overall demand for all commodities will likely grow at a rate never seen before.

2 THE WORLD HAS SOME SERIOUS PROBLEMS WITH THE SUPPLY OF COMMODITIES

At the same time that there is this significant and ongoing increase in the demand for commodities, the world is beginning to encounter serious supply constraints for many of them. For example, the volume of rock a mining company has to dig through to find one ounce of gold today is a multiple of what it was only a few years ago; today a miner creates more than 20 tonnes of waste just to produce one wedding ring. Most of the biggest gold mines in the world, many based in South Africa, are seeing supply dry up. Hardly surprising when you consider they have already been dug to a depth of 3–4 kilometres.

This phenomenon is occurring for nearly every metal we use: copper, zinc, platinum, gold, silver and so on. We are finding it harder and harder to find new supplies of all these things – in fact, there are perfectly sensible analysts who have predicted that new silver production will basically stop as soon as 2020. The same is true in the oil market, where companies are having to go to extraordinary lengths to find new oil and many energy experts believe that the 'cheap', which is to say relatively easily accessible, oil is now essentially gone. The oil price plummeted from a peak in 2008 on the back of a glut of cheap oil from US shale production but has more than doubled from its last low in early 2016. I would argue that there is a fair amount of evidence that the era of cheap oil may well now be behind us.

We are also inevitably running into supply constraints with 'soft' commodities (things that grow) as the world exhausts supplies of arable land, fish and fresh water in a bid to feed so many billion people. This will only get worse as people in the developing world increase their meat consumption, as livestock farming leads to far higher water and land consumption than growing crops.

Basic economics tells us that where demand for something is increasing and supply is decreasing or fixed, then the price of that something must go up. This should be fairly obvious. If more people want something but there is less of it available, they will have to offer more money than the next person to get hold of it. This goes some way to explaining why virtually every commodity in the world has seen a significant increase in price in the last few decades. This being the case, we can conclude that the fundamental, structural (inherent) trend in commodities will be for their prices to increase.

3 THE SUPPLY OF NEW PAPER MONEY DRIVES UP PRICES

There is, however, another reason why commodity prices (in terms of paper currency) look set to carry on rising, and I would argue that it is just as important a driving force.

As we have mentioned several times already, in recent years governments all over the world have been producing vast quantities of new money. The Americans have more than tripled the outstanding supply of US dollars in the last three years. If you triple the supply of money but the supply of things is basically fixed, then the price of those things should triple, albeit with a time lag.

This is another reason why the dollar (and yen and euro) price of almost all 'stuff' has increased rapidly in the last few years. While governments all over the world continue to pursue a policy of money printing (or 'inventing', as I prefer to call it), commodity prices – if priced in those currencies – will generally trend up strongly.

It should be obvious that for those of you whose salary in paper currency is fixed (which is the case for most people), this is very bad news for your standard of living. If your salary this year is the same as last year but bread, eggs, milk, petrol and so on have increased in price by close to 20 per cent, it should be clear that you will suffer a reduction in your *real* standard of living. This is precisely what has been happening all over the world for several decades. The great news is that there is something you can do about it: you can own commodities. I describe this as 'owning inflation'.

Luckily for us, developments in financial products in the last few years have made owning commodities easier and cheaper than ever before. As already discussed, it wasn't that long ago that it was actually very hard to buy financial exposure to commodities. You had to have a reasonably large sum of money and a private banker. This is no longer the case, which is extremely good news.

One of the main reasons we can now own commodities is thanks to the development of the next – and arguably the most important – category of investment vehicle: funds.

Funds

For the majority of people, funds are the most relevant (and appropriate) investment vehicle. This is because a fund enables you to own
a large basket of several of the other financial products discussed in
this chapter. Buying the right funds at the right price will make a
huge difference to your life. So what are funds and, more importantly,
what are the 'right' funds to buy?

Funds were created several decades ago for a very logical reason.
We have already referred to the term 'diversification', which is simply the investor's version of 'not putting all your eggs in one basket'.
Early on in the creation of financial assets, particularly shares, it was
clear to anyone with common sense (and it has since been shown
academically many times) that splitting your money between several
investments is inherently less risky than having all your money in one
investment. This should make sense to you intuitively.

It was also the case that many early potential investors were excited
about investing in more than just one business area or 'sector'. Why
restrict themselves to owning one oil company if they could invest in
several oil companies as well as a number of agricultural companies,
railway companies, pharmaceutical companies, defence contractors
and so on, all at the same time?

Equally, as we have already suggested, why restrict themselves to
assets from only one region of the world? By owning a wide variety
of companies from a wide variety of countries, not only would they
spread the risk, but they would also give themselves exposure to as
many exciting parts of the world economy as possible.

It is clear that many people with money to invest were interested
in owning a large number of shares in a large number of sectors and
countries. The only problem for most people was that there was usually a reasonably large minimum investment required in order to buy
any given share. This meant that, in the early days of the stock market,
only very rich people were able to own a large number of shares in
a large number of sectors. They were the only ones who were able
to spread their risk and benefit from owning a greater number of
potentially successful companies – yet another reason why the rich
found it relatively easy to stay rich.

If you had to invest a minimum of $1,000 in each share, for example, you would obviously have needed $10,000 to invest in ten shares – or $30,000 to own each of the 30 stocks in the Dow Jones, an 'index' of 30 of the biggest companies in America. In the early days of the stock market, this was a huge amount of money for one person to invest. Diversification of any kind was, therefore, only possible for people who were already extremely wealthy (and was precisely how most of them invested).

The genius of funds

Investment funds were created to solve this problem. The idea was simply to pool money from many investors, who were each interested in owning a large cross-section of investments. This large pool of money would then be able to invest in a cross section of investments. If 10,000 people invested an average of $10,000, for example, you would have a fund of $100 million, which could then buy dozens or even hundreds of different shares. In the UK, for example, the Foreign and Colonial Investment Trust was founded in 1868 to 'Help the "investor of moderate means" have "the same advantage as the large capitalist".'

Everyone who bought shares in that fund would then nominally (theoretically) own that proportion of *all* the shares owned by the fund – even if that theoretical investment in each share was far less than the minimum amount they would ordinarily be permitted to own directly.

The other advantage for investors was that the company offering the fund for sale would take care of the administrative burden of owning the dozens or hundreds of shares.

As you can imagine, given the many advantages in terms of diversification and administration that funds gave investors, the idea caught on. Today there are numerous investment companies offering many thousands of different funds. Companies that offer a range of funds are known as fund managers, asset managers, investment managers or hedge funds. These terms all mean basically the same thing (although hedge funds are slightly different). You may or may not have heard of companies such as BlackRock, M&G, Jupiter, Fidelity, Henderson, Invesco, Standard Life Aberdeen and so on, or seen them advertising – particularly in early April around the annual ISA deadline. There are thousands of these fund management companies around the world running hundreds of thousands of funds.

Active and passive funds

As funds have become more popular as an investment over the years, two main categories of fund have developed: active and passive. Active funds are funds where an individual (known as a fund manager) tries to use his or her skill to pick the best shares (or other assets such as bonds or commodities) to make the best return possible for investors in that fund.

A fund of this type will usually be limited to investing in a certain type of asset class. For example, it might be a 'European equities fund', in which case the fund manager would be limited to buying European *shares*. This limitation on what the fund manager can invest in is called a 'mandate'. The mandate on any given fund describes the type of assets in which that fund manager can invest. This is something I don't like about many active funds, as it means that, if the mandated asset class has a bad year, the fund manager is basically unable to get your money out of those assets and put it into something safer. Active funds also tend to be relatively expensive, as you will have to pay for the 'clever', well-paid fund manager to invest in the 'right' shares, bonds or commodities, depending on what type of fund you have purchased.

As with any finance profession, some fund managers are excellent and well worth this premium (as we saw when I presented some of their returns earlier in the book). However, there is a wealth of research that says that, on average over the long run, passive funds outperform active (after accounting for costs).

Which brings us to the second type of fund: passive funds are where a fund management company copies the performance of an index (see below). These funds are sometimes referred to as tracker or index funds (because they 'track' an index). A good example would be a tracker on the FTSE 100. If you were to buy into such a fund it would aim to replicate as closely as possible the performance of the FTSE 100 index. If you were to invest in a FTSE tracker, your money would essentially be divided between the 100 shares in the FTSE index. This is a crucial advantage of being in a fund. You yourself would not be able to own all 100 stocks in the FTSE index unless you had a great deal of money and a great deal of time to devote to investment.

These days even the super-rich will tend to use a tracker or index fund to own the FTSE 100 stocks, as they would see too much of their potential return eaten up in fees if they actually bought all of the stocks in the FTSE 100 Index individually. Paying for 100 separate transactions in order to end up owning all of the companies in the index is clearly not ideal when you can pay once to own a tracker fund and have basically the same exposure. A fund is also much less work, as you can imagine.

Passive funds are a cheaper way to invest than active funds and are a much easier (and cheaper) way to get exposure to a large number of shares than buying those shares individually.

Indices or tracker funds

At this point, it is important to explain what an index is. An index is simply a method of measuring a stock market in some way.

You will most likely have heard of the FTSE 100, since it is referenced by the British press every day.*

The FTSE 100 is an index and is simply an invention of the London stock market; it adds up the price and size of the biggest 100 companies in the UK in order to generate a number, which is known as the 'level' of the FTSE 100.

The point of this is to give investors all over the world a snapshot of how well the British stock market is doing and, to a certain extent, how well the British economy is doing. The FTSE 100 does not represent the entire British economy, but it is a good proxy since the top 100 companies tend to represent about 80 per cent of the entire value of the stock market, and a reasonably large percentage of the value of the UK economy as a whole.

---

* The media's traditional 'Today in the markets' spots generally tell you what the FTSE 100 and the pound are doing each day and are, therefore, no use whatsoever to anyone in my view. This reality was perfectly captured in the 1990s TV comedy *The Day Today* by the marvellous character 'Collaterlie Sisters'. Please do take a moment to look her up on YouTube if you fancy some light relief!

The FTSE 100 index does not tell the whole story about the economy because there are hundreds of other, smaller companies listed on the London stock market, as well as thousands of 'private' companies (i.e. companies not listed on the stock market), operating in Britain. The UK's top 100 companies also do a great deal of their business overseas. Nevertheless, to some extent this index is a useful indicator of the state of the UK economy.

Every country in the world that has a stock market has several stock market *indices*. They were originally created and managed by the companies in charge of those stock markets, for example the New York Stock Exchange in America or Deutsche Börse in Germany. Examples you may know include: the Dow Jones 30, which is made up of a selection of 30 of the largest companies in the USA; the NASDAQ and S&P 500 (also in the USA), both of which have a much broader composition than the Dow Jones; in Japan the Nikkei 225; in Hong Kong the Hang Seng 40; in Germany the DAX 30; in France the CAC 40, and so on.

It is important to realize that indices are somewhat arbitrary constructs. Each national stock exchange chooses to include different numbers of stocks in their main index and cuts their market up in a variety of different ways, providing other additional indices for the investor to look at.

Despite being arbitrary, indices are very useful. If you want to make sure that you own the hundred biggest companies in the UK, 500 of the most important companies in the USA or the 40 largest companies in France, you need look no further than those indices to find out which companies you need to own. There will also be a tracker (or passive) fund for that index that will leave you the proud owner of shares in all of those companies for one transaction fee. I hope you can see that such funds are potentially exciting investment vehicles and a great financial innovation.

You might also be interested in owning a number of smaller companies from the countries above. As you might imagine, smaller companies tend to grow faster than larger ones. It is generally easier for a company with £100 million worth of sales or profits to grow that number by 10 per cent than it is for a company with £10 billion worth of sales or profits – and certainly easier for them to grow by 50 per cent.

Faster-growing companies will often have faster-growing share prices, which means you may have the opportunity to make higher returns with successful smaller companies than with very large companies. For this reason, many investors like to have exposure to smaller companies as well as larger ones. Most countries, therefore, provide an additional smaller company index. This is why we have the FTSE 250, FTSE SmallCap and AIM (Alternative Investment Market) in the UK, and why there are similar mid- and small-cap indices in other countries. The FTSE 250 includes the next 250 companies after the biggest 100 companies found in the FTSE 100 index. Collectively, all 350 companies are called the FTSE 350. Pretty simple stuff.

In the past, the long-standing, well-known indices were calculated by the information divisions of the various national stock markets. In recent years, independent financial information firms such as Reuters and Bloomberg have created their own indices for a wide variety of assets, as have certain divisions of investment banks like Barclays and Goldman Sachs. What this means is that you can now find indices and their related funds for pretty much any asset or country in the world: bonds, commodities, big companies, small companies, and stock market sectors such as banks, telecoms or pharmaceutical companies.

The reason this is important for our purposes is that as a private investor you are generally able to 'buy' these indices through a related passive fund. There has been an explosion in the choice available for the private investor in recent years. If you have a strong view on the UK economy, then you can buy a FTSE 100 index fund. Equally, if you think biotechnology companies are likely to have a good time, you can own them via a biotech index. If you feel that Singapore has a bright future, you can 'own' Singapore.

Within reason, you can own almost anything that occurs to you. If you read an article explaining why something has a bright future (graphene, thorium, tungsten, water, coal mining in Bangladesh, Brazilian oil, property in Montenegro, diamonds – the list is very, very long), you will often be able to buy something that gives you financial exposure to that theme. Don't forget, however, that you will need to buy into that something at the right price.

You can also make money when things go down

Another thing to be aware of is that (as counter-intuitive as it might seem) if you think something will fall in value, you are often able to make money out of that too. This is called 'shorting'. Essentially, shorting is a bet that something will go down instead of up.

For example, if you believe that the German stock market will suffer due to a eurozone crisis, you can 'short' it. To do this, you buy a product that will make you money if the German stock market falls. Shorting is another great thing to be aware of. Many people have never heard of it and most have no idea that anyone can do it. You just need to know how. It should be noted that shorting is quite a risky and specialist activity and not to be entered into lightly but it is well worth knowing that it is possible at the very least.

The great thing about indices and index funds then is that they enable you to own or short hundreds of different shares even if you only have a small amount of money to invest – and you can generally do this with relatively low fees and pretty tax efficiently too.

Smart beta

Something that has occurred since I wrote the first edition and is worth touching on briefly is the development of so-called 'smart beta' funds. These aim to give you the low cost and breadth of a passive or tracker fund but with the improved performance you would hope to achieve with an active fund. They do this by weighting the investments held within the fund using various clever metrics – hence '*smart* beta'.

As an example of how this works, one problem with many tracker funds is that they are what is called 'market cap weighted'. This means that the bigger the company is within an index, the larger it is as a percentage of that index and, therefore, as a percentage of any tracker or index fund that attempts to replicate the index. As a result, any money you invest into such a fund owns a much bigger chunk of the big companies than of the small companies.

To explain a bit and keep the maths relatively easy: if you were to put £10,000 into a FTSE 100 tracker fund today you would end up with roughly £1,100 worth of Royal Dutch Shell, £700 worth of HSBC and £550 of BP, but less than £100 each in the smallest companies in the index such as EasyJet, Admiral and Just Eat. The point is that 'market cap weighted' indices like the FTSE 100 (and S&P 500) mean that you end up with a *much* heavier exposure to big companies than small ones.

This can be problematic for your performance because big companies, by their very nature, are ones that have already succeeded and gone up a great deal in price, while small companies, all other things being equal, are often the ones that could be amazing investments as they grow.

By owning a 'normal' tracker fund, you will very likely end up having far too much of your money exposed to companies that have already seen a huge uplift in their share price – and far too little of your money with the ones that could be tomorrow's success stories. Smart beta funds attempt to get round these sorts of problems. One of the simplest ways they do this is with what is called an 'equal weighted' fund. You have probably guessed by now that an *equal weighted* FTSE 100 fund would just be one that owned 1 per cent of each of the 100 companies in the FTSE rather than 8 per cent in Shell and 0.1 per cent in the minnows of the index.

Over time, an equal weighted index of the FTSE 100 or S&P 500 may outperform a market cap weighted index. (To be fair, whether it does or not will depend on the prevailing mood of equity markets at the time. In recent years winners have continued to win for an unprecedented period of time, as seen in the massive size of companies like Apple, Alphabet (Google) and Amazon.) But equal weighting isn't the only game in town here. There are many other ways to weight the components of a fund – for example by using the sorts of financial ratios we looked at earlier in the chapter when we discussed equities. New smart beta funds using dividend yield or other valuation metrics can show a meaningful improvement in annual returns over older, simpler passive funds.

Smart beta funds aim to give you the performance of an active fund for the fees of a passive fund, and you should certainly consider them once you are ready to invest.

The annoying complexity of fund names

The distinction between passive, active and smart beta funds is probably the most important thing to understand about funds. As you start to look into funds as an investment, however, you will encounter a bewildering array of other names for the different types. These include: open-ended and closed-ended funds, open-ended investment companies (OEICs, pronounced 'oiks'), unit trusts (UTs), mutual funds, investment trusts (ITs), SICAVs and exchange traded funds (ETFs).

It is not necessary to have an in-depth understanding of precisely what all of these terms mean, and it is certainly not worth getting confused. There is a fair amount of overlap between the different types. It is enough simply to understand that there are a number of different types of fund that have developed for historical reasons.

How to buy funds and what you pay

What is important to understand about these different types of fund, however, is how they are bought and sold – and what you will pay to buy and sell them. Different types of fund are traded and charged for in different ways. This is the main thing you need to think about. As you will recall from our examination of compound interest in Chapter 3, the cost of owning something is key because small changes can mean large differences to your cash pot over time. Funds are basically purchased in one of two ways: they are either traded on the stock market, like a share, or they are not. We need to understand these two broad categories because the way they are traded and charged for differs.

Once you have an ISA or SIPP account with a good stockbroking firm, you will be able to invest any money that you have paid into that account in a huge variety of different things. This includes thousands of shares from stock markets all over the world as well as thousands of different funds, both active and passive. It is perhaps worth reiterating that if you have an ISA account at most high street banks you will most likely not enjoy this flexibility and choice.

When you buy or sell a share in your ISA or SIPP account through a stockbroker, that broker will charge you a commission. In the old days this commission was usually a percentage of the money you invested and could often be as much as 1.5 per cent of the value of what you were buying or selling, usually with a minimum charge such as £50.

For example, if you called your broker and instructed them to buy £1,000's worth of a share, you would have ended up with £950's worth of that share and paid the broker £50 as their commission for performing the transaction for you. If, however, you had purchased £5,000's worth of that share, you would have paid £75 commission and ended up with £4,925's worth of stock.

You can see that, for those who had a large amount to invest, commission that was charged as a percentage quickly became an annoyingly significant amount of money. Imagine someone selling £50,000's worth of shares (as you will be doing in a few years' time). At 1.5 per cent commission, they would be paying a commission of £750. It is also worth understanding that, with a 1.5 per cent fee to buy and sell, the investor would need to see a return of at least 3 per cent before they started to make any real money. Actually, as many of you will now realize, in an environment with 5 per cent or more inflation, the investor would need to see that share appreciate by at least 8 per cent before they were making a real return. Again, this shows us how important fees are.

Broadly speaking, it is no harder for a stockbroker to buy or sell £100,000's worth of a stock than £1,000. It *is* harder for a stock-broker to trade very large quantities of a share, but few private individuals would have enough to buy or sell to cause such problems. Unsurprisingly, customers who were investing significant amounts felt pretty hard done by, paying such large commissions in order to execute relatively simple trades.

As the financial services industry became more competitive, the more forward-thinking brokerage firms started offering their customers better terms to trade, such as commission rates with an upper cap. The advent of online trading in the 1990s then enabled the very best firms to start offering their clients even more competitive rates, given that the cost to them of offering a computer-based online service was much lower than having to pay large numbers of staff to deal with clients over the phone. Today it is possible to buy and sell shares online for as little as £5.95 – a vast improvement over a fee of several hundred or even several thousand pounds and part of the revolution in financial services that is one of the main themes of this book.

High-percentage commissions still exist if you wish to call a bro-ker and instruct them to buy or sell shares for you over the phone but it tends to be only older, technologically limited clients – or very wealthy individuals who have large numbers of shares to trade – who persist in doing this, given just how much more expensive it is.

So, if you want to buy a share or anything that trades on the stock exchange in the same way a share does, you will pay whatever com-mission rate your stockbroking firm charges. With costs to do this as low as they are today, this is great news.

Funds that trade like shares

As explained above, certain types of fund trade on the stock exchange like shares. The main ones of this type that you need to know about are Exchange Traded Funds and Investment Trusts. ETFs are almost all pas-sive funds. You can buy an ETF based on the FTSE 100, on gold, on the Australian dollar, on the CAC 40, and so on and so on. There are thou-sands of ETFs based on thousands of assets. Investment trusts, by contrast, tend to be active funds run by a fund manager with a particular focus such as smaller British companies or Japanese equities (Japanese shares).

This means that whether you want to own 100 of the largest UK companies, a basket of shares from all over the world, a portfolio of commercial property assets, or a fund that specializes in American technology shares, you can get that exposure and often only pay the commission charged for buying a share.

As explained above, today if you are with a good stockbroking firm you will usually buy and sell shares (and funds that trade like shares) from as little as £5.95 up to about £15 per transaction. In fact, there are a number of firms in the UK market with whom you will only have to pay £1.50 per transaction, if you set up regular auto-mated monthly payments into certain funds or shares. The UK market has come a long way in the last few years in this respect, but this is something that only a tiny percentage of the population are taking advantage of. Investors from the 1980s would find it hard to believe that it is possible to buy and sell shares for as little as £1.50, and this fact demonstrates the thinking outlined in Chapter 3: 'Today's financial products are better than ever before.' If you know where to go, the difference between the best financial accounts and products available today and those of only a few years ago is like the difference between a sports car and a horse and cart. Sadly, many financial services companies in the UK, and certainly most of the high street banks, continue to sell 'horse and cart' type products because many people don't know where to find the 'sports cars'. This is another reason it is perhaps understandable that so many people think investment is a mug's game.

One final thing to be aware of in terms of how exchange traded funds and investment trusts are priced is that there is sometimes also an annual management fee (the annual management charge, or AMC) on top of the commission you pay. This is incorporated into the price of the fund you are buying and thus won't be explicitly stated when purchasing, but it will be detailed on the website of whomever you are buying that fund from. As an example, a fund I own has an annual management charge of 0.4 per cent. This, plus a dealing commission, is often still a cheaper way to invest than buying funds that are not traded on the stock exchange.

Funds that do not trade like shares

We are now aware that there is a huge range of funds that trade like shares. There are also many thousands of other funds that do not trade like shares. These funds are usually what are called open-ended investment companies (OEICs) or unit trusts.

Just as with funds that trade like a share, you can buy an OEIC or unit trust on an incredible range of investments. There are funds which give you exposure to UK shares, UK bonds, European smaller companies, commodities, Russian shares, Latin American shares and so on. We will worry about what kind of investment we would like exposure to later; for now, let us look at what the cost of owning an unlisted fund is (i.e. the cost of a fund that does not trade like a share). Again, one of the key reasons so many people have bad experiences when investing is that they have bought products without understanding what percentage of their money they are losing to fees and charges.

Charges and fees

There are basically three types of fee or charge you will need to be aware of when considering whether or not to buy an unlisted fund (one that doesn't trade like a share): the initial charge, the Annual Management Charge (AMC), and the Total Expense Ratio (TER) – now more frequently called the Ongoing Charges Figure (OCF). There are further types of fee – exit and performance charges – but these are quite rare.

> It is crucial that you understand all relevant fees and costs before you invest in anything.

This way you can minimize the proportion of your hard-earned cash that gets eaten up by fees. As ever, many people have no idea what these fees are when they walk into their high street bank and ask to see a financial adviser. As a result they can end up paying too much in fees, making it harder to achieve a good return on their money.

1 INITIAL CHARGE

Traditionally, companies offering unit trusts and OEICs would charge you a percentage of your money when you originally bought the fund. For a long time, this was as much as 5 per cent of what you wanted to invest, and sometimes it was even more than that (especially for a 'hot' sector. There were many Internet and technology funds in the dot-com boom that charged very high fees upfront, leaving financial professionals to 'make hay while the sun shines'). Say you were lucky enough to have your full ISA allowance at the time, of over £10,000 to invest, and you decided to buy one of these funds, you might have paid more than £500 for the privilege. If you were using a financial adviser to decide which fund to buy, you would have been paying their fees on top. Contrast this with what you would pay if you made your own decision about which fund to buy and put that money into an exchange traded fund, as described above. Through a good stockbroker, you could pay as little as around £10, that is, just the dealing commission – or even only £1.50. At worst, you would pay £10 plus the annual management fee that some listed funds carry (generally this will not be more than 0.5 per cent). On £10,000 the difference, therefore, would be as much as £800 – or 8 per cent of your money! Without wanting to labour the point, if you pay away 8 per cent more of your money in fees than is necessary, and assuming inflation is at least 5 per cent, you will need whichever investment you have chosen to return 13 per cent before you see any *real* return. This disastrous reality is one of the reasons many people have historically struggled to make a decent return on their money. And remember that real inflation is also quite possibly higher than 5 per cent. That is to say that the reality is even worse than this example.

Many funds still charge these onerous initial fees but if you have an account with a good stockbroker, you will usually be able to buy an unlisted fund with a zero per cent initial fee because they will waive it. There will be charges for some of the more popular funds, even at a good stockbroking firm, but they will be significantly lower than the fees you are likely to be charged by other providers. If you have made your own decision about which fund to invest in, you will also have removed the layer of fees levied by a financial adviser. Altogether, this can have a meaningful impact on your returns.

It is worth noting that these days the better financial advisers are actually able to get you into some funds more cheaply than you might be able to do yourself, as they are able to buy in bulk for their clients. This can make using a financial adviser worthwhile – assuming you know how to find a good one who isn't trying to charge you 3 per cent or more, like some of the worst (and biggest) ones still do! Beware of any finance company that will not tell you what percentage of your money they charge each year. In fact, please report them to the Financial Conduct Authority (FCA) as there are still a number of large and pretty well-known companies engaging in this kind of sharp practice.

2 ANNUAL MANAGEMENT CHARGE

In addition to any initial charge on a fund, nearly all funds will charge you an annual fee to cover the costs of running the fund. This number will be quoted in the fund's literature. Crucially, the annual management charge (AMC) does not tell the whole story. When you are considering the purchase of a fund, you should always find out the total expense ratio or ongoing charges figure.

3 Total expense ratio or ongoing charges figure

This number includes a few additional costs that the AMC does not. Many fund management groups do an impressive job at putting the Total Expense Ratio or Ongoing Charges Figure (TER/OCF) in the smallest of small print. In fact, during a recent visit I made to a UK high street bank, the financial adviser struggled to even find the TER for a fund my friend owned. I found this quite outrageous, and further evidence of just how few people in the UK market understand what they are paying when they buy a financial product. That adviser had obviously never been asked the question!

There is no need to understand in detail what goes into the TER/OCF, but you should check what percentage it is so you know how much of your money will be eaten up every year. Obviously, the lower it is the better.

To be clear – the OCF *includes* the AMC. A fund with a 0.9 per cent annual management charge and a 1.15 per cent OCF has an *additional* 0.25 per cent of costs in it which tend to be the audit and accounting costs and the costs of the custodian and depository firms who legally look after the assets in the fund.

A key point to make here is that, by law, any performance numbers that the fund publishes are *after* the OCF charges have been taken out. If a fund publishes that it made 10 per cent this year and has an OCF of 1 per cent, it actually made 11 per cent of investment return.

4 Exit and performance charges

There are two other charges you may encounter, although they are both relatively rare. An exit charge is what it sounds like: the fee you will pay when you sell the fund. Thankfully, they aren't very common these days, although many mortgage products still have them.

Performance charges tend to be found in the hedge fund industry and at the racier end of the fund universe. Quite simply, a performance charge is an extra percentage of your money that will be paid to the fund manager, usually only if your fund goes up by more than a certain percentage. There is nothing wrong with a performance charge, as long as the return that triggers it is sufficiently high and the charge itself is sufficiently low.

Accumulation and income funds

One final aspect of funds to be aware of is the difference between accumulation and income funds. Shares often pay a dividend. If you own shares in a company, that company will pay out a proportion of its profits to its shareholders, usually twice a year. This is the dividend.

As we have seen, bonds also pay a percentage return, known as a coupon. Dividends and coupons are collectively described as 'income'. If you own a fund that generates income from dividends or coupons, you can choose to have that income paid out to you in cash (as would be the case in an income fund) or you can elect for that money to be ploughed back into units in the fund you own. This is called 'accumulation'.

Very often you will be able to choose between income or accumulation versions of the same fund. Unless you need the money, for example if you are retired, it is best to choose to own the accumulation fund. Ploughing the income earned back into your fund will maximize the effect of compounding on how your money grows and is hugely important as a result.

Insurance products

I would describe another category of investment vehicle as 'insurance products'. These include a range of different products, which are usually structured by insurance companies and then sold to the public directly through their own sales network or via third parties such as high street banks, building societies and financial advisers. Within this category I include the type of endowment product that was sold to large numbers of people in recent years as a way of building money to pay off their mortgage. The nomenclature here is slightly confusing because the word 'endowment' also describes money left to a non-profit institution such as a university or charity, usually by a wealthy individual. Here, however, we are concerned with the mortgage product.

The other main category is investment bonds, of which there are several types you may have heard of. These include: with-profits bonds, distribution bonds, guaranteed income and growth bonds, stock market bonds and property bonds.

The point here is that these products are very similar to funds, with the main difference being their tax treatment and the costs you are likely to pay to own them. Because they are considered to be insurance products, the government taxes them differently from funds. Depending on your tax situation, this can be advantageous, but I would argue that, unless you are wealthy enough to be saving/ investing more than your monthly ISA allowance, you are generally best off avoiding these products.

One reason for this is that these products tend to give you far less flexibility in terms of what you will end up owning than you can achieve with funds or many of the other investment categories that you can own as part of your ISA account. To quote the CISI (Chartered Institute for Securities and Investment):

> Nowadays almost all of the funds offered within investment bonds can be bought directly as unit trusts or OEICs, which are much more flexible. Money can be withdrawn from a unit trust or OEIC at any time without penalty.

Another reason, to return to what is by now a familiar theme, is that these products tend to be expensive and their costs rather opaque. Again, the CISI themselves say:

> Charges applicable to investment bonds are not always easy to understand ... [IFAs] who sell investment bonds can receive up to 6–7% or even 8% initial commission. These high initial commissions are seen as the primary reason why some unscrupulous advisers might recommend investment bonds when an alternative investment product may be just as good or better.

I have had personal experience of this. I was lucky enough to be able to buy a flat in central London in my mid-twenties. When I went to see an IFA to help me with my mortgage situation, not only did he suggest a product with what I deemed to be excessive commission charges, he wanted to charge me an additional £500 for having suggested the product in the first place. I flatly refused to take his advice and made my own arrangements. Again, it is not my intention to disparage all financial advisers by any means, and I acknowledge that this is anecdotal, but it is important to know that you can avoid these sorts of charges – and quite possibly do a better job with your financial situation as a result – if you are willing to take a little time to understand what the other, better options are or if you use a more ethical and fairly priced financial adviser.

Foreign exchange

Many of you reading this book will have heard of the foreign exchange (or forex/FX) market. It is quite simply the global market in different currencies. You will have encountered the 'retail' forex market every time you have gone on holiday and needed to buy euros, dollars, rupees, or whatever else you needed for your travels. ('Retail' in finance is used to describe a financial service provided to the private individual rather than a company or professional investor.)

As you can imagine, there is a huge need globally for companies, governments and all sorts of other organizations and individuals to change money in order to be able to buy and sell things across borders. Because of this, the forex market is by far the biggest market in the world. The number given on Wikipedia at the time of writing is that around $4 trillion a day is traded and this number very likely underestimates the reality – particularly when you consider how large a black market there is in foreign currency transactions too. This vast scale is unsurprising when you think that nearly every single product (oil, cars, agricultural products) or service (telecommunication, banking, legal) that crosses a border necessitates a foreign exchange transaction. In addition, there is an enormous amount of trade in foreign currencies for purely speculative (financial) reasons.

As with any other market, the prices of the assets involved move up and down a fair bit. In the forex market, the 'assets' are the currencies of hundreds of countries.

A country's currency will lose or gain value against other currencies, based on a combination of what is happening in that country and what forex traders expect to happen to that country in the future, just as a share price will move based on what people think that a company is doing and will do in the future.

A share will tend to go up in value if the company is doing well and if people believe that it will continue to do so. A currency will do just the same if people feel the same about the country behind it. A good example, when I wrote the first edition of this book in 2012, was the strength against nearly every other world currency of the Australian dollar (AUD) and the Canadian dollar (CAD). Anyone lucky enough to visit Australia in 2007 and then visit again in 2012 would have seen the incredible increase in the value of the dollar. In 2007 a British tourist would have received around 2.5 AUD for every one of his or her pounds, whereas in 2012 he or she would only have got about 1.5 AUD.

Put another way, if a British tourist had purchased a large number of Australian dollars in 2007, held on to them and then converted them back to pounds reasonably recently, he or she would have made a return of around 40 per cent – not bad.

There is always a bull market somewhere

The same sort of return could have been made in a large number of other currencies. One of the great things about the foreign exchange markets is that 'there is always a bull market somewhere'. One currency's strength is, inherently, another currency's weakness, so, no matter what is happening in the world economically, there is always the chance to make money in the forex market if you know what you are doing.

Just as we have seen with other investments, a superb thing about the forex market today is that there are ways for the private investor to participate in it that did not exist until quite recently. One of the main ways that private individuals can participate in the forex market is by using spread betting, which we mentioned previously. There are also exchange traded funds available for a large number of currencies, perhaps a simpler way for the 'average punter' to get exposure. That said, trading foreign exchange can be quite complicated and is not for the faint-hearted. For the majority of people reading this, simply owning assets from all over the world will give you useful exposure to a large number of the world's currencies, without you having to worry about learning the 'black magic' of forex. We will look at how to do this in the chapters that follow.

Derivatives

The penultimate category of financial product for us to address is derivatives. These are without question the most complex and 'professional' of investment products, and arguably not appropriate for the vast majority of individuals as a result. One of the main reasons for this is that with derivatives it is possible to lose a great deal more money than you start with. This is one of the reasons why the famous investor Warren Buffett described them as 'financial weapons of mass destruction', although he also sees derivatives as a potential threat to the entire global economic system.

The term 'derivatives' encompasses a large number of different products, most especially 'futures' and 'options'. It is perhaps easiest to think of a derivative as a bet between two people about what the price of something will be in the future.

The oldest derivatives in the world are agricultural futures. Merchants and farmers of rice in Japan, and wheat and other similar crops in Europe and the USA, came up with the clever idea of agreeing a fixed price for an agreed quantity of a crop at some time in the future. This helped the farmer to budget, given that he was then guaranteed a certain amount of money no matter what happened to the price of his crop throughout the year. It also helped the merchants to manage their inventories because they knew what price they would be paying, and what quantity of grain or rice they would be receiving from the farmers they were trading with.

The derivatives market has come a long way since agricultural futures and is now a complicated and sophisticated market within which you can make bets on a vast number of financial instruments, commodities, and even left-field things such as who will win a presidential election. Because of their complexity and the high risks associated with them, very few people should get involved in buying and selling derivatives, at least until they have spent a good amount of time learning about financial markets generally – and derivatives specifically.

That said, it is possible to make a very large amount of money in a short space of time if you trade derivatives successfully – arguably more so than with any other type of financial instrument. For those who are interested in getting involved with the derivatives market, the best way to trade them as a UK-based individual is by using a spread betting account. We will look at how to do this in more detail later in the book.

Crypto assets/blockchain

As you will see in what follows, I was already very much aware of an emerging financial asset called 'bitcoin' when I wrote the last edition of this book in 2015. Despite being reasonably close to it as a story at the time, I decided that it was still a little too marginal an asset class for me to include in that version of the book.

In writing this third edition, I confess that I have been sorely tempted to do the same again – that is to say, to leave bitcoin, crypto assets and blockchain out of the book completely. I have my reasons for this stance, as you will see. However, given the enormous press attention that the sector has had in the last year or two, I concluded that I really should include a section on it for the sake of completeness. At this stage of proceedings, given how relatively mainstream it has become as an asset class – or, at the very least, how ubiquitous it has become on everyone's social media feeds, I think that to ignore it completely would be doing you a disservice.

Below I have done my best …

- To provide a basic explanation of the asset class
- To give you evidence for why I feel vaguely qualified to comment on it (although I would stress that I do not hold myself out as an expert on the subject)
- To come to some sort of useful conclusion about how to think about it and what to do about it in the context of 'owning the world'.

What are bitcoin/crypto/blockchain?

A full description of what precisely bitcoin, crypto assets and block-chain actually are is well beyond the scope of this book. I would argue that the space is the most complicated and controversial of financial asset classes in existence. Explaining what they are in any great detail would add far too many thousands of words to this book and, more importantly, waste many hours of your time – entirely unnecessarily in my view. There are plenty of other books and resources out there which can give you the detail if you are interested (I have included some of these in the bibliography). We don't need to go down the rabbit hole of any massively detailed explanation of what they are in order for you to achieve the goal I wish you to achieve in reading this book – developing the confidence to get your financial affairs in order – I'm a big believer in the merits of the 'fastest route from A to B'. Nevertheless, I will do my best to summarize what they are as briefly as possible.

From single- to triple-entry bookkeeping/accounting

Perhaps the best 'plain English' description of what they are that I have seen is that they are a technology that enables triple-entry bookkeeping (or accounting). To explain: for most of human history, humans were hunter-gatherers and any trade that did occur took place under a barter system. As a result, trade was pretty limited, and humans didn't really make any forward progress in terms of becoming wealthier or more technologically sophisticated for tens, arguably even hundreds, of thousands of years.

Then, a few thousand years ago, some smart folk in what is modern-day Iraq (the Sumerians, as it happens) invented a transformational technology: something called single-entry bookkeeping (or single-entry accounting – the terms are basically interchangeable). This simply meant that they figured out how to write down that person X *owned something* and/or that person X *owed* person Y something.

Archaeologists have found clay tablets dating back to several thousand years BCE which recorded the fact that a certain individual owned a certain quantity of an agricultural crop. Although this may not seem like much of a breakthrough, it was actually completely transformational for humanity and for our ability to grow economically and technologically.

As the website Hacker Noon (hackernoon.com) has put it:

> Once you can keep track of who owns what, trading starts to happen
> at a much larger scale. That's why the kings and queens of ancient times
> could build castles and establish professional armies and create great
> wonders of the world ...

The problem with single-entry bookkeeping was that you had to trust the person who was keeping score. Any unscrupulous scribe in a position of power could very easily alter the record to enrich his friends or family at the expense of the rightful owner of any given property. If the lesson of history is to be believed, this is very often precisely what happened – leading to a great deal of strife and bloodshed.

Fast-forward a few centuries and we find that various human cultures had upgraded this single-entry accounting system to a version 2.0: logically enough, we call this *double*-entry bookkeeping. Double-entry bookkeeping is the foundation of modern accounting and, without exaggeration, modern civilization. There would be no nation states, no large buildings, bridges, roads, cars, planes, boats, drugs or supermarkets had humans not invented the fundamental technology of double-entry accounting. (Think about this next time you describe accountants or accounting as 'boring'. Actually, none of the most important or fun things in life would exist without them or it – truly.)

The way double accounting works is pretty obvious to us twenty-first-century geniuses, not least because we have the benefit of hindsight. In essence, rather than some arbitrary class of aristocratic scribe or record keeper being in charge of keeping a record of everyone's wealth, there were now two records kept – credit and debit or asset and liability. Crucially, these records were also now invariably kept by an independent third party who could mediate between creditor and debtor and ensure that both sides fulfilled their obligations. The independent third party has been through various guises since the system was invented (think of the moneylender Shylock in Shakespeare's *Merchant of Venice* as one example), but the two main institutions that underpin any double-entry system are governments/nation states (and, by extension, their militaries – a point we will come back to) and banks.

Enter triple-entry bookkeeping

The double-entry system has underpinned virtually all human devel-opment since roughly the Middle Ages. With the arrival of bitcoin in 2009 we may have moved into an era of *triple-entry* bookkeep-ing – the point being that the technology behind bitcoin embeds the 'trusted third party'/intermediary element of the double-entry system (the bank or government) *within the technology itself*. It does this by encoding the necessary information in a distributed ledger called the 'blockchain'.

The 'ledger' incorporates a record of every transaction that has taken place, and the fact that it is 'distributed' (i.e. doesn't sit in one place but is essentially in little pieces of code in thousands of places all over the world) theoretically make the system robust. The security and trust elements to do all of this are enabled by advanced cryptog-raphy (writing and solving complex codes) – which is why bitcoin is described as a 'cryptocurrency'.

As you might imagine, the ability to remove banks and govern-ments from financial (and other) transactions is potentially highly transformational, arguably even revolutionary in scope. Given this fact and given the vested interests involved, the arrival of crypto-currency and blockchain has been met with a very wide range of reactions depending on the audience in question. Unsurprisingly, futurologists and techno-anarchists are delighted and see the emerg-ing technology as a catalyst for a bright future where the power of nation states is severely limited and handed back to 'the people'. Gov-ernments, central banks and the banking establishment are less sure, not least given how useful such technologies are to criminals and 'rogue states' – another key consideration in the debate.

As best I can remember, I first became aware of bitcoin in about 2013 when I met the finance journalist and comedian Dominic Frisby. I had long been a fan of his work as *MoneyWeek* magazine's resident expert on precious metals and was delighted to meet him face to face when he interviewed me for his 'Bulls and Bears' podcast. A year or so later, I became aware that Dominic was crowdfund-ing a book on the subject of bitcoin via the literary crowdfunding site Unbound. I was one of the people who contributed to getting the book published. *Bitcoin* was published in November 2014 and was therefore one of the earliest relatively mainstream books on the subject.

My point in recounting this story is to emphasize that I have been aware of bitcoin as a technology for several years, have given it a fair amount of thought in that time, and did not just dismiss it out of hand as has been the case with a reasonable number of folk who work in more mainstream financial markets. Even before I was offered the chance to contribute to Dominic's book on the subject, I had heard and read a fair bit about it – else I would certainly not have contributed to Dominic's crowdfunding effort, as you might imagine. Aside from Dominic's book – which I read with interest the moment it was published – I also have a number of friends and acquaintances who have previously held high-profile jobs at top investment banks and investment funds who have become involved with crypto and blockchain companies.

As a result, I can say that I have followed developments in this area with interest for more than five years. Part of my reason for doing this is that the overriding idea of this book – 'owning the world' – is to ensure you have exposure to *all* major asset classes. I look at this in more detail in Chapter 10. The primary question to answer in this section of the book then, as far as I'm concerned, is whether or not I include bitcoin and/or crypto assets more generally as one of those *major* asset classes alongside shares, bonds, cash, commodities and property as part of an 'own the world' approach to investment. The simple answer, as far as I'm concerned, is yes – but with meaningful reservations.

My belief is that any money you allocate to it should be thought of just as you might think about investing in one single risky share or similarly speculative investment and not as a core pillar of owning the world. In practice, this means that you might consider investing 1, 3 or – at the maximum – 5 per cent of your wealth into the space.

Bitcoin or bitcon?

My reason for this stance is quite simple: while it is certainly a fascinating and explosive emerging market and technology, the whole area reminds me of the dot-com boom of the late 1990s when I saw at first hand precisely the same thing that I have seen in the last year or so with crypto assets – huge press exposure, a massive frenzy of interest, and a whole slew of people who have never invested before in financial products of any kind being sucked into the space in the hope of getting rich quickly.

When the same thing happened in the dot-com boom of the late 1990s, the vast majority of people lost a great deal of money and it was a tragic thing to watch. Without wanting to be excessively gloomy, I think it is worth explicitly acknowledging that when people lose their entire life savings or are declared bankrupt, it can and does have exceptionally serious and unpleasant ramifications for them and for their families. This is serious stuff. For every resilient individual who is able to shrug their shoulders, dust themselves down and look to rebuild their now decimated finances from scratch again, there are people whose lives are destroyed and, in some cases, even lost (there were several thousand additional suicides on both sides of the Atlantic following the dot-com crash of 1999/2000 and the financial crisis of 2008/9 – this should not be forgotten).

The trouble with the current maelstrom of interest in crypto for me is that it is just like the dot-com boom of nearly 20 years ago but almost certainly considerably worse, for the following reasons:

1 THE SHEER SCALE OF THE PRICE INCREASE MEANS THAT PRICES ARE MORE LIKELY TO FALL THAN RISE OVER TIME

We have already seen how powerful the idea of mean reversion is in finance. The more extreme a relatively short-term price move has been in any financial market, the further that price will be away from the long-run mean and the more likely it will be to revert to the mean as a result (i.e. fall). Any asset that goes from less than $1 to nearly $20,000 in less than a decade (as bitcoin has) is more likely to be above the mean and more likely to revert downwards than continue on upwards – eventually, at least. This is no doubt a big part of why the price of bitcoin has already fallen to just over $6,000 at the time of writing. As billionaire investor

Jim Rogers has put it: 'I've seen a lot of bubbles in my career, but bitcoin is in a league of its own.'

Here's a somewhat prosaic example of how extreme this has been. In 2010 a software developer named Laszlo Hanyecz purchased two pizzas for 10,000 bitcoins. This was about $40 worth of bitcoin at the time. At the peak bitcoin price in December of 2017, the bitcoins he used to purchase those pizzas would have been worth not far off $200 million. Those are expensive pizzas. I recount this example for two reasons: first, to illustrate the sheer scale of the price move with a real-world example; second, to make the point that these sorts of move arguably invalidate the technology as a viable *currency* for the time being at least. One of the key requirements of a functioning currency is that it is relatively stable and not too volatile against things you might want to buy or trade. This cannot be said of bitcoin as this example shows.

2 SOCIAL MEDIA

The dot-com boom happened at a time when social media didn't exist and even email was in its infancy compared to today. A key reason for the extreme price movement in crypto assets in the last few years has been the extraordinary role played by social media. Never before in history has it been possible for such a relatively large proportion of the world's population to get excited about one investment. Facebook has over 2.2 billion users. This is unprecedented and means that 'the madness of crowds' can and has been stronger for bitcoin and crypto than for any other financial asset in history. Never before have so many people with no knowledge of financial markets been sold a financial product in the way they have in the last few years. Vast numbers of people have 'invested' for the worst reason of all – because it is going up and they see other people making money (theoretical or paper money at least – the money won't be real unless they take profits at the right time. I fear that most won't – just as with the dot-com boom). The problem with this is that this effect can be just as powerful on the way down as it was on the way up as everyone panics and sees those around them start to lose money rather than make it.

3 THE AREA IS ENTIRELY UNREGULATED AND THERE IS A PLETHORA OF DUBIOUS 'EXPERTS' INVOLVED

Part of the reason why interest has been so widespread is that the area is entirely unregulated. In most countries, it is illegal to promote most financial assets directly to individuals, for example via a social media platform such as Facebook. Even though I have had a 20-year career in financial markets, am authorized and regulated by the UK's financial regulator, and have had to pass several exams and undertake annual ongoing training over the years to get into that position and stay there, there are still incredibly strict rules that govern my ability to make recommendations of regulated financial assets such as shares, funds and other types of market investments.

This isn't the case for bitcoin and crypto assets. The space is unique in this regard. Anyone can set themselves up as an 'expert' and make wild promises about how you are 'guaranteed' to make 'life-changing' returns or 'thousands of per cent a year' (I have seen all of these claims on my social media feeds in the last few years). If I made those claims about regulated financial markets, I might soon be facing time in jail, yet regulators on both sides of the Atlantic have been exceptionally slow to stop people from doing just that in the crypto space. Many (likely most) of the 'educators' in the space holding themselves out as 'experts' and making such claims have few if any financial qualifications or any previous professional experience of financial markets. I have lost count of the number of times someone has jokingly told me that a friend of theirs with no previous experience of financial markets has suddenly become an online crypto 'expert'.

Their lack of experience or qualifications notwithstanding, many of these people have looked as though they knew what they were talking about, either because they have been selling Ponzi schemes which have yet to collapse – of which there are many – or simply because the market was going up indiscriminately as they plied their trade. This has been far less the case as the market has collapsed throughout 2018. As Warren Buffett has said: 'Only when the tide goes out do you discover who has been swimming naked.'

The other problem with crypto being entirely unregulated means that much of it is a complete Wild West/bandit country in terms of what people are actually buying. In the dot-com boom of the late 1990s, tech companies raising money on the US or European stock markets were at least functioning within the constraints of a stock market – something that has been regulated and operated within a strict legal structure for approaching two centuries. To quote Jim Rogers again:

> There have been plenty of bubbles I have seen in my life but this one is
> a little strange, because at least when the dot-com bubble was around,
> those were companies that said they had a business.

During the dot-com boom, people may have taken complete leave of their senses in terms of what they were willing to pay for highly speculative early-stage companies, but those companies had at least been vetted by a raft of professionals in some shape or form and were actually doing something commercial, or trying to. Even if pets.com was a terrible business model which haemorrhaged money on every bag of pet food it shipped, it was at least genuinely trying to sell pet food to customers via the Internet. Its business plan and accounts had been given consideration by bankers, financial analysts, accountants and auditors. Its various legal contracts had been verified by lawyers and it was not permitted to raise money from investors on the US stock market without sign-off from the US regulatory bodies who would have given consideration to all of the above.

People have quite rightly criticized regulators on both sides of the Atlantic over their numerous failures in the dot-com boom and during the subsequent global financial crisis of 2008 onwards. There is no question that they have far from a perfect track record. That said, I don't think it is that hard to argue that *some* regulation is better than none at all. Despite those crashes and plenty of high-profile company failures and scandals over the years, the system does actually function most of the time for thousands of perfectly sensible companies, in dozens of countries and across every sector of the economy, and has done for generations.

The same cannot be said of the crypto space. In the crypto world, people with entrepreneurial ideas looking to raise money have used a structure called an Initial Coin Offering, or ICO. Depending on what source you consider, there have been as many as 4,000 Initial

Coin Offerings in the crypto space in the last few years raising billions of dollars of real money.

To quote *Forbes* magazine:

> ... insider trading and dirty deals are flagrant. One coin-offering creator told Metastable Capital's Naval Ravikant, the CEO and cofounder of AngelList: 'If you agree to buy tokens at the ICO and support the price, then 30 days later, we'll secretly sell you any leftover tokens at a lower, pre-agreed price,' recalls Ravikant. That's a felony on Wall Street. In the cryptocurrency Wild West? 'These are the kinds of deals being cut left and right.' ...*

To show just how ridiculous the ICO space can get, Zack Brown of Columbus, Ohio, in the USA has managed to raise over $135,000 with his 'Useless Ethereum Token' despite writing in large letters on the landing page of the site:

> You're going to give some random person on the internet money, and they're going to take it and go buy stuff with it. Probably electronics, to be honest. Maybe even a big-screen television. Seriously, don't buy these tokens ...

Other crazy crypto coins include:

- Dogecoin, which started as a joke and is nominally worth over $300 million at the time of writing
- Potcoin – a coin for the cannabis community
- Legends Room coin – a coin for users of a Las Vegas strip club
- Coinye Coin – originally launched for fans of the rapper Kayne West but shut down when he sued them for trademark infringement.

There are many more similar examples and there are numerous scams out there. Sadly, because these things are not regulated, people who should be nowhere near these sorts of investments are investing

---

* *Source:* www.forbes.com/sites/laurashin/2017/07/10/the-emperors-new-coins-how-initial-coin-offerings-fueled-a-100-billion-crypto-bubble/#1cc7ec546ece

and, in the worst examples, buying these things on credit cards or increasing their mortgage to get on board.

4 Crypto assets are impossible to value

Another point here when comparing the crypto market with more conventional investments is that they are impossible to value in any fundamental way. Earlier in this chapter, we looked at the idea of using a P/E ratio and similar financial ratios to look at the value of a company and in Chapter 5 we looked at ways to value the property market including ideas such as rental yield or the ratio of income to house prices. Later in the book, we will have a look at some other valuation techniques as applied to the other asset classes, including cash, bonds and commodities.

The point here is that it is not possible to use these fundamental valuation tools on crypto assets. They don't have revenues, profits or balance sheets. The only pseudo-fundamental valuation methods I have seen in order to try to establish a price target are more or less spurious ideas about what the whole crypto space 'should' be worth in aggregate.

Lots of proponents of the space point to the fact that crypto is 'only' worth x billion dollars at present and that if it became 'only' 3 or 5 or 10 per cent of all financial assets, then this implies that there is massive upside. Advocates of this analysis articulate wildly bullish price targets for the whole space, saying that each bitcoin will be worth as much as $300,000 or even more than $1 million (from just over $6,000 per coin as I write) and that there will be a tidal wave of new millionaires created by bitcoin and by numerous other crypto assets.

Crypto assets may well end up comprising a meaningful percentage of financial assets, but I believe that there is reasonable uncertainty about whether or not this will happen. It is by no means inevitable as many commentators in the space repeat more or less constantly and without qualification – something I believe could be very damaging financially for a large number of the people who listen to them.

Even if crypto assets do become more mainstream and take significant market share away from the share, bond, cash, property and commodity markets that have served us more or less well for centuries, it is likely that the majority of the crypto assets which exist today will go to zero. Crypto advocates argue that blockchain will be just as big as the Internet and, as a result, will create vast amounts of economic value, produce the next wave of success stories like Apple, Amazon, Facebook, Google and so on, and make many people very wealthy in the process as a result.

I don't necessarily disagree with this contention, but what I would say is that hindsight is 20/20. It is easy to point to the handful of companies that now have valuations of several hundred billion dollars but it would have been vastly harder to have picked that handful of companies in 1999. People investing in the dot-com boom in the late 1990s had a far higher chance mathematically of investing in companies that then went bust or fell to a tiny shadow of their former selves than in the tiny minority of companies that are now enormous household names, for the simple reason that there were considerably more of the former than the latter and this is what happens in investment.

How would you have known in 1999 that Google was the one to own rather than Excite, Lycos, America Online or Yahoo? Or that Apple, which was not yet in the mobile phone business, would end up dominating that market and destroying the incumbent and seemingly indestructible giants of the day: Nokia, Ericsson, Motorola, Siemens and so on. Facebook was five years away from even existing in 1999. My point here is that even bitcoin or ethereum – the best-known assets in the space and arguably the 'safest' and most 'blue chip' as a result – could very well be the AOL and Nokia of crypto investment and disappear entirely in the reasonably near future. The overriding winner in the crypto space might not even exist for another decade for all we know.

This is a view held by some of the smartest investors in the world. UK billionaire investor Jim Mellon has said that he believes bitcoin itself is going to zero. He has a multi-decade track record of calling several discrete markets well enough to become a self-made billionaire – including markets as tough as commodities, mining and resources, emerging markets and, more recently, biotech. I suspect his prediction of zero will prove to be a little bit aggressive given how many bitcoin enthusiasts will hoover up inexpensive bitcoin as it falls, but it is nevertheless interesting that people of his calibre hold this view and he is certainly not the only one. Some of these characters may have a vested interest in talking down crypto assets, for sure, but many of them do not. In my experience, the people predicting that bitcoin will go to zero tend to have a long track record of massive investment success to the tune of having becoming billionaires or leading some of the biggest and most successful entities in the world. The ones saying that each bitcoin will be worth millions of dollars invariably do not.

I would make another related point, which is to say that it seems more than likely to me that the winners in this space will very likely be the crypto divisions of those multibillion-dollar companies that have already been the winners of the last 20 years or more. Much to the chagrin of the visionaries and techno-anarchists who hope that crypto will change the world by taking power away from elites, big corporates, central banks and governments, I suspect that those very elites, corporates, central banks and governments are likely to be the big winners in the space in the next few decades. JP Morgan, Goldman Sachs, Apple, Facebook and central banks and governments all over the world are making significant commitments to blockchain technology projects. They have matchless human resources, very deep pockets and, in the case of the corporates, enormous lobbying power with the relevant authorities.

5 DECENTRALIZATION MAY NOT REDUCE THE POWER OF NATION STATES

To counter this argument, friends of mine who are passionately committed to the crypto space have argued that, because cryptos are decentralized and distributed, governments and regulatory authorities will not be able to co-opt them. If the technology behind a transaction sits as electrons on thousands of computers all over the world, then the Federal Reserve, ECB or UK Treasury can't have jurisdiction over it. I have to completely disagree with this analysis. While governments continue to have a 'monopoly of violence' within their national borders, which I believe they very likely will for centuries to come, they will be able to make holding any crypto asset they like illegal for their nationals to use if they so desire. If it becomes illegal to transact in bitcoin in the USA or Europe, it won't matter that the technology is decentralized and distributed because you can't decentralize or distribute the human being that wants to use it. Governments are perfectly capable of arresting and imprisoning individuals who use bitcoin if they so desire.

There is plenty of precedent here. As I have written elsewhere, ownership of gold by private individuals was illegal in the USA from 1933 to 1974. The reasons behind this prohibition were essentially the same ones that might make the US or other authorities consider outlawing the use of certain crypto assets if they feel threatened. In a similar vein, I would remind the reader that there are three countries in the world that tried to switch from using US dollars to transact their oil sales to dealing in a gold-backed version of their own currency since the USA came off the gold standard in 1971. Can you guess which those countries were? The answer is Iraq, Libya and Iran. Go figure. My point is simply that when the US- and dollar-led global currency system sees threat, the USA will be swift to act with legal and/or lethal force, and I see no reason why this will change in future.

Crypto fans point to the fact that the space 'will be bigger than the Internet boom' as a reason to invest. I would say that they may well be correct but remind readers that people who invested in the Internet boom in 1999 had something like a 90 per cent chance of losing money and you might wait a while to see how things play out before committing a meaningful percentage of your hard-earned savings. The same phenomenon has happened throughout history. Most people who invested in railways in the 1840s lost their money. Many who invested in the 1860s or 1880s made a killing and became the millionaire 'robber barons' of late industrial America. The same happened with electricity, television and radio, and the automotive and aviation industries. It doesn't pay to be early unless you are incredibly lucky or incredibly smart and there is potentially even more uncertainty this time around, given that we don't know how powerful governments and regulators all over the world are going to react. As ever, patience is a virtue and time is one of your biggest allies in investment.

6 THERE IS UNCERTAINTY OVER THE TAX POSITION

Another problem with crypto assets as an investment is that there continues to be some meaningful uncertainty over how they are treated from a tax perspective. HMRC in the UK seems to be doing its best to clarify precisely how the various assets should be treated in terms of income or capital gains tax, for example, but I still see plenty of disagreement on social media with one supposed expert saying one thing and then another, frequently an accountant, saying something very different. At the very least, the picture is certainly complicated, and I think that many people who have invested in the space in recent years with no understanding of such things are at risk of being seriously caught out in the future. Part of the whole approach to investment which I outline in this book is to keep things as simple as possible, including from a tax perspective. As far as I'm concerned, any exposure to crypto assets introduces another level of complexity in this area set against using the tax-sheltered accounts which are available for all of the other asset classes.

Other structural problems with crypto

One final broad point I would like to make about the crypto space is to highlight that when I look through the breathless excitement about how 'world changing' it is, there seem to be several other potential structural problems with the practical application of the technology that are highlighted by critics, as outlined below.

I IT USES FAR TOO MUCH ELECTRICITY

Even now, the production and use of bitcoin alone uses about the same quantity of electricity per annum as the entire economy of Switzerland. This is with a tiny fraction of the world's population using it and this is for only one of thousands of crypto assets. Estimates are that if bitcoin were handling the same transaction volume as Visa, it would gobble up the entire global electricity supply.

Crypto enthusiasts point to a bright future where amazing technological breakthroughs in renewable energy have given us unlimited free energy. I very much hope that does happen, but I think it is some way off and the electricity problem may therefore be meaningful for the development of the crypto market in the more immediate future and for some time to come.

2 It would 'break the Internet' if used at scale

A similar point that is made by the 'bears' reasonably frequently is that the blockchain which keeps the record of transactions required for the technology to work is so large that it simply couldn't work with our current Internet capacity – and certainly not using smartphones on wireless networks. Just as with the energy point above, without a transformational technology which may or may not be forthcoming, something like bitcoin could never be used by several billion people making everyday purchases. The system is just too data hungry and unwieldy as a result.

To be fair, my reading on the subject leads me to believe that this isn't the most valid of criticisms. Without wanting to go into too much detail, there are already scaling solutions for bitcoin such as something called the Lightning Network, which enables transaction volumes comparable to existing networks such as Visa or Mastercard.

3 It isn't secure enough yet

Anyone who has followed the space for some time will see headlines every few months about how some entity has been hacked and millions or even hundreds of millions worth of crypto-currency have been stolen. There are numerous examples of this: Mt Gox in 2014, when $473 million worth of bitcoin was stolen; DAO in 2016, when $50 million worth of ether was stolen; and even as recently as January 2018, when a Japanese crypto exchange was hacked and over $500 million stolen.

Perhaps even more importantly, I would also argue that individuals themselves have to learn a great deal and spend an annoying amount of time implementing relatively complicated security measures to ensure that their own personal holdings in crypto assets are secure lest they fall foul of hacking on a smaller scale. Either that or they use a 'trusted third-party' crypto service provider, which, to my mind, rather invalidates the point of the whole technology and makes it little different from using a bank or broker for more conventional assets, except that there is no regulation.

4 It is insufficiently robust against war and/or natural disaster

Related to these last three points about electricity, network bottlenecks and problems with security is a concern about how robust the technology would be in times of war or a massive natural disaster such as the eruption of a supervolcano, a massive solar-flare, or an enormous earthquake somewhere like California. To be fair, the only way to destroy bitcoin itself completely is to destroy every single node (i.e. record of the blockchain) – records of which sit on computers all over the world. A bitcoin enthusiast friend of mine has made the point that if we suffer a natural disaster big enough to take out every computer in the world with a record of the blockchain, our financial system will be the least of our worries and I think his point is well made.

Summary

I don't dispute for a moment that crypto assets and blockchain technology might very well create enormous economic value eventually, and make lots of people very wealthy as a result – I just think that for the time being there is far too much uncertainty for it to be considered as one of your key investment pillars in 'owning the world' alongside shares, bonds, property, cash and commodities without significant reservation.

If you are excited by the possibilities of crypto assets, by all means consider making an investment but realize that this will be highly speculative. This is fine for, say, 1–5 per cent of your investible capital but everywhere I look on social media I see people who *only* have crypto investments, having never thought about their ISA, pension or precious metals situation. Many such folk have even borrowed on credit cards to 'invest' in crypto because they have so comprehensively bought into the idea that they can and will 'get rich quick'. I've seen individuals on social media articulate their excitement about being able to 'retire' after investing £500. It is all rather depressing for anyone who witnessed precisely the same thing 20 years ago during the dot-com boom. It seems that human beings are doomed to forget the lessons of history. By all means consider a speculative investment in a crypto asset or assets if you are so inclined, but please do not make it a core pillar of your savings and investment, for the time being at least.

I would come back to a common theme that repeats through the book – that, over a lifetime of investment, the investment tortoise generally does a great deal better than the investment hare. There are two centuries of evidence to that effect.

You don't need to chase an asset that might offer you a 'once in a generation' opportunity to 'get rich quick' but which might go to zero. That having been said, I feel that there is a chance that bitcoin itself might end up playing a similar role to gold in the very long run (i.e. providing an alternative to fiat currencies), and it is for this reason that there may be merit in holding a small amount of your wealth in it against that possibility.

As such, my personal view is that if you only have a few hundred or a few thousand pounds to invest, you will probably be best served by simply investing in bitcoin and ignoring all of the other crypto assets given how much uncertainty surrounds their future. If you do decide to do this, please do ensure that you spend a good amount of time learning how to buy and store it securely.

In conclusion

Having read this chapter, you should now, I hope, feel more confident about what financial products are out there in the world. I would repeat that you do not need to have an extremely detailed understanding of financial products, but a basic grasp will be hugely helpful.

Now you have that basic grasp, it is time to look in more detail at the precise steps you will want to take to get your finances humming.

PART 3

How to put your knowledge to good use

- Now that you know the basics, how do you put this knowledge to use?
- How can you go about 'owning the world'?
- What do you need in order to take things further?

8
Where do we go from here?

'It takes as much energy to wish as it does to plan.'

Eleanor Roosevelt

So far we have:

- looked at why you need to take action with your finances
- explained how this is easier than you might have thought, thanks to compound interest, great financial products, ongoing global growth and high real inflation
- shown how you might free up some money to invest
- looked at which accounts are the best in terms of quality and value
- explored the range of financial products you need to understand a little about
- explained how to keep costs low by using the right accounts and products, and why this is so important for your long-term financial success.

Having covered this ground, we are now ready to look in more detail at what you might own – and how you might own it – in order to really kick your finances into gear. The next three chapters, then, are going to look at three fundamentally important topics:

1 Mapping your route

In Chapter 9 we are going to look at working out how much you need to live on. As with many things in life, if you don't have a specific target to aim for, then you are unlikely to hit anything. The budgeting process we will look at isn't that complicated, but it is arguably the first step towards achieving financial freedom and an important process to go through as a result.

Chapters 10 and 11, however, are probably the most important ones in the whole book. They present two basic approaches to investment that you might use to take it from here: 'keeping it simple' and 'taking things further'.

2 Keeping it simple

Many of you will have read this far and will I hope now be keen to get your money working for you. But maybe you aren't interested in spending much more time learning about money and finance. This book may well have been the limit! You want to invest the money you have managed to free up for your ISA account but you don't want to spend time keeping up with finance and current affairs, reading more books on the subject or learning in any more detail about things like shares, bonds and commodities.

If this describes you, then you will want a simple plan that you can set up and maintain with a minimum of fuss and effort but which still does a very good job with your money. In Chapter 10 we will look at how you might construct just such a plan. You are going to use what you have learned so far about investment, the world economy, financial accounts and funds to put an excellent structure in place for your money. You should see the logic behind the steps I am going to suggest you take and feel confident in them because of what you have read so far.

We will look at this in detail below, but for now it is perhaps worth summarizing the approach briefly: the 'keeping it simple' approach involves you setting up a direct debit to pay money each month into funds that will benefit from global growth and inflation.

Even though you will not have to invest a great deal of time, taking this approach will still give you a high probability of making life-changing returns and protecting your downside. Again, using your own common sense to interpret the information that follows should give you confidence that this will be the case.

I would argue that the 'keeping it simple' approach is also the one you should take if you are just starting out with investment or don't have a particularly large amount of money at the moment. For what it is worth, I would suggest that if you have less than about £50,000 then you should stick to the simple approach for the time being. This is simply because trading in and out of positions, and the work that goes in to buying individual shares successfully, is not really worth the effort with anything less than about £10,000 or so per share. Once you *have* built a bigger pot you might consider using the 'keeping it simple' strategy for 80 per cent of your money and start trading more (perhaps even buying some individual shares) with the remaining 20 per cent. This is part of what we will look at in Chapter 11.

I appreciate that many people might find the above paragraph exasperating – £50,000 may seem like a vast amount of money. I can understand this sentiment, but I would argue that even if you are only on the average UK salary, if you manage to invest 10 per cent or so of your monthly income in your ISA account (using the 'keeping it simple' strategy), then you have a good chance of getting to £50,000 in less than ten years.

If this seems like a horribly long and pointless amount of time and makes you feel like giving up, I would encourage you to stop for a moment and think about where you were and what you were doing ten years ago. If you are anything like me, it will seem like that time has gone past in the blink of an eye. I would repeat that investment is a marathon, not a sprint. As I said right at the beginning of the book, this is not a 'get rich quick' scheme – but you will get rich.

Wouldn't it be better to start on the road as soon as possible, with the exciting prospect of building this sort of pot over the next few years? Remember that your progress in growing your money speeds up over time, thanks to compound interest. Getting from zero to £50,000 does take a while, but if you continue to invest successfully then getting from £50,000 to much bigger numbers should only take the same again. It is crucial, however, that you get on the road to start with.

The good news, if you have less than £50,000, is that, for now, you won't have to spend too much time thinking about finance or doing any more work. If, however, you are lucky enough to have a reasonably large amount of money already and feel willing to get more involved, you might consider taking things further.

3 Taking things further

The 'keeping it simple' approach we will outline in Chapter 10 should yield great results for your personal finances. It will more than likely constitute a significant improvement over any arrangements you had in the past and it is a particularly appropriate strategy if you are just starting out.

You may, however, decide that you place sufficient value on your financial future that you want to be more hands-on with all things financial going forwards. You will want to 'take things further', especially if you have significant assets already.

I would hope that you have found many of the points we have discussed so far entirely logical and reasonably easy to grasp. Topics such as the importance of keeping costs down, the amazing possibilities that result from compound interest and the importance of diversification are not that complicated and, once you know about them, can help you significantly improve your financial situation.

Dare I suggest that some of you may even be excited about finance now that you have seen what a difference you can make with relatively easy wins? Making money from your money is very liberating, and I would hope that you might be interested in continuing to learn more about finance and investment.

To repeat the quote from Alexander Green that introduced Chapter 2:

> No one cares more about your money than you do. With a basic
> understanding of the investment process and a bit of discipline, you're
> perfectly capable of managing your own money ... By managing
> your own money, you'll be able to earn higher returns and save many
> thousands ... in investment costs over your lifetime.

If you fall into this category and are eager to learn more, then Chapter 11 will provide you with a road map to really rev up your understanding of finance. The main difference between those of you who want to keep things simple and those who want to take things further is that the former method involves choosing some funds and automatically paying money into them each month. After that, there is very little additional work to do. You just have to let it ride, and you will never have to think about what the markets are doing or when the best time to invest is.

Those of you who choose to take things further, however, will spend more time looking at your investments and making decisions about what to buy and sell, and when to do so. You will begin a journey to learn more about financial markets and how to invest in shares, bonds, property, real estate, commodities and so on.

I hope as many of you as possible choose to take things further today, if you already have the means, or further down the road if you are just starting out. At the very least, I urge you to read both chapters. Doing so will mean you are best placed to decide which of these approaches is best for you personally and they should get you excited about the vast opportunities that lie ahead.

9

Mapping your route

'If you don't know where you're going, you might wind up someplace else.'

Yogi Berra

Working up a budget is perhaps one of the most important steps you will take on your road to financial success. It is probably fair to say that many people do this in some shape or form, but it is probably not controversial to suggest there are that three things that relatively few people do:

1 Make a sufficiently *detailed* budget – throw in everything but the kitchen sink ...
2 Budget for your dream life – plan for the life that you actually want rather than the one you have today
3 Stick to a budget once you've made it.

Human nature dictates that we are all pretty bad at point three, and I am certainly no exception. I would be the first to suggest that trying to moderate your intake of overpriced coffees or spend less on having fun each weekend is often doomed to failure. Nevertheless, if you can manage the first two points at least, I genuinely believe you can start moving your mindset in the direction of sticking to a budget. Even if you miss by some margin, you will still be closer to success than you would be had you not gone through the process.

As such, I suggest you work up one budget that is realistic for you today, based on your current income. Then make another one that is what you would need to live the life of your dreams, as a source of inspiration and something to aim for. Once you have done this, you can set about doing some basic sums to work out how much you need to save to give you the best chance of achieving the latter. In Table 9.1, you will find an example of how you might work out a reasonably detailed budget. Not everyone needs to cater for all the items on this list, but putting together a similar document for your own particulars will give you a really good idea of where you stand.

It seems likely that the large majority of readers will have access to a spreadsheet program. I would highly recommend taking the time to build a spreadsheet that looks something like the example in Table 9.1. You can then enter your expenses into the relevant column. Car insurance tends to be annual, for example, whereas utilities are monthly or quarterly, but you might think about weekly expenditure for nights out or grocery shopping. It is entirely up

Table 9.1 Calculating your expenditure

	PEF Budget Calculator	Daily	Weekly	Monthly	Annually
MUST SPEND	Rent/mortgage, council tax				
	Groceries, household goods				
	Transport: commute				
	Utilities: electricity, gas, water				
MIGHT SPEND	Car/other travel				
	Childcare				
	Cleaner				
	Clothes				
	Cosmetics, toiletries				
	Credit card				
	Eating out: bars, cafés				
	Entertainment: books, cinema				
	Gifts				
	Gym, sports				
	Haircut, beauty				
	Holidays				
	Household: larger items				
	Insurance: car, contents, life, pet				
	Internet				
	Medical: dentist, prescriptions				
	Mobile phone				
	Other: opticians, subscriptions				
	Pets				
	School/university fees				
	TV: licence, streaming services				
	TOTALS				

to you how you work things out, but I find that if you take the time to fill in all the columns so that you get an idea of what everything will cost you daily, weekly, monthly and annually then it will ensure the very best visibility where all things financial are concerned.

Many of you will know how to make the spreadsheet work so that something inputted annually is divided by 12 automatically to produce the monthly number, and by 52 for the weekly number. This means that you can easily produce a spreadsheet that gives you all the numbers you need. If you don't know how to do this yourself in Excel or another spreadsheet program, you might consider finding a nearby teenager because they almost certainly will.

As suggested above, it is worth taking the time to do this twice: once for your realistic expenditure at the moment given your current income and once for your dream life. How much would the mortgage or rent be on your dream home, for example? Or, in an ideal world, how much would you like to be able to spend on amazing holidays each year?

Once you have worked out the two sets of numbers, you will have a good idea of how to manage the income you have today (which must include an allocation of at least 10 per cent to investment) and what you would ideally like to have in the future. This second lot of numbers can then serve as a target to aim for. Please feel free to use the table included here to help you with this process.

An alternative to building your own spreadsheet, especially nowadays, is to use one of the excellent budgeting tools or apps you can get online or for your smartphone. I particularly like youneedabudget.com but there are many options available, many of which are free. I would highly recommend spending one rainy Sunday afternoon finding one that you like so you can work out how to free up 10 per cent of your monthly income for investment and what you might need to live the life of your dreams.

You can't get to your destination unless you know where it is.

Annuity rates today are about 5 per cent. At the most basic level, this means that when you retire, whatever lump sum you have in your pension can be exchanged for an annual income equivalent to about 5 per cent of that lump sum. This is why I make the point that if you want an income of the average UK salary of about £26,000 a year at retirement, you will need a pension pot of about £500,000 (at 5 per cent). If you have worked out that your dream life requires an annual income of, say, £80,000, then at an annuity rate of 5 per cent, you will need a pot of around £1.6 million (target income/annuity rate).

At first sight, this probably seems rather depressing or daunting, to say the least. You might be wondering how on earth you are going to build a pot of more than one-and-a-half million pounds. There are a few points I would like to make in response to that concern.

First, as we saw in the section on compound interest, with a long-term commitment to doing the best with your money you really can aspire to turn relatively small amounts of money into large amounts. All you need is time (I would say at least ten years), a modicum of knowledge and a bit of effort in terms of taking care of the necessary administration.

Second, and to link to the first point, the example above is looking *only* at passive income – that is to say the 'perfect world' scenario of you being able to live your life entirely funded by the money you make from your money. In reality, we will all likely spend several decades of our life working in some shape or form. This is important because your active income (the money you are paid for your work) will obviously make up a huge component of the costs of your dream lifestyle during the decades you work. It can also, if you are sensible and take the right steps with a decent percentage of your earnings, vastly increase your likelihood of building the 'scary' seven-figure retirement pot we are talking about.

Third, while today's annuity rates may only be 5 per cent, by the time you have got through the material that follows and vastly improved your understanding of matters financial, you should aspire to return more than 5 per cent on your money. I feel that it is unlikely that I, personally, will ever buy an annuity product (unless it is a legal requirement when I retire). This is because, as you might imagine,

I have great confidence that I can manage my financial affairs to get a return of a good deal more than 5 per cent per annum when I retire. My 'pot' will be in a wide range of investments, which, taken together, should provide me with a much higher income than 5 per cent – and do so reasonably safely.

It should be clear that if I can consistently make 7, 8 or even 10 per cent, my pot need only be half the size it needs to be at 5 per cent. As we have seen, these sorts of returns are entirely possible: simply buying a rental property at the right time in the cycle will give you reliable long-term returns at these sorts of levels. Equally, buying shares in a good business at the right price will more than likely give you these sorts of returns, if you hold those shares for the long term and for their income in the way that many top investors do.

Finally, to go back to the notion of active income again: I personally hope to carry on making some kind of active income well past traditional retirement age. In common with all of the 'old' people I respect, I aim to continue working in some shape or form well into my seventies, or possibly even eighties (as long as I still have my critical faculties!). I am well aware that I am unlikely to be in any kind of high-powered, full-time employment but on the basis that 'every little helps', some kind of income in retirement will help to lower the amount of money I need to squirrel away and/or the returns I will have to achieve consistently on that money to live my dream life.

Hopefully you can see that if, for example, I am able to pull in £10,000 a year as a DJ or cabaret singer in my seventies (!) and return about 6 per cent on my savings, and my dream income is £40,000 a year (given I would hope to be based somewhere cheap and hot, where that kind of money goes a long way – Croatia, perhaps), my pension pot need only be £500,000 (£40,000 – £10,000 = £30,000 of income from my investments; at 6 per cent, I therefore need £500,000 [£30,000/0.06] to live my dream life).

We all have different aspirations and plans. I would hope that what you take away from this chapter is the notion that having a think about precisely where you want to get to financially and, by extension, what you will then need to do to get there, will be hugely helpful in making your money work for you. As the renowned author Fitzhugh Dodson said: 'Without goals, and plans to reach them, you are like a ship that has set sail with no destination.'

Now we have dealt with where we are going, let's finally turn our attention to how we might get there.

10

Keeping it simple: 'owning the world'

'The most powerful tool an investor has working for him or her is diversification. True diversification allows you to build portfolios with higher returns for the same risk. Most investors ... are far less diversified than they should be. They're way overcommitted to ... stocks.'

Jack Meyer, *Smart Money*

I am aware that I've used this quote from Jack Meyer before, but I believe its message is important enough to bear repeating, especially given how impressive Meyer's track record as an investor is. Think back to our two crucial investment themes from earlier in the book: the world economy keeps on growing and there is significant real inflation in the world. It should come as no surprise to you that if you are going to take the simpler, more 'formulaic' approach to investing, you will want to ensure that you quite simply 'own the world' and 'own inflation'.

This is our big-picture starting point. We will now look in more detail at why we want to take this approach and how we might achieve it as efficiently as possible, given the financial accounts and products available today.

The other key feature of the 'keeping it simple' investment approach we look at in this chapter is that you will be paying whatever money you have decided you can afford into your investments *regularly every month* with a direct debit. Investing every month has two significant benefits. First, it is easy for you to set up and requires a minimum of effort going forwards. You will not have to make complex decisions about when to put your money to work. This will maximize your chances of actually doing something with your finances sooner rather than later.

The other key benefit of investing regularly each month is that it results in what is known as 'averaging in' or 'smoothing'. Obviously, the price of any financial asset or market goes up and down over time. By investing each month, you improve your chances of buying in at a good average price and you ensure that you do not put a large amount of money in something just ahead of a crash. If anything you own does crash, by averaging in each month you will then pick it up when it is cheap in the months that follow that crash. Doing this removes a huge amount of stress and hassle and is key to keeping things manageable.

So let us look at the big picture first ...

The advantage of owning the world

When I talk about 'owning the world' I mean:

- You should own a wide variety of investment products or assets. In the long run you will want to have cash, shares, bonds, commodities and property, not just one or two of these.

- You should aim to own assets from all over the world, not just one geographical area such as the UK or the USA.

You will recall from earlier in the book that the world economy as a whole continues to grow. You will also remember how important it is to be diversified. Owning the world means that you end up being diversified both geographically and by asset class.

But what does this mean?

Geographically diversified

'Geographically diversified' simply means that if one part of the world is having a difficult time, perhaps Europe or the USA, you still have a good chance of making money because you have exposure to another part of the world that is going up a great deal, for example certain emerging markets or Japan. Every year, different parts of the world are stronger than others.

Rather than trying to work out where the best place for your money will be next year, which is difficult and time-consuming, it is easiest just to be invested in every major part of the world. This means that you benefit from the consistent growth of the world economy as a whole. Bear in mind that the world has only really ever had 'down' years across the board in times of major war.

One of the biggest mistakes people make with their investments is that they tend, in the main, to own assets from their own country. This means two things: firstly, that when that particular country or geographical area has a difficult time, their investments there will struggle. Secondly, that they miss out on the potential for explosive growth that comes with owning what some would deem to be more exotic parts of the world.

It is worth noting that stock markets in many of the faster-growing areas of the world can double or even triple over quite short periods of time. With that sort of performance, you don't need to have a large share of your money exposed to these markets in order to enjoy a material impact on growing your wealth and achieving the sorts of numbers we saw at the beginning of this book.

There is no guarantee that this will continue. The trend might even reverse, and growth in the USA and the UK might one day again be better than in places like China, India and Brazil (at the time of writing this third edition of the book this is basically the case – underscoring the point).

The key point here is that you may not want to spend too much time trying to work out what is going to happen. A simpler approach is just to ensure that you have exposure to the world as a whole. As the world keeps growing and developing, this approach will give you the best chance of benefiting from that growth.

I would repeat that the only time the world as a whole has failed to grow has been in times of major wars. If we are unlucky enough for the 'Third World War' to happen in our lifetimes, your investment performance might be the least of your concerns. Having said that, without wanting to sound horribly cynical, smart money has usually found that even wartime can be reasonably lucrative. Even in the case of another world war, there will be opportunities for the informed and enlightened to keep their money safe and possibly even to grow it.

Leaving aside that rather depressing possibility, however, in the more normal run of things, 'owning the world' simply means that you want to end up with exposure to everywhere: the UK, Europe, the USA, Japan and the rest of Asia, as well as various emerging markets. You will want to own assets in as many places as possible so that you catch those doubles and triples over the years, and benefit from the explosive growth of the global middle class. In an ideal world, you might also own a wide range of types of company – large and small – in all of these regions.

One of the reasons relatively few people pursued this sort of strategy in the past is that it used to be very hard for a private individual to invest like this. It is also the case that relatively few financial advisers have a grasp of how to do it or even why it is a good idea for all the reasons we looked at earlier in the book. Not that long ago, this strategy realistically wasn't possible for a private individual. Today you can get closer than ever before to this sort of asset allocation without paying crazy fees – even if you only have a small amount of money to start with.

Diversified by asset class

'Diversified by asset class' means that in those dreaded crash years when *shares* (equities/stock markets) fall off a cliff, as most of them did in 2000 and 2008, for example, you won't lose a vast chunk of your money like everyone else. You'll actually have a good chance of having a positive year (or at least a far less negative one than most people) because, even though your shares might have fallen in value, you will own *other* assets such as property, bonds, gold, silver, oil and other commodities. Many of these will have held up very well in a bad year for shares. The reason this happens is due to a phenomenon called 'negative correlation'.

It is often the case in investment that certain types of asset tend to go up when others go down; that is to say, they are negatively correlated. This relationship in real life is never exact, but if you own a wide variety of types of asset rather than, say, just shares or just property, you have a much better chance of seeing your money continue to grow if there is a stock market or property crash, for example.

Gold went up in value every year from 2000 until 2011. What a shame that the vast majority of people in the world did not own any. Before that, shares had gone up virtually every year for a decade or so, whereas gold went sideways or down for a long time. In 2007–9, stock markets around the world crashed by more than half but oil hit an all-time high in 2008 and gold was up nearly 20 per cent in 2009.

In the long run, it is much easier to own a mixture of assets so that you have a better chance of owning something that goes up when another type of asset crashes.

To summarize: the holy grail here is your money being put to work with the minimum of effort but the maximum exposure to the world as a whole. Ultimately, you will want to be the proud owner of a wide variety of assets – shares from all over the world, cash, commodities, bonds and property – so that you will benefit from global growth, wherever it is, in the future.

The advantage of owning inflation

You will also want to ensure that you invest a good percentage of your money each month so that you can protect yourself from real inflation. The best way to do this is to own the monetary metals (gold and silver) and a wide range of other commodities. This will mean that, unlike almost everyone else, you will actually gain from inflation in the price of 'stuff', rather than suffering a decrease in your living standards.

It is my belief that monetary metals are in a multi-year bull market (against fiat currencies at least), primarily because of the money-printing actions of the world's central banks. As long as central banks around the world keep printing (or rather inventing) more money, precious metals and other 'things' will continue to go up in price over time (if not in a straight line).

> Exposure to monetary metals and commodities will enhance your overall performance without complicating matters or being prohibitively expensive.

If central banks stop printing money and put interest rates up in the years ahead, this will change, but while they continue to pursue the policies of the last several years we will need to invest accordingly. Some readers will note that gold and silver have fallen a great deal in the last few years, but I do not see this as affecting any of the points I make in this chapter. As we shall see, gold went up 24-fold in the 1970s but pulled back around 50 per cent in 1975. Nothing ever goes up without periodic corrections but if you are well diversified you can hold on to your allocation and continue to perform – and if you invest regularly you will also enjoy a good averaged price over time.

The smartest investors use this approach

Before I continue, I would like to point out that I am most certainly not the first person to advocate this method of investing. This broad approach has been used with excellent results by some of the smartest investors in the world for several decades. About owning a wide cross section of investments, famous US investor Harry Browne has said: 'Over broad periods of time, the winning investments add more value to the portfolio than the losing investments take away.'

Meanwhile, award-winning British wealth manager Tim Price has called diversification the 'only free lunch' in investing. As I said in the first section of this book, I think the best thing to do is to invest with the smartest investors in the world or, failing that, invest like them.

There are a number of particularly good books that highlight the strength of this strategy. One of these is *The Ivy Portfolio* by Mebane Faber and Eric Richardson, which focuses on Harvard and Yale

Universities' investment funds. Harvard and Yale both have very large (multibillion pound) investment funds called endowments. The Yale fund returned an average of 13.5 per cent per annum for the 20 years up to June 2014. Meanwhile, Harvard's fund returned 12.3 per cent per annum over the same period. *The Ivy Portfolio* studies how these funds achieved such impressive and consistent returns and concludes that it is a result of their wide diversification across asset classes.

Don't forget what these sorts of numbers mean for your wealth

It is worth flagging that, thanks to the power of compound interest, if you had been able to invest in either of the Harvard or Yale funds in 1985 you would have made around *40* times your money by 2008. This is based on making just *one lump-sum investment*. If you had been paying money into funds with this sort of performance every month, as I am suggesting you do, the number could be significantly higher.

This should remind you of a previous point about compound interest. As we have already seen, paying just a few hundred pounds each month into a fund that is consistently making these sorts of returns really will result in you having at least a million pounds at retirement, and possibly far more. Hundreds of pounds regularly invested at these rates of return becomes millions of pounds. In my opinion, this reality should be drummed into the head of every student from the moment they arrive in secondary school.

Jack Meyer ran the Harvard Fund from 1990 to 2005. During the last decade of his tenure, the endowment earned an annualized return of 15.9 per cent. We have already seen what he has to say about investment (but why not hammer the point home!):

> The most powerful tool an investor has working for him or her is diversification. True diversification allows you to build portfolios with higher returns for the same risk. Most investors ... are far less diversified than they should be. They're way overcommitted to ... stocks.

Being American, Meyer is referring to US investors and US stocks but the same holds true for those in the UK who have too many British assets, and German investors owning only German stocks, and so on. Sadly, it is not possible for private individuals to invest in the Harvard or Yale funds, but more than ever we are able to invest like them.

An example: the Permanent Portfolio

A similar approach to that taken by Harvard and Yale is called the 'Permanent Portfolio'. It was created in 1981 by investment adviser Harry Browne (and outlined in his book of the same name). Just like Harvard and Yale and their funds, Browne's idea was that, if you own a diverse range of assets, you should always have something that performs well.

He highlighted the existence of four basic stages in an economic cycle: prosperity, inflation, deflation and recession. He then advocated holding 25 per cent each of shares, gold, long-term US bonds and cash to give you a chance of benefiting from each of these stages.

Browne's allocation was a very simple way of 'owning the world'. The main reason for this simplicity was that financial services were far less sophisticated in the early 1980s when Browne was writing than they are today, so things had to be kept simple or you wouldn't be able to implement the ideas as an investor. Table 10.1 shows how this structure performed from 1981 until the end of 2017 and an illustration of the return you would have made from a starting pot of $50,000.

The key thing to look at here is just how seldom the strategy loses money. It has had only five negative years out of 37! This strategy even had a positive year in 2008, when financial markets all over the world were crashing horribly. Despite this downside protection, the average annual return over 37 years is 7.5 per cent. This might not sound like much but when compounded reliably over a lifetime of investment this is more than enough to generate significant wealth. It is also worth noting that 7.5 per cent is obviously a good deal higher than the interest rate you might get on your current account or cash ISA, but the key point I am trying to make here is that this diversification can significantly protect your downside when investing.

This is something that is poorly understood by most people when they fear that *any* kind of market investment is too risky and opt for a wealth-destroying cash ISA instead. I would also explicitly note that – again – the numbers in Table 10.1 are based on *one* investment at the beginning of the period. Investing regularly would generate far bigger numbers over time – hundreds can and do become millions.

TABLE 10.1 The Permanent Portfolio: investment returns (USD) (1981–2017)

						$50,000.00
Year	Stocks	Gold	Long bond	Cash	Port-folio %	Cash
1981	-4.1	-32.8	1.8	14.0	-5.3	$47,357.97
1982	22.1	12.5	38.5	10.7	21.0	$57,287.54
1983	22.0	-14.3	-0.7	8.5	3.9	$59,506.07
1984	6.0	-20.2	14.6	9.6	2.5	$60,993.06
1985	32.8	6.9	34.2	7.6	20.4	$73,412.07
1986	17.5	22.9	24.9	6.2	17.9	$86,543.10
1987	3.9	20.2	-7.9	5.9	5.5	$91,306.20
1988	15.9	-15.7	8.1	6.7	3.8	$94,750.65
1989	31.4	-1.7	20.2	8.5	14.6	$108,556.01
1990	-2.1	-2.2	4.9	7.8	2.1	$110,830.19
1991	31.3	-10.3	17.3	5.7	11.0	$123,001.85
1992	7.4	-6.2	6.8	3.6	2.9	$126,554.04
1993	10.1	17.7	18.3	3.1	12.3	$142,088.80
1994	2.0	-1.9	-11.9	4.2	-1.9	$139,376.28
1995	38.2	1.0	33.7	5.7	19.6	$166,754.28
1996	24.1	-4.9	-4.8	5.1	4.9	$174,879.21
1997	34.1	-21.5	15.4	5.2	8.3	$189,393.46
1998	30.7	-0.2	16.7	4.9	13.0	$214,071.27
1999	22.4	0.1	-15.0	4.8	3.1	$220,658.00
2000	-12.5	-5.5	20.5	5.9	2.1	$225,300.10
2001	-12.0	2.0	3.4	3.7	-0.7	$223,648.58
2002	-22.7	24.8	16.7	1.7	5.1	$235,097.73
2003	29.1	19.5	1.0	1.0	12.7	$264,865.75
2004	10.7	5.4	9.2	1.3	6.6	$282,459.28
2005	5.7	18.4	8.7	3.1	9.0	$307,797.12
2006	15.3	23.0	-1.5	4.7	10.4	$339,720.66
2007	6.0	31.3	10.3	4.4	13.0	$383,998.74
2008	-37.1	5.5	41.2	1.5	2.8	$394,653.31
2009	27.1	24.0	-25.5	0.2	6.4	$420,022.58
2010	15.4	29.7	5.3	0.1	12.6	$473,060.78
2011	2.0	10.2	29.9	0.1	10.5	$522,905.21
2012	16.1	7.0	2.3	0.1	6.4	$556,148.09
2013	32.6	-28.3	-14.9	0.1	-2.6	$541,570.64
2014	13.4	-1.5	29.7	0.0	10.4	$597,841.58
2015	1.3	-10.5	-3.3	0.0	-3.1	$579,384.89
2016	11.6	8.6	0.9	0.3	5.4	$610,395.96
2017	21.9	13.7	11.5	0.9	12.0	$683,543.82

Source: Solent Systematic Investment Strategies

Another example: the Gone Fishin' Portfolio

A similar strategy, aimed at the private investor, can be found in another of the books I alluded to earlier: *The Gone Fishin' Portfolio* by Alexander Green, investment director of top investment network The Oxford Club.

The 'Gone Fishin' Portfolio' is basically a slightly more complicated and American-centric version of our 'keeping it simple' method. Green shows his readers how to set their money up so that they can own a wide range of assets with the minimum of effort, just as we are going to in this chapter.

For those of you who wish to pursue the keeping things simple approach in this chapter but who are prepared to invest the time to read one book on the subject, I would highly recommend this one, as it will give you a deeper understanding of the value of this approach.

How to own the world and own inflation

So we are going to own the world and own inflation. We will now look in more detail at how we might do this. Before we do, however, let us answer an important question ...

If this is such a great approach to investment, why isn't everyone doing it?

The first thing to say is that many of the smartest and wealthiest investors in the world *are* doing this. Many of the wealthiest individuals, families, academic institutions and investment companies invest like this, including people like the Rothschild family and Harvard, Yale, Oxford and Cambridge universities. But the most obvious answer as to why relatively few other folk are is one we have seen before: most people don't spend enough time, or even any time at all, learning about finance. As a result, they have no idea how to invest in a wide variety of assets from all over the world. It is also fair to say that relatively few financial advisers are sufficiently up to speed on this knowledge, nor would have a good idea of how to put this together for their clients in a cost-effective way even if they were.

Perhaps more importantly, it used to be nearly impossible to own the world as a 'normal' private individual. Until relatively recently, you would have needed to be a multimillionaire to get such a wide investment exposure (yet another reason why many of the rich have remained rich through history).

To own a wide range of financial assets from all over the world, which is what you are aiming to do, you had to own a large number of funds. There were two problems with this:

1 Unless you had a very large amount of money, costs were prohibitive. Too much of the money you were trying to invest would be eaten up in fees, resulting in poor performance. In fact, to a great extent this is still true for many people given how expensive some financial advice and the wrong financial accounts and products can be (costs you are learning to avoid or reduce).

2 In addition, you can no doubt imagine that owning a large number of funds was a real pain administratively. The 'keep it simple' strategy aims to make things easy enough so that this doesn't take very much of your time. We do not want to spend hours and hours keeping on top of the administration involved in owning dozens of different funds.

However, in recent years it has finally become possible to get the exposure we want easily and cheaply.

Three steps to keeping it simple

In order to implement the 'keeping it simple' approach, consider taking the following steps:

1 Open an ISA account with a quality stockbroking company

Using the correct ISA provider will ensure that you pay lower costs than you might using a high-street bank or lower-quality firm. It will also mean that you are able to invest in a much wider range of investments. As we have seen, both of these points are important in order for you to succeed financially. As I said in Chapter 6 when we first looked at ISA accounts, you can find my thoughts on which are the best providers online rather than here in the text of the book, given that these things change over time.

2 Set up a direct debit to your ISA account

We have already looked at how you might find a certain amount of money to invest each month. Once you have worked out what you can afford, you can set up a direct debit instruction with your ISA provider. They will usually give you a choice of which day of the month funds will automatically be transferred from your current account to your ISA account.

3 Split your money between 'owning the world', owning inflation, and cash

We will look in more detail in a moment at precisely how you might own the world and own inflation. An important consideration is what percentage of your monthly investment you allocate to each. In general, I would suggest that you allocate 60 to 70 per cent of whatever you are able to invest monthly into owning the world, 10 to 20 per cent into owning inflation, and keep the rest in cash.

Keeping a certain amount of your savings in cash is a good idea for three reasons: first, as we have already seen, cash cannot fall in (notional) value. The only risk to cash is inflation eating it up. Second, it is always good to keep some cash available in order to take advantage of investment opportunities that might arise in future. Third, you also need to hold cash to be properly diversified, given that it is one of our asset classes.

Although what we are looking at in this chapter is a method of investing that does not require you to learn much more about finance, I think it is very likely that you will have some excellent thoughts of your own about where you might invest that money at some stage in the future. You will want to have some cash on hand to take advantage of those thoughts.

Alternatively, sometime in the future you might use that cash to make any number of exciting purchases without having to sell out of any of your other investments. Whatever happens, it is likely that you will be glad that you have kept some of the money you are saving every month as cash.

It is also worth noting that many experts in personal finance suggest that, when you start saving, you should keep 100 per cent of your savings in cash until you have built up a 'rainy day' pot, which can cover you for a certain amount of time if you were to lose your job. Different commentators advocate different sums of money but the convention seems to be anywhere from one month to six months of salary. What you decide to do in this respect is entirely up to you. I would suggest that if you feel safe in your job you might consider three months sufficient.

In other words, I am suggesting that you do not begin to invest money into the financial assets we are looking at in this chapter (such as investment funds or precious metals) until you have first cleared any expensive (non-mortgage) debt and have saved at least a month's salary to keep as cash, and possibly more. Once you have done this, however, you can start allocating some of your monthly savings to investment.

Given the percentages I suggested above, Table 10.2 details how you might split your money between the three categories of the 'keeping it simple' approach – owning the world, owning inflation, and cash – depending on how much you are able to save.

TABLE 10.2 How you might split your money

Total to invest each month	Kept in cash (10%)	Potential allocation to a fund or funds	Invested in those funds (%)	Total added to ISA each month	Possible allocation to precious metals	Investment in precious metals (%)
£50.00	£•	£50.00	100%	£50.00	£•	0%
£100.00	£10.00	£90.00	90%	£100.00	£•	0%
£150.00	£15.00	£135.00	90%	£150.00	£•	0%
£200.00	£20.00	£180.00	90%	£200.00	£•	0%
£250.00	£25.00	£225.00	90%	£250.00	£•	0%
£300.00	£30.00	£270.00	90%	£300.00	£•	0%
£350.00	£35.00	£315.00	90%	£350.00	£•	0%
£400.00	£40.00	£260.00	65%	£300.00	£100.00	25%
£450.00	£45.00	£305.00	68%	£350.00	£100.00	22%
£500.00	£50.00	£350.00	70%	£400.00	£100.00	20%
£550.00	£55.00	£395.00	72%	£450.00	£100.00	18%
£600.00	£60.00	£440.00	73%	£500.00	£100.00	17%

(*Continued*)

TABLE 10.2 (*Continued*)

Total to invest each month	Kept in cash (10%)	Potential allocation to a fund or funds	Invested in those funds (%)	Total added to ISA each month	Possible allocation to precious metals	Investment in precious metals (%)
£650.00	£65.00	£435.00	67%	£500.00	£150.00	23%
£700.00	£70.00	£480.00	69%	£550.00	£150.00	21%
£750.00	£75.00	£525.00	70%	£600.00	£150.00	20%
£800.00	£80.00	£570.00	71%	£650.00	£150.00	19%
£850.00	£85.00	£615.00	72%	£700.00	£150.00	18%
£900.00	£90.00	£610.00	68%	£700.00	£200.00	22%
£950.00	£95.00	£655.00	69%	£750.00	£200.00	21%
£1,000.00	£100.00	£700.00	70%	£800.00	£200.00	20%
£1,050.00	£105.00	£745.00	71%	£850.00	£200.00	19%
£1,100.00	£110.00	£790.00	72%	£900.00	£200.00	18%
£1,150.00	£115.00	£785.00	68%	£900.00	£250.00	22%
£1,200.00	£120.00	£830.00	69%	£950.00	£250.00	21%
£1,250.00	£125.00	£875.00	70%	£1,000.00	£250.00	20%
£1,300.00	£130.00	£920.00	71%	£1,050.00	£250.00	19%
£1,350.00	£135.00	£965.00	71%	£1,100.00	£250.00	19%
£1,400.00	£140.00	£960.00	69%	£1,100.00	£300.00	21%
£1,450.00	£145.00	£1,005.00	69%	£1,150.00	£300.00	21%
£1,500.00	£150.00	£1,050.00	70%	£1,200.00	£300.00	20%
£1,550.00	£155.00	£1,095.00	71%	£1,250.00	£300.00	19%
£1,600.00	£160.00	£1,140.00	71%	£1,300.00	£300.00	19%
£1,650.00	£165.00	£1,135.00	69%	£1,300.00	£350.00	21%
£1,700.00	£170.00	£1,180.00	69%	£1,350.00	£350.00	21%
£1,750.00	£175.00	£1,225.00	70%	£1,400.00	£350.00	20%
£1,800.00	£180.00	£1,270.00	71%	£1,450.00	£350.00	19%
£1,850.00	£185.00	£1,315.00	71%	£1,500.00	£350.00	19%
£1,900.00	£190.00	£1,310.00	69%	£1,500.00	£400.00	21%
£1,950.00	£195.00	£1,355.00	69%	£1,550.00	£400.00	21%
£2,000.00	£200.00	£1,400.00	70%	£1,600.00	£400.00	20%
£2,050.00	£205.00	£1,445.00	70%	£1,650.00	£400.00	20%

There are a couple of points to note about this table:

- The table goes up to £1,650 in the 'Total added to ISA' column, purely because this is just below the amount you are permitted to save in a new ISA account each month at the time of writing, given the annual allowance of £20,000. I acknowledge that only very high earners can afford to save this every year but please don't be put off by that.
- Our method for owning inflation is to invest in precious metals (we will look at why in more detail shortly). I am a strong advocate of investing in both gold and silver where possible. In a bid to keep dealing costs low, however, I don't think you should invest in silver as well as gold unless you are able to save quite a substantial amount of money. Owning gold alone will ensure that you own inflation for the time being.

So let us now look in more detail at how we might own the world and own inflation.

Owning the world

As we've already said, when we talk about 'owning the world', we mean that you would ideally own a good range of assets with truly global exposure. Having come this far and read the section on funds, you might already have an idea of how it might be possible to own the world in this way: you will hopefully remember that you can buy a tracker or index fund for a vast range of different types of asset (assuming, of course, that you have an ISA provider that offers such a range).

For illustrative purposes, one method of owning the world would be to buy one fund for each geographical area, and one or two for each asset class. You could buy a FTSE 100 tracker to own UK shares and an S&P 500 tracker to own the USA, for example. You might then do the same for Europe, Asia, Latin America and Africa, and then use other funds to get exposure to real estate, commodities and the bond market.

Again, having read this far, you may realize that this approach can only work if you have a significant amount of money to invest. This is because every time you buy a financial product, you pay a fee. To get truly global and diversified asset exposure this way will obviously require you to buy a large number of funds.

An example at this point might be instructive. Table 10.3 lists the funds we might consider buying in order to end up owning the world in a reasonably comprehensive way.

This is just an example purely for the purposes of illustration. Plenty of professional investors might argue that it is actually a conservative number of funds to own when aiming for a truly global and diversified exposure. A purist might argue that there are no 'hot' sectors or thematic funds within this structure (such as tech, biotech, pharmaceuticals, agriculture, energy and so on). But the point I am trying to make still stands. Each time we buy a fund we have to pay commission or other fees and have added to our administrative burden as an investor. The approach suggested below would, therefore, only be suitable for someone with a large amount of money and time to invest.

That lucky individual could quite simply split their money up between a large number of funds and sit back and watch their money grow through the economic cycle no matter what the economy is doing, as per Harvard and Yale's endowment funds. In the future, when you have built a seven-figure pot of money and are confident in your financial knowledge, you might well aspire to invest in this way. For most people, however, owning 26 or even more funds in order to own the world simply isn't practicable. We need to think of a more suitable method.

One fund to own the world

The more suitable method, for the time being, is to look for one fund – or a small number of funds – which gives you as much exposure as possible. This approach keeps things simple administratively and keeps your costs as low as possible. Thankfully, in the relatively recent past it has become possible to find just the sort of products you might use to do this.

TABLE 10.3 One way you might use funds to own the world

Shares	Large Cap	Mid & Small Cap	Dividend
UK funds	1	18	23
US funds	2	19	24
Europe including Switzerland	3	20	25
Japan	4	21	26
China	5	22	n/a
Rest of Asia	6	n/a	n/a
Latin America including Brazil	7	n/a	n/a
Russia and Eastern Europe	8	n/a	n/a
India	9	n/a	n/a
Africa or frontier fund	10	n/a	n/a
Middle East	11	n/a	n/a
Bonds			
Global bond fund to include government and corporate bonds	12		
Real estate (property)			
Global real estate fund	13		
Commodities			
Agricultural commodities fund	14		
Energy commodities fund (oil, gas, etc.)	15		
Industrial metals (copper, zinc, platinum, etc.)	16		
Precious metals (gold and silver)	17		

Earlier in the book, and in this chapter, I explained how I would not name my favourite ISA providers given the dynamic nature of that advice. As you might imagine, the same holds even truer for fund products. At the time of writing there are a number of funds in the UK market that you might use to own the world. No doubt more will be offered by the best financial services companies in the months and years ahead.

As such, please do consider having a look at our website for suggestions as to the best specific fund products you might consider putting in your ISA to own the world.

Owning inflation

You will no doubt remember that 'stuff' goes up in price when there is inflation. In fact, inflation *is* an increase of the price of stuff if you think about it. These are two sides of the same coin. In the vernacular of investing, 'stuff' is better known as 'commodities'. If we want to own inflation, we just need to own some commodities. We have already looked in some detail at the case for commodities in Chapter 7.

Before we go on, it is worth noting that once you have invested money in a fund to own the world as per the last section, you should already have a reasonable degree of natural exposure to commodities (and global currencies for that matter) by virtue of owning a fund which includes some commodities or will have exposure to companies that are involved with commodities in one way or another.

This is good news but, in my opinion, the exposure you get through this is not as much as you will want to have going forwards, for all the reasons we have already considered: governments inventing money; resource scarcity in the face of population growth; and increased demand for raw materials. While so many governments continue to create vast amounts of money out of thin air and the developing world continues to grow and urbanize, you will want to have more exposure to commodities.

The simplest way to do this is to own precious metals. Gold and silver benefit from many of the positive metrics associated with commodities in general, but they have an important additional benefit: they have historically been seen as money.

Why gold and silver are the best commodities to own: they are money

'Gold is money. Everything else is just credit.'

John Pierpoint (JP) Morgan

While I have confidence in commodities in general, industrial and agricultural commodities are famously volatile and when the global economy slows down they can suffer severe falls in price. A good example is copper. Copper is a metal, just as gold and silver are, but its use is basically 100 per cent industrial. As such, if the world is manufacturing fewer cars or building fewer skyscrapers, the copper price can fall drastically. We have seen this in recent years as commodity investors around the world have taken to worrying about the Chinese economy slowing down (China has been a huge consumer of copper for obvious reasons).

Gold and silver are not immune to the same phenomenon, and they will periodically fall by a meaningful percentage. The crucial difference between gold and silver and all other commodities, however, is that they have been used as money for several thousand years. The two metals have industrial and retail applications (for example, in jewellery and antibacterial products) but an increasingly large part of the demand for both of them derives from their use as a financial asset – that is, as money.

Given the general commodity exposure you will have by virtue of owning the world, I firmly believe that the best assets for you to buy to gain *additional* exposure to commodities – and therefore to 'own inflation' – are precious metals. Unlike all other commodities, they benefit from both industrial demand and monetary inflation. They are relatively easy to buy and have a strong individual investment story, which we will look at next.

Please note that all the points I make about gold hold doubly true for silver. Silver tends to amplify whatever gold does. If the price of gold goes up by 10 per cent, silver will tend to go up by two or three times that amount. This is also true when the price goes down, which is why the prudent investor will usually own more gold than silver. In order to understand why gold and silver are particularly important to own beyond the general upward trend in commodities we have already outlined, we must first look at exactly what 'money' is.

What is money?

It might seem ridiculous to have a section explaining what 'money' is but I would contend that most people actually don't understand enough about what it really is – and this has a significant negative impact on their ability to *make* it. I hope, therefore, that you will persevere with what follows and trust that it is important in helping you grow your real wealth.

To really get to grips with what money is, we need to go back in time quite some way to understand why it was invented. In early human societies the 'economy', such as it existed, was a barter system. An individual with food would exchange some of that food for clothing or a weapon, for example. This system enabled early human societies to significantly improve their productivity through specialization: one group could focus on food production (farmers, fishermen) and another on the production of other relatively vital goods such as clothing (tanners, weavers) or tools and weapons (blacksmiths).

As you can imagine, the barter system had severe limitations. A farmer who wanted new clothes or shoes for his family would have to find someone with those products available who, at that precise moment in time, wanted what the farmer had just produced. This was particularly problematic if you consider how perishable and seasonal most of the farmer's products were and how difficult they were to store and transport.

As a result, several thousand years ago some bright spark came up with the idea of using something as a *medium of exchange* and *store of value* – what we now refer to as 'money'. It is important that we think for a moment about what qualities were required for the function early societies required money to perform. These qualities are reasonably self-evident and, at a fundamental level, have not changed over time.

Whatever they chose to use as 'money' needed to be:

1 PORTABLE

A key feature was the ability to carry enough of it with you. Portability had been one of the major problems with the barter system: a farmer needed to herd animals into town, or bring a wagon full of crops just to have enough to exchange for something reasonably 'expensive' such as a plough or some good boots. Portable money also enabled people to travel further than ever before, secure in the knowledge that they would be able to buy vital supplies far from their homes rather than having to face the uncertainty of hunting or foraging for food and fresh water.

2 REASONABLY READILY AVAILABLE, YET RELATIVELY SCARCE

There would have been no point in choosing to use something which was virtually impossible to find or that would require a large percentage of the population to work to produce. It is probably for this reason that precious gemstones, despite coming to be highly valued, were never used as a common currency for day-to-day transactions such as buying food. On the other hand, choosing something that was extremely common (timber or pebbles, for example) would have resulted in the use of something insufficiently portable. To use the example of timber, people would have simply chopped trees down to the point of then having to carry a pointlessly large amount around with them – and this would be no better than a barter system.

3 DURABLE

For something to act as a store of value it was crucial that it would last for long periods of time and not be fragile or easily damaged. There would be no point in using something that would rot away or easily be broken in two, for example. Gold and silver perform this function particularly well.

4 FUNGIBLE AND DIVISIBLE

To really work, money also needed to be divisible into reliable units. Some early societies in the Pacific Islands used seashells and feathers as money. Problems would arise when one islander had a particularly large seashell or unusually beautiful feather: how much more was a big seashell worth than a small one when exchanging it for a quantity of fish, for example? More advanced societies ensured that the size and weight of their money was standardized to avoid such issues. In other words, their money was 'fungible'.

When you consider the above requirements, it is unsurprising that Professor Niall Ferguson says, in his superb book *The Ascent of Money*: 'Metals such as gold, silver and bronze were ... regarded as the ideal monetary raw material.'

Precious metals were made into coins as early as 600 BCE, possibly earlier. Metal coins were then used pretty much universally for several centuries before the next major development: the arrival of paper money.

Paper money

For the first few hundred years of its existence, paper money was very simply an IOU: it came about because another bright spark realized several centuries ago that, rather than taking the high risk and paying the significant costs (soldiers, ships, sailors) of transporting large amounts of precious metals over long distances, it would be easier to leave the physical metal in a vault somewhere safe and instead use a piece of paper representing that metal to perform transactions. These pieces of paper became the original bank notes. This is why it says on a British bank note: 'I promise to pay the bearer on demand the sum of ...' What this originally meant was that someone holding a one 'pound sterling' note could go to the Bank of England and demand one pound (weight) of 'sterling' silver (containing 92.5 per cent pure silver) in its physical form. As I write, you would be able to exchange £1 for 1/190th of a pound of silver. That is to say that the pound is now 190 times less valuable than it was originally in real terms – a pretty good illustration of what inflation does to your money over time!

The point here is that gold and silver have been used as money by countless human societies over thousands of years for all the reasons above. Precious metals came to be used almost universally because, more than any other raw material in existence, they possessed these key characteristics: portability, relative availability, durability, divisibility and fungibility. It is precisely because they possess these characteristics that precious metals constitute a superior 'money' to paper – or, for that matter, to zeros invented by a government in a computer or, in my opinion, to emergent cryptocurrencies such as bitcoin.

Why you should own gold today

For the first few hundred years of its existence, paper money was only ever an IOU backed by a precious metal somewhere. In 1971, faced with the enormous cost of the Vietnam War and unable to pay America's creditors in gold bullion (i.e. real money), President Nixon suspended the convertibility of the US dollar into gold, and America's creditors had to accept being paid back in paper dollars. The result was that the price of gold (in paper dollars) went up by a factor of 24 over the following nine years – from $35 to $850.

Certain commentators in recent years have been saying that gold is 'in a bubble' because it has gone up approximately five times in eight years. This is very simplistic analysis. History teaches us that big structural bull markets can go up far further and for far longer than this. Saying that something has gone up a lot is not a real analysis of whether it is in a bubble. There are strong arguments to suggest that this time the rise in the price of gold could be even more dramatic than in the 1970s. When considering the gold market today, it is perhaps more instructive to look at the following six factors:

1 This bull market is a fraction of what happened in the 1970s

As I have mentioned above, the 1970s bull market in gold was a vastly higher percentage increase than we have seen this time around. We are nowhere near it today.

To repeat: between 1971 and 1980 the gold price increased from around $35 to $850. That is to say it went up by a factor of approximately 24. The current bull market started at about $250 in 1999. If the gold market achieved the same growth in *this* bull market as it did in the 1970s, this would imply a price of $6,000 ($250 x 24). However, the price at the time of writing is around $1,250.

It is perhaps worth noting that Britain's ex-Prime Minister Gordon Brown sold most of the UK's national reserves while he was Chancellor of the Exchequer – at around the $250 level. It might be tempting for anyone reading this to say that 'hindsight is 20/20' and suggest that Gordon Brown can't be blamed for failing to see what would happen in the gold market. I would argue differently. There were ways of looking at gold's value that positively screamed that it was cheap, and there were plenty of commentators at the time who highlighted the likely long-term value of gold.

One such commentator was Jim Rogers, whose track record of correctly calling every major market theme since the 1970s (and resultant delivery of 4,200 per cent growth at George Soros's Quantum Fund) should have suggested that he was well worth listening to. As we shall see, just as with all asset classes, there are ways of working out whether gold is inherently expensive or cheap over the long run.

2 The demand for gold (and silver) is rising

In the 1970s bull market there was a tiny fraction of the possible buyers there are today. Buying came almost entirely from 'sophisticated', 'professional' investors and from Europe and the USA. There were no exchange-traded funds in gold, and essentially no other gold funds. In terms of private individuals, only the very richest people in the developed world could be involved in the market, through their private bankers. The market was a physical market and you owned ingots or coins in a vault.

In fact, for much of the twentieth century it was illegal for private individuals to own gold, even in the West. In the USA, private individuals were not permitted to own gold from 1933 to 1974! As an aside, some readers may be aware that world-famous stock market investor Warren Buffett is pretty regularly on record being negative about gold. It is perhaps worth explicitly noting that his great mentor, Ben Graham, was never able to invest in gold given it was illegal to own for the whole of his professional life. As a result, he never included gold in any of his models (the models Buffett learned from the very beginning of his career) and never lived through the two periods in the last 40 years where gold has performed exceptionally well. I believe this goes some way to explaining Buffett's disinterest in the asset class.

With China and the USSR under communist rule, effectively no one in either of those enormous countries could invest in gold either for most of the twentieth century. The only people permitted to do so were a tiny elite in the ruling parties who were able to travel and to keep wealth outside of their country, in Swiss banks for example. The situation today is radically different, with authorities in China proactively encouraging their vast population to own gold through a national advertising campaign.

In addition, in the 1970s developing countries with massive populations – such as India, Brazil and Indonesia – were all immeasurably poorer than they are today, putting gold as an investment out of the reach of all but the tiniest minority. Today these countries have affluent middle classes totalling hundreds of millions of individuals – a number that is growing all the time.

There was some government or central bank buying from many developing countries but remember how incredibly poor they were compared to the USA and Europe at that time. They were tiny economies, and so even a concerted effort on any of their parts to buy gold was fundamentally irrelevant to the global market and to the price of gold.

Even in the developed world it was very hard for the private individual to own gold compared to today.

> Today people all over the world can buy gold with the click of a mouse button.

As a result, the potential market is a significant multiple of what it was in the 1970s.

Despite this reality, even now the actual allocation of overall investment assets to gold is small. Even after the significant uplift in the price
in the last couple of decades, gold as a proportion of total invested
assets is actually at historical lows. It currently stands at less than 1 per
cent – compared to 3–5 per cent historically. If, as I suspect will be the
case, gold takes back its long-run share (or more) of invested assets globally, this will constitute nothing short of a tidal wave of money chasing
an ever-shrinking supply of the yellow metal. The implications of this
for the price are extremely positive. Figure 10.1 illustrates this point:

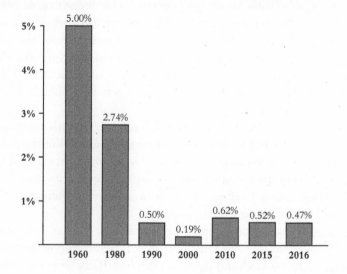

FIGURE 10.1 Gold percentage of global financial assets (1960–2016)
Source: Dan Popescu and BMG Group Inc.

This fall in the percentage allocation to gold has happened because
of how much paper money has been printed all over the world and
ended up in shares, property and bonds.

There is another important consideration when looking at the
demand side of the gold equation: the resurgence of gold buying by
many central banks (those outside Europe and the USA that actually
have any money left).

China has been selling dollar assets and buying gold more or
less quietly for several years and has purchased more than a trillion

dollars' worth if some estimates are to be believed (they are also the world's biggest gold miner). It is perhaps also worth mentioning that China has been extremely active in other commodities, acquiring vast amounts of agricultural and resource assets in Africa and Latin America. The Chinese would seem to have the same view of 'stuff' as we are outlining in this chapter.

China is not the only country to have been a substantial net buyer of gold. Many central banks have been adding to their gold reserves where possible – including Mexico, Russia, South Korea, Taiwan, Singapore, the Netherlands, Indonesia, Turkey and many more. As a whole, they became net buyers of gold in the second quarter of 2009 and have been buying increasing quantities more or less ever since. This net central bank buying of gold from all over the world should be positive for the gold price in the long term, all other things being equal.

3 The dollar price of gold doesn't tell you much

Another consideration here is that looking at the US dollar price of gold is a terribly simplistic approach to working out its value and a little like using an elastic ruler given how variable the value of the dollar is. A better way of looking at establishing gold's value is to compare it to other key assets over time.

GOLD VERSUS OIL

A great way of measuring the value of something like gold is to look at its ratio to things like oil, property and stock markets. The average ratio of the gold price to a barrel of Brent crude (oil) since 1970 has been about 16:1. At the time of writing this is roughly where they are trading. This would indicate that gold is in no way 'expensive'. For gold to be expensive, using oil as a valuation tool, that ratio would need to double, as has been the case on several occasions in the past. Such a change implies that oil could halve and gold double in price, or a mixture of the two. Since I originally wrote this paragraph in the previous edition of the book, oil has indeed halved in price, demonstrating in a small way the predictive power of looking at these kinds of ratios (although it has bounced since then).

GOLD VERSUS HOUSE PRICES

Another useful ratio when considering either property or gold prices is the ratio of gold prices to house prices. Figure 10.2 shows the average cost of a UK house, priced in pounds.

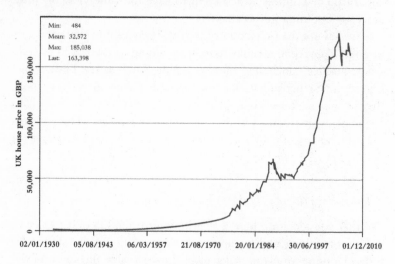

Min:	484
Mean:	32,572
Max:	185,038
Last:	163,398

FIGURE 10.2 Average UK house price (1930–2010)
Source: moneyweek.com/3465/gold-price-and-uk-house-prices-04909.

You will remember that the purchasing power of the pound has fallen by about 90 per cent since 1971 and that this, more than anything, accounts for the increase in the *nominal* price (if not *real* value) of UK property. Gold has been a much better long-term store of value compared to the pound. If we look at the price of UK houses *in terms of ounces of gold* – Figure 10.3 – we can draw some interesting conclusions.

We can see that 2002 was a terrible time to sell gold, since it was as cheap as it had ever been historically compared to house prices. Without wishing to sound like a broken record, I really would love to know if former UK Prime Minister and Chancellor Gordon Brown and his advisers were looking at charts like these when they took their decision to sell the UK's gold. I suspect not, which illustrates how criminally incompetent politicians can be when making these sorts of decisions.

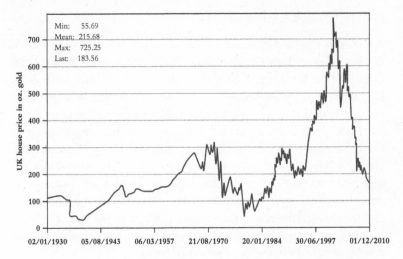

Min: 55.69
Mean: 215.68
Max: 725.25
Last: 183.56

FIGURE 10.3 Average UK house price in ounces of gold (1930–2010)
Source: moneyweek.com/3465/gold-price-and-uk-house-prices-04909.

The point here is that the smart money will always be looking at *relative value* in the long run. Folks like the aforementioned Jim Rogers could never guarantee that a British house costing 700 ounces of gold was inherently the wrong price, but they could say that there was most certainly a very good chance that it was. You can't escape mean reversion in any market over time.

People are forever suggesting that you 'can't time the market'. I would argue that if you are prepared to spend a little while looking at the relative value of a wide variety of assets, you have a good chance of making better long-term decisions about your finances. Figure 10.3 tells you that the smart money sold property in 2006/7 and purchased gold. If UK house prices get back down to less than 100 ounces of gold, as they have done in the past, this implies either that gold doubles from here or that UK house prices halve. My best guess is that it will be a combination of the two and they will meet somewhere in the middle, at which point a UK house will be good value again and a bar of gold will be inherently expensive. Whatever happens, people who sold property to buy precious metals in 2006/7 may be able to sell their precious metals and buy a much nicer house than the one they sold a few years ago.

GOLD VERSUS STOCK MARKETS

Another metric used by the smart money is to compare gold to a stock market index such as the Dow Jones Industrial Average. In 2012 the Dow Jones was trading at around 12,000 and it has more than doubled since then – a testament to the power of investing. With the gold price at $1,600, the ratio of gold to the Dow Jones was therefore about 7.5:1. This ratio has been as low as 2:1 on more than one occasion in the last century and was nearly 1:1 in the early 1980s. If we were to see a 2:1 ratio again, this would imply the possibility of gold increasing to $12,000 per ounce with the Dow at current levels – or, a good deal more likely given current circumstances, a crash in the Dow and a slightly less extreme rise in the price of gold. In recent years the Dow has gone up and gold has gone down, which just means that the rubber band is stretched even more tightly than before.

I am not alone in believing that we could see a 2:1 ratio again. Many of the financial commentators who best predicted the gold bull market and the financial crisis of the last few years see the endgame as a likely return of the gold-to-Dow ratio to 2:1, or worse (read 'better' for gold investors).

Their views are seen as controversial; however, the mainstream financial commentators who argue that they are crazy to believe the Dow and gold could ever trade to those sorts of levels are the very same people who argued against gold in the past, were wrong the entire time and missed a 500 per cent move as a result.

In my experience, few of these commentators do the comparative analysis against the other assets we are looking at here. Many of the conditions that we are discussing are the same conditions that caused such a ratio to be reached in the past. If anything, many of the arguments for seeing a 2:1 ratio again that I am outlining here are more pertinent today than they have been on the previous occasions this has occurred.

I think there is a decent chance that people who see the 2:1 ratio as beyond the realms of possibility will prove to have been suffering from a nasty dose of anchoring (see Chapter 5). As you should be able to see, these ratios suggest that we are not yet near 'bubble' territory for gold. There is still vastly more money in other assets and there are compelling reasons why much of that money could be chasing gold in the months and years ahead. That having been said, there is an argument that some of that money might be chasing bitcoin and other crypto assets which many believe can and will serve a similar purpose to gold in future. It is for this reason that I suggested in Chapter 7 that a small speculative investment in bitcoin may be appropriate.

4 Interest rates

Another argument for continued strength in the gold price concerns global interest rates. Although you will by now be well aware that I expect the global bond market to drive interest rates up in the years ahead, real interest rates today are basically at a 300-year low. Real interest rates are negative in nearly every corner of the world, as real inflation is usually higher than the interest rate.

Bear in mind that one of the biggest negatives about holding gold is that you do not earn any interest. When interest rates are high, owners of gold miss out on this return. Economists call this the 'opportunity cost' of owning gold. This is the main reason gold performed so weakly in the early 1980s. At that time, Paul Volcker was chairman of the Federal Reserve and instituted high interest rates in a bid to control inflation. Inevitably, a great deal of money left gold, chasing what were historically high interest rates it could now earn elsewhere, and the gold price fell.

With the negative real interest rates we have today, there is no such downside to owning gold and, given where real inflation is, nominal interest rates have room to increase by several per cent before interest rates are no longer a bullish argument for gold.

5 The supply of gold and silver

We have, hopefully, established quite a strong case for the growth in *demand* for gold. Let us now turn our attention to supply.

Simply put, it is falling significantly. It is getting harder and harder to find and extract gold. Earlier in the book I highlighted the fact that finding one wedding ring's worth of gold involves mining no less than 20 tonnes of rock today. The world's biggest mines (in places like South Africa) are finding it harder and harder to extract gold and their production is going backwards. To give you an idea of just how scarce gold is, a little-known but interesting fact is that all the gold in the world ever mined could fit into two Olympic swimming pools.

There are strong arguments to suggest that there is likely to be much more demand for gold in the future. At the same time, the supply picture for gold is far from rosy. As I have mentioned before, one of the fundamental truths of economics is that when demand for something is rising yet the supply of that something is fixed or falling, the price has to rise.

6 The supply of paper money

There is one final factor to consider: the supply of paper money.

I hope you will forgive the repetition, but we should by now be familiar with the fact that the supply of paper money all over the world is increasing at quite a clip. If there are three times the number of dollars in the world and the same amount of gold, then, all other things being equal, the price of gold in dollars should be three times higher before you even begin to consider the demand and supply figures outlined above.

In fact, the supply of dollar money has grown so much since it was last linked to gold in 1971 that the implied price of gold today 'should' arguably be tens of thousands of dollars. I'm not saying the price will get there any time soon, but it is an interesting ratio and underscores the potential in the long term.

Before we move on to the next section of this chapter I want to repeat the important point that pretty much everything we have said about gold is relevant to silver. Silver has traditionally played the same monetary role as gold, and I see no reason why it will not continue to do so.

In fact, the outlook for silver is arguably significantly more positive than for gold. There are a number of reasons for this. First, silver has significantly more industrial uses than gold and so there is more non-monetary demand for it. It is also worth noting that there is roughly 16 times more silver in the world than gold. This implies that the long-run price of silver should be roughly one-sixteenth of the price of gold. With gold now trading at around $1,250, silver 'should' trade at around $78. It currently trades at around $16.

An update on precious metals for the third edition

Anyone who read the original edition of this book, listened to interviews I have given in the last few years or seen me speak at an event, will know that I have regularly been on record espousing the merits of having a fair chunk of your savings in precious metals, as per this chapter.

This has opened me up to a measure of criticism, given that the gold price peaked in late 2011 and has since fallen in value by around a third. Silver, which I have also continued to recommend as a key component of an investment strategy for those with a bit more money to invest, has more than halved from its peak. Given this reality, one Amazon reviewer wrote: 'The author's enthusiasm for commodities and particularly precious metals including gold and silver seems to reflect hubris over past trading successes and naive theories of monetary inflation, rather than realistic prospects of future returns. Since the book was written, gold prices have experienced sharp falls.'

There is much to say on this subject. Most importantly, I think this sort of criticism of my thoughts on commodities and precious metals in particular illustrates just why you should own them. Too often, people fall into the trap of thinking they know how to asset-allocate: when to own shares, when to own precious metals, when to own bonds. I would argue that for most people this is more 'hubristic' than allocating a sensible part of your long-term investment strategy to each of these asset classes, including one as important as precious metals.

The whole point of 'owning the world' (for someone who wants a 'find it easy to sleep at night', 'set and forget' strategy, at least) is that your money is nicely diversified across the main asset classes and geographies every year – *no matter what*. This has a proven track record of working in the long run, because you will not get decimated in a disastrous year such as 2000 or 2008, and are more likely to make reasonable financial progress year after year. The fact that the gold price has experienced sharp falls since 2011 is neither here nor there and focusing on this misses the point of the book and the method (the set and forget method, at least).

The price of gold *is* down since 2011, although, as we saw earlier in the book, it has still averaged 11.3 per cent per annum in sterling terms over the last 15 years. I hope you would agree that this compares reasonably favourably with your current account or cash ISA. I would also stress that equity markets are up very strongly, and anyone following an 'owning the world' strategy overall will have benefited handsomely from this. In another year – possibly in the not too distant future – gold will be up a great deal and equity markets will be down. The point here is that there is a great deal of evidence that having *consistent exposure to all asset classes* works in the long run – at least it has done for a very long time, across all phases of the economic cycle.

If you ensure that you own a good mix of shares, bonds, hard assets and cash, you will end up with a more stable, safe and reliable portfolio than the majority of people who have not diversified. You may worry that owning such a wide variety of assets makes your portfolio too neutral to perform successfully, but history and evidence show us that this isn't true. As Harry Browne, famous investment author and creator of the Permanent Portfolio discussed earlier in this chapter, wrote: 'Over broad periods of time, the winning investments add more value to the portfolio than the losing investments take away.'

More important, however, is the fact that by adopting this diverse approach you are very unlikely ever to lose a great deal of money. You will most likely not suffer in a year like 2000 or 2008, when so many people lost their proverbial shirts. Not losing a significant amount of money in any given year is very important – particularly if you're about to retire and are at risk of losing a huge percentage of the pot you've spent a lifetime building. While this may seem obvious, relatively few people understand the 'break-even fallacy', which really solidifies the point.

The break-even fallacy

To explain: say you asked the question 'If you lose 50 per cent on an investment, how much would it then have to rise by to get back to where it started?' Many people would say that the answer is 50 per cent. This seems logical. If something falls by 50 per cent, then surely it must have to rise by 50 per cent to 'break even' (get back to the level at which it started).

The real answer, however, is that it needs to then rise by *100 per cent*. If this seems wrong to you, then let's quickly look at the numbers. Say you owned a share that was worth £100. If there is then a big stock market crash and it falls 50 per cent, it will then be worth £50. If your share now rises 50 per cent from that level (£50), the share will only get back to £75, as 50 per cent of £50 is only £25. This means that to get back to £100, the share will have to rise by 100 per cent (100 per cent of £50 is clearly £50).

This is why it is so important to minimize your losses in investment and why, in the words of famous US investor Warren Buffett:

> 'Rule No. 1: Never lose money. Rule No. 2: Never forget rule No. 1.'

As we have seen, a proven way of lowering the risk of ever making a big loss is to own a wide variety of assets from around the world – in other words, to 'own the world'.

The tortoise beats the hare ...

It is important to note that this approach is unlikely to give you 30 per cent or 50 per cent years. The aim is to grind out an average performance of high single-digit to low double-digit or so percentage returns over a lifetime of investing, and to minimize the risk of losing a big chunk of your money in a 'crash' year.

Some years you might only make or possibly even lose 2 per cent at a time when lots of other people are crowing about how they've made a 'killing' in the stock market (or in something like bitcoin perhaps). You might feel a little stupid as a result, but this is precisely when you should stick to your guns. The people who are succeeding in the stock market in such a year are generally the ones who will lose half of their money or even more in a year like 2008 or 2000.

Over a lifetime of investing, the tortoise will generally beat the hare because of the break-even fallacy. The tortoise will certainly be more likely to have a juicy seven-figure sum at retirement, so please resist the siren call of the 'I've made a killing' crowd (a call that has been particularly loud in the last couple of years as stock markets have hit new highs again and again and in the mad frenzy of the bitcoin and extended crypto asset world).

I hope that this will reassure any of you worrying that you have 'underperformed' in the stock market because some of your money has been invested in precious metals each month. Over time, the fact that you were a tortoise in the year or two when the hare was running particularly fast will very likely have been a blessing in disguise.

Over a lifetime of investment, making 'boring' single-digit returns and protecting your downside will provide you with a far better result than owning something that goes up 50 per cent one year and falls 40 per cent the next. Slow, boring and steady – and not losing money – wins the race!

The other great thing about the tortoise approach is that you don't have to keep on top of the world of finance or spend a great deal of time thinking (worrying) about where to invest and whether there might be a stock market crash this year. You don't have to worry about whether you should be investing in Asia, the USA or Europe – or in bonds, commodities, real estate or shares – because you will simply own a good mix of all of them.

As we have seen, it is only in the relatively recent past that this method of investing has become possible, thanks to innovations in the financial services industry. It is just a shame that relatively few people understand why it is a great approach or how to implement it.

To be clear, this is what I suggest for the vast majority of people who don't want to commit any time or effort to developing an in-depth knowledge of finance. I call it the 'keeping it simple' strategy. Of course, people who are willing to learn a great deal about finance and current affairs *can* expect to make more specific asset allocation decisions and very possibly outperform any 'set and forget' strategy – but this comes with a big health warning: it takes real skill and you need to put a good deal of work in. We will discuss this in more detail in the next chapter.

This is the primary reason that I am still entirely comfortable sticking to my belief that you should allocate a meaningful percentage of your money to gold (or, indeed, both gold and silver) and do so regularly each month. Even when gold is down from its peak, you should have a sensible percentage of your money in it at a nicely averaged entry price. The evidence, over the last 40 years or so, has shown that this is a good approach, and nothing the price has done since 2011 changes that reality.

For what it's worth, I think gold and silver will surprise the bears in the not too distant future and will remind us all why it should be a key pillar of any 'set and forget' investment strategy. Gold went up by 2,400 per cent between 1971 and 1980, but in the mid-1970s it corrected by nearly 50 per cent. People who panicked and sold at that point missed out on the enormous gains of 1976–80. I feel that we are in a similar situation today. Figures 10.4 and 10.5 might help to illustrate the point.

FIGURE 10.4 The price of gold and the 1970s pull-back
Source: Plain English Finance

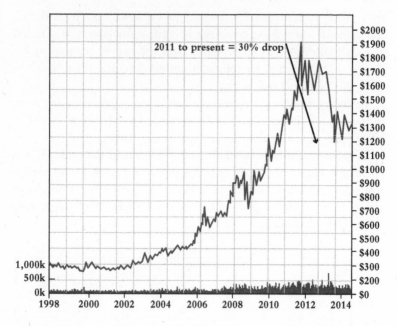

FIGURE 10.5 The price of gold and the present-day pull-back
Source: Plain English Finance

To me, the move from late 2011 until now looks very similar to the move between 1975 and 1977. Time will tell whether the price powers ahead as it did in the late 1970s, but, whether it does or not, precious metals will remain a key component of our keeping it simple strategy.

If you would like to read about these various arguments and more besides in detail, I can highly recommend Jim Rickard's excellent book *The New Case for Gold.*

How to own precious metals

We have outlined in some detail why we need to own inflation and how the best way to do this is to own precious metals. This is relatively easy and inexpensive to do. With the 10–20 per cent of your monthly investment funds you have left after investing in an own the world fund as per the previous section, you might consider buying some precious metals.

In the first edition of this book, I advocated investing in precious metals by using stock market-listed exchange-traded funds (ETFs). Since then, however, I am increasingly of the view that the best way to get exposure to precious metals is to actually own physical gold (and/or silver) rather than via a fund or ETF.

A concern I always had with precious metals ETFs is that there is about 50 times as much 'theoretical' gold in the world as physical gold. Without getting bogged down in too much detail, this means that a 'paper' claim on some gold somewhere is arguably not as secure as actually personally owning gold (or silver) yourself.

The more I thought about this, the more I wanted to suggest that people own actual, physical precious metals. There are a number of ways to do this. Again, because this is a dynamic area, rather than include specific recommendations on how you might go about buying precious metals here, please have a look at our website for more up-to-date information about my views on the best ways to buy gold and silver.

A few final considerations

There are a few further things to consider when adopting a 'keeping it simple' strategy:

Lump sums

If you already have a lump sum you would like to invest (a very good idea) and if you want to keep things very simple, then you might consider dividing that sum by ten or 12 and pay one-tenth or one-twelfth of it into your chosen investments each month for the next few months, along with what you intend to save monthly. We already saw how investing every month like this achieves 'averaging in' or 'smoothing', which is why taking this approach is a good idea. It will reduce the risk that you invest a big lump of cash days before a market crash. Don't forget, however, that you should already suffer far less from any kind of market crash than most, given your geographical and asset diversification.

Rebalancing

Imagine you invested £3,000 in gold and silver at the beginning of a year, paid £6,000 into your chosen 'own the world' fund and kept another £1,000 in cash. This would imply that you had allocated 30 per cent of your money to gold and silver, 60 per cent to owning the world, and 10 per cent to cash.

Now imagine that your gold and silver go up by 20 per cent (combined) over the course of that year, your world fund increases by 10 per cent and cash by 0 per cent (as interest rates are basically 0 per cent). This would mean that one year later you would have £3,600 in gold and silver, £6,600 in your 'own the world' fund and £1,000 in cash. The crucial thing to understand here is that your percentage allocation to each asset will have changed slightly. You will now have £11,200 in total and it will be split as follows: 32.1 per cent gold and silver, 58.9 per cent in your world fund and 9 per cent in cash compared to your target split of 30/60/10 per cent.

Obviously, the percentages have not changed by a huge amount, but over time, if you did nothing to deal with this situation, you could end up with a split that is some way away from the 30/60/10 that you are looking for.

The solution to this is something called 'rebalancing'. Once a year or so, you would look at the proportion of assets you hold and sell the ones that have gone up most to buy the ones that have gone up least (or fallen). In the example above, if your target is 30/60/10 then this would imply you would like to own: £3,360 of gold and silver, £6,720 in your world fund, and have £1,120 in cash. All you would need to do would be to sell £240 worth of gold and silver, put half of it into your world fund and keep half in cash.

This approach ensures that you stick to your target asset allocation but it also means you are automatically taking some profit from your best-performing assets, and using that profit to buy other assets at a relatively cheaper level.

The more mathematically minded of you will have noticed that, if you are buying assets every month in the right proportions, the percentage changes at the end of the year are likely to be small, unless there have been some very big moves in a short space of time.

You will not need to worry too much about rebalancing if you are following the methodology of monthly investment. Nevertheless, I would argue that you should just check your percentage allocation at least once a year to make sure things haven't moved too far away from your target. This is the only real work you will ever need to do after you have set things up with this approach.

'Past performance is not indicative of future results'

Many of you will have seen this phrase in the literature of financial services companies. Depending on the type of firm you are dealing with or the product you are considering, it is usually compulsory for it to appear.

I have serious misgivings about the usefulness of this statement. If past performance is no guide to future results, then how would we pick football teams, why would we choose a certain brand of car over another, and why might we decide to vote a government out of office at election time?

The reality is that past performance *can* be indicative of future results. We do, however, need to be careful how heavily we rely on it and must ensure that we use it as only one among many possible indicators of future performance. In my opinion, sound analysis of what is going on around us is generally more useful for predicting what might happen in the future than focusing overly on performance numbers. Past performance is no doubt something we should be aware of and keep an eye on, but I would contend that solid analysis and logic will trump it every time.

I would hope that after reading this far you would agree that the strategy I have outlined in this chapter is based on just such solid analysis and logic. There is a great deal of evidence to support the ideas of owning the world and owning inflation – and we have seen how you can do this effectively and cheaply.

In summary

If you remember the magic of compounding, you will hopefully see that if you pay as much money into your investment accounts as possible and leave that money there for as long as possible, you will achieve the biggest result in terms of building your money. The more money you invest and the more you leave invested, the more 'free' money you can generate from compounding (interest on your interest, or return on your return).

You will have to make your own decisions about when and for what reason you withdraw money from your ISA or other investment accounts, but the longer you leave it before upgrading your car or taking that exotic holiday, the more cars and amazing holidays you will be able to buy in the not too distant future – and the more comfortable your retirement will be in the long run. As my economics teacher said to me in my first ever economics lesson, economics is essentially all about:

> 'Jam today or more jam tomorrow.'

As you might imagine, it is my firmly held opinion that if you follow the logic outlined in this chapter you will have done an extremely good job of setting up your financial affairs, particularly for someone who doesn't want to invest any real time or effort.

You will ...

- be well diversified geographically and in terms of assets – you are invested in the world
- stand to benefit from the inflationary policies of central banks all over the world while many other folk see their purchasing power gradually destroyed
- achieve this cheaply and effectively.

For those of you who want to get your house in order with relatively little effort, I believe this is a great approach to take. It will give you an excellent chance of making a good amount of money from your money. As we have seen, it has worked for the likes of the Rothschild family and Harvard and Yale for decades.

In reasonably short order you should see a significant impact on your finances. Your money will start making you money. If you stick with the plan for several years, your money will very possibly end up making you more than you could earn by working – the ultimate goal. By getting your financial affairs in order you give yourself the best chance of building a pot that could make having a mortgage or any other kind of debt a thing of the past.

I can't say that this approach will always make money. You may well experience the odd down year, as there is no certainty in investment. What I can say with a degree of confidence is that it is highly likely that this strategy will grow your real wealth over time (as demonstrated by Table 10.1: The Permanent Portfolio). If the material you have read so far has succeeded in its job, you will hopefully find the ideas sufficiently compelling to agree with this assessment.

A very important final point

The above notwithstanding, I want to make a very important final point: although I am confident that the approach outlined in this chapter is a good one, there really is no substitute for taking a proactive approach to looking after your money. Arguably, this has never been truer than today.

There are some very serious and frankly rather frightening structural changes going on in the world today, not least the possibility of rampant real inflation. If you really don't have the inclination to spend a bit more time learning about finance, then please do implement the ideas in this chapter. In order to give yourself the very best chance of surviving and thriving, however, I would strongly recommend that you take further steps to improve your understanding of finance. Once you open the Pandora's box of learning about money, there is a good chance you might even find it fun and interesting.

Whatever happens, you will certainly give yourself the best chance of spotting a big trend or change in the way the world economy is working. This will minimize your chance of being caught out in a crash and maximize your chances of investing in the right places. Taking responsibility for your own financial affairs will also save you a great deal of money in fees and costs, which can have a significant impact on your finances as a whole, as we have seen. Chapter 11 aims to point you in the right direction in terms of how you might most effectively go about improving your financial literacy and to give you some examples of what can be achieved and how to proceed.

So that is the 'keeping it simple' approach. Create some financial surplus as per Chapter 5, get your accounts set up as per Chapter 6, invest as per the last two chapters, and get going. If you are someone who wants to 'keep things simple', that is it. I hope you have found what you have read to be compelling and I hope that you will take action to revolutionize your financial affairs.

If, as I hope, you are interested in 'taking things further' and maximizing your chances of doing an even better job with your money then please continue to the next chapter. At the very least, it is well worth a quick look at what follows, even if you see yourself as one of the 'keeping it simple' crowd.

I I

Taking things further

'How you go about investing is vastly more important than which
stocks you buy.'

Porter Stansberry, founder of Stansberry & Associates

In the previous chapter, we looked at how you might invest success-fully using what we've looked at so far – but without any particularly strenuous ongoing work. It is my belief that the investment method outlined in Chapter 10 is a great approach if you would rather not spend significantly more time learning about money and finance. It will ensure that you pay low fees, end up with an excellent spread of assets and have a high chance of making consistent *real* returns (after accounting for true inflation). This strategy can yield wonderful results in the long run thanks to the power of compounding.

Automation best for most?

There are actually a number of compelling arguments to suggest that keeping things simple as outlined in the last chapter is potentially the best approach to investment for most people. For many folks, remov-ing yourself from the equation can have a very positive effect on your likely investment returns. The following explains why this is the case.

As you know by now, the S&P 500 index in the USA is a good proxy for 'the stock market'. It fell from 1,500 in October 2007 down to the rather spooky and biblical level of 666 in March 2009 (that is a 56 per cent collapse – ouch!). Since then, however, it has then gone from 666 all the way back to around 2,750 as I write (that is more than a 300 per cent recovery – nice!).

The problem is that human nature is such that, if you had tried to time your investments to take advantage of these moves, you would almost certainly have got it wrong. In fact, the situation is worse than that: there is a high probability that you would have sold low and bought high and timed your investments about as badly as it is pos-sible to. Why is this? It's because we are hard-wired psychologically to get this wrong.

We humans are pack beasts. We pay a disproportionate amount of attention to what everyone else around us is doing. Much as we fight it, very few of us have the knowledge or self-confidence to be truly contrarian. When the market bottomed at 666 in March 2009, nearly everything you would have read or seen in the news would have gone on about how risky stock market investment is and how much money everyone had just lost. As a result of the fear, woe, pessimism, anger, general wailing and gnashing of teeth, you would have been highly unlikely to have considered putting your hard-earned savings into the stock market. Everyone would tell you you'd be crazy to even consider it: 'Brrr. Too risky! Look what just happened!'

Even more insidiously, as the market recovered from the bottom – 10 per cent up, then 20 per cent, 30 per cent, 40 per cent and all the way up to 300 per cent (today) – it would have been perfectly natural for you to say to yourself (pretty much every month): 'Damn! I must have missed it now. I'm too late.' You would then not have invested.

After a year or two of this, the next thought you might have had would probably be something like: 'Oh dear. I really must sort this investment thing out. Look! The market is up 300 per cent. It just keeps going up. My mate has made a fortune. I've been avoiding it the whole time and missing out. Right. That's it. I'm in.'

You know the rest. Just as you decide it is time to get back in, along comes the next dot-com or Lehman's style crash and you get absolutely flattened and spend the next decade licking your wounds. The cycle repeats. This really happens. Time and time again. It is human nature. We are hard-wired to do this.

The solution for many people is to take themselves out of the equation. Most folk should ignore the news completely and automate their investments. Do not try to second-guess what is going to happen. Do not try to time the market and start thinking 'I should buy this now or sell that now.' Do not ask supposed 'experts' what they think either. Just invest what you can afford, every month, without fail, into something sensible such as the method suggested in the last chapter and do this until such time as you want to live on the proceeds (a time that will hopefully arrive sooner than most people dream is possible if you do this).

In our example of the S&P 500 above, had you been automating your payments monthly, you would have bought in at 1,500 just before the crash (ouch) but then every month after the crash too (at levels along the lines of 680, 750, 850, 930, 1,000 and so on, all the way up to 2,750 – lovely!).

The net result of this approach is that you should grind out consistent and meaningful returns (far higher than interest rates) through the economic cycle, no matter what is happening. Thanks to Einstein's eighth wonder of the world – compound interest – the tortoise then thrashes the hare and you will end up with more money than you thought possible.

Stick to your guns

As long as you are doing something sensible with your money, another key consideration when you take this approach is to *stick to your guns* and to invest for the long term. I would argue that doing this is far easier once you understand a bit about finance – because you will have more confidence in what you are doing and be less likely to sell out of things in a panic when the headlines are screaming about 'massive crashes' or whatever else.

When doing speaking events, I quite often say that, in the long run at least, investment success is truly 90 per cent about administration and only 10 per cent about what you invest in (within reason). If you have actually made the effort to set up an investment account with a good-quality company, optimize your ISA and pension arrangements and set up the necessary regular direct debits, you will be 90 per cent of the way to investment success. The final 10 per cent is about choosing something sensible to make those payments into, *automating* and *sticking to your guns*.

To illustrate this point: Professors Elroy Dimson and Paul Marsh of the London Business School have shown that investing in UK smaller companies has achieved an annual return of no less than 15.4 per cent going back as far as 1955! You read that right: 15.4 per cent a year for 60 years!

Making that sort of return on the money you save and invest will make you wealthy really rather quickly – particularly if you're using an ISA account so you don't even incur any tax liability. You may well become an ISA millionaire over the course of a few years.

There is a problem, however: although this performance track record over no less than 60 years is amazing (and almost entirely unknown by the vast majority of people other than a small minority of folks in the City), the 15.4 per cent returns didn't come smoothly every year. Some years smaller companies powered ahead by 30 per cent or even 40 per cent or more. On several occasions between 1955 and the present day, however, they *fell by more than 50 per cent.*

These falls are so extreme that most people holding UK small caps will tend to lose faith, give up in fear, crystallize their 50 per cent loss and then never invest in the space again – a terrible result all round and nowhere near the 15.4 per cent annual return they could be making, particularly when you consider the points I made about human psychology above. This is why having confidence in what you are doing and sticking to your game plan is so important, but it is also why I believe owning the world works. With global, multi-asset investment you are incredibly unlikely to see those sorts of horrendous falls in your investments and more likely to stick with them as a result.

All of the above having been said, this chapter is for anyone who would like to contemplate being more proactive about their investments. If you think you have the psychological strength, discipline and appetite for a good deal of work, you may prefer to learn more about finance rather than set and forget.

Given how dynamic today's financial world is and how big a subject investment is, for some people it may be worth taking a more proactive approach to looking after your money, particularly if you have a reasonable sum to invest. Learning more about finance and investment will mean that you increase your chances of growing your money more quickly, while simultaneously making you confident that you can do so relatively safely.

Given what a huge subject finance is and how it is constantly changing, this chapter is absolutely not intended to be a comprehensive guide to everything you need to know in order to become a successful investor or trader. Such a guide would have to run to thousands of pages and would need updating weekly, possibly even daily.

What I do hope to achieve in this chapter is to:

- highlight some of the key concepts you will want to understand to get up to speed on finance
- point you in the direction of some top-quality resources that should help you get to grips with these concepts
- give you some examples of what can be achieved if you do.

Three important goals

Once you have finished this chapter, you should be on the road to knowing how to make decisions about asset allocation, how to invest in individual assets and how to 'trade'.

1 Learn how to make decisions about asset allocation

Throughout the book, I have stressed how important it is to invest in a wide variety of assets. The previous chapter outlined a largely formulaic way of achieving this. If you are prepared to get to grips with further aspects of finance, you will get to the stage where you can finesse your asset allocation in order to take advantage of phases where one asset is performing more strongly than the others.

Armed with a reasonable knowledge of basic financial analysis, economics and economic history, you will be capable of making big-picture decisions about when certain assets are more likely to perform better than others. As an example, anyone with a good grasp of relative value between the various asset classes might have decided to be heavily weighted towards precious metals from 1971 until about 1980, towards equities from the early 1980s until about 2000, and then back to precious metals from that point until today. This approach would have resulted in very high returns indeed for no less than 40 years.

Many people argue that making these calls successfully is impossible. This is certainly a fashionable view in the finance industry: 'hindsight is 20/20' and it is surely unrealistic to think that anyone can time markets as successfully as in my example above.

I politely disagree. As I have said several times, you will never be able to make these sorts of calls with perfect timing, but without question there are ways of comparing the main asset classes that highlight when one of them is more likely to be good value. We have already seen some of these methods, for example comparing the gold price to the price of oil and the level of the stock market. This weighing up of the long-term value of various assets or markets is sometimes referred to as 'life-cycle investing'. For the knowledgeable, patient and confident investor, this approach can and does yield superior results. The only caveat to this statement is that it does require a great deal of time and skill and as a result is not for everyone.

One of the reasons relatively few people succeed in making big-picture asset allocation decisions is quite simply that relatively few people take the time to understand and look at all asset classes, or even to work out how to invest in them. I would argue that this is true for nearly all private individuals and many professional investors. That said, there are plenty of examples of professional investors who have made these calls over the years. Increasingly, you are able to find out who these people are and follow their advice, often entirely free of charge.

Optimal asset allocation also changes with your age

One of the universal rules of sensible investment is that you should become more conservative with your investments the closer you get to retirement. When you are young, you can afford to be a bit racier in a bid to grow your money as quickly as possible and you can cope with a little volatility along the way. At the most basic level, this implies owning more shares and fewer bonds, all other things being equal.

> As you get older you should be thinking more about the return *of* your money than the return *on* your money.

There would be nothing more tragic than having a nasty negative year in your late fifties, for example, and losing a large amount of the pot you have worked so hard to build. Having a down year in your twenties or thirties will mean you lose less money in total (given that your pot is smaller at that point) and you have far more time to make it back. Losing 40 per cent of £10,000 at the age of 28 is clearly a great deal less of a problem than losing 40 per cent of £1,000,000 at the age of 60 as you go to retire. Generally, this means that as you approach retirement you will ensure that you keep more of your money in bonds and cash, and less in shares.

As you gain a deeper understanding of these things, you will be able to make your own decisions about how to allocate your money between shares, bonds, commodities, cash and real estate – and how this should change as you get older. This is not easy by any means but the more you learn, the better chance you will have of getting it broadly right over the years, and this will have a positive impact on your ability to make great returns while also minimizing risk.

2 Know how to invest in individual assets

Once you have learned a bit more about finance, you might also consider investing in individual assets (rather than just funds). Armed with the knowledge that follows, you may well soon feel confident enough to choose an individual share or commodity that you think has a particularly bright future.

I have owned a fair few things over the years that have gone up 100 per cent or more. A few years ago I made over 160 per cent profit in just over eight months in silver. I also sold a share that had gone up 350 per cent in about 18 months. (I sold it early because I wanted the funds at the time, and sadly this share is now up 675 per cent from my purchase price. There's no point in crying over spilt milk, however – and the next opportunity is always out there somewhere, which is a thoroughly uplifting and liberating way of thinking.)

Obviously, these sorts of gains don't happen all the time and there are always losers to contend with (I've had my fair share of those, to be clear) but, as you can imagine, you don't need too many of these successes over the years in order to grow a large enough pot for the target lifestyle you have drawn up a budget for (see Chapter 9).

However, you are unlikely to experience these sorts of returns if you stick to the basket of funds recommended as part of the 'keeping it simple' strategy. Finding and investing in big winners (and avoiding losers) requires more knowledge, but it is still not that difficult to get to the point where you might start to have a go at this. You just need to be prepared to learn a little and ensure you are using the right resources.

3 Learn how to trade

Once you have had a look at the material that follows, you will be more likely to start 'trading'. That is to say, you will consider more regular purchases and sales of financial assets – and you will hold them for a shorter period of time than if you were following the 'keeping it simple' method described in the previous chapter. If you manage to do this successfully, it can have a significant positive impact on your returns, as we shall see.

Once you are able to use certain techniques to improve your chances of buying the right assets at the right time – and to buy low and sell high (or even sell high to buy back low) – you stand to make significant returns. This isn't easy but, as we have already seen, there are methods of investing that achieve consistent returns, particularly if you understand certain valuation metrics and are willing to think globally and about a diverse range of assets.

One thing worth bearing in mind when thinking about becoming more of a 'trader' than an 'investor' is that, in my opinion, you should *only use part of your capital to trade*. This is related to the earlier point about asset allocation. Even if you have a reasonable amount of money to look after and feel confident that you have learned a great deal about exciting trading strategies, I would suggest that you continue to keep a large portion of your money in more conservative, longer-term investments. Another tragic scenario in investment, which many people fall foul of, is deciding to use all their investment capital for more aggressive, exciting short-term trading strategies. This was one of the reasons so many people lost so much money in the dot-com boom of the late 1990s and, sadly, at the time of writing this third edition, I am seeing the same thing happen all over again in the crypto and blockchain space. Everywhere I look on social media, I see people who are obviously using all their savings and, even worse, sometimes even borrowing on their credit cards or taking on more mortgage debt to invest in crypto. These are also usually people with no previous experience of all the other asset classes who have never before invested in shares or funds, for example. It pains me that so few people ever seem to learn the lessons of history, even such relatively recent history.

It is perhaps helpful to think of 'trading capital' as another one of the fundamental components of your asset allocation strategy. Even if you think you've become quite good at short-term trading, it might be an idea to allocate your money something like this:

- 40 per cent longer-term investments in shares and share funds
- 25 per cent in precious metals and other commodities
- 10 per cent in bonds
- 10 per cent in real estate (not including your primary residence)
- 15 per cent to 'wing around', trading more risky assets (perhaps small, higher-risk shares, or trading forex and other assets with a spread betting account).

The above is just a broad-brush example, and there are many other ways you could allocate your money. As a UK resident, you can use a spread-betting account to have lots of fun with trading. You might, therefore, allocate the 'wing around' percentage of your capital to this. A small minority of people (after putting in a great deal of work) can make extraordinary returns with spread betting (something like 90 per cent of people lose money). But I would argue that even they should still only use around 15 per cent of their overall pot for that purpose. Any profits they make can then be used to buy more of the other asset classes listed above. This is far safer than using a larger percentage of your capital to spread bet – or invest in crypto assets for that matter.

Reinforcing the point of 'taking things further'

There is a chance that as you read this chapter for the first time, much of the information and terminology will seem alien and quite possibly rather daunting and complicated. To a certain extent, the ideas *are* rather complicated. Getting up to speed on finance in any detail is no walk in the park. I still stand by the assertion I made at the beginning of the book: that you will be able to make a hugely positive difference to your finances in less than the time it took you to learn how to drive, because

I believe reading chapters 1 to 10 (and setting your affairs up as recommended by the 'keeping it simple' strategy) qualifies as taking less time than learning to drive.

The journey to true financial literacy, as advocated by this chapter, however, is a longer road and one that continues for your whole life as an investor, but it is one I hope you are at least prepared to consider. You may find some of the ideas rather complicated to begin with but if you are willing to persevere and, most particularly, to immerse yourself in the resources suggested, you should find you start to understand these concepts reasonably quickly. The benefits of doing so can be life changing.

So now let us turn our attention to the basic ideas and resources that will help you to achieve the three goals above.

Four key concepts for investment success

It is my belief that there are four key concepts you need to think about for consistent investment success:

1 You will want to understand a fair amount about human psychology, as it relates to investment decisions.
2 You must be able to perform basic 'top-down' analysis: working out big themes that help you to asset allocate most effectively. (To do this requires a basic grasp of current affairs, economics and economic history.)
3 You should be able to perform basic 'bottom-up' analysis to choose specific assets and make sure you buy them at the right price. (To do this you will need to gain a basic understanding of both fundamental and technical analysis.)
4 You will want to arrange your financial affairs with various third parties so that you are able to invest cheaply and tax efficiently in *all* the main asset classes *and* receive a constant stream of possible investment ideas.

If you can get moderately up to speed on these four things, you have a very good chance of making returns that are higher than those of many professional investors – and higher than what many people think is possible. I would argue that relatively few people are up to speed on all four of these, even many finance professionals.

It is a relatively rare person who thinks explicitly about human psychology, has a basic grasp of economics and economic history, follows current affairs, respects and has at least a basic understanding of both fundamental and technical analysis *and* knows how to arrange their affairs so that they can invest in all major asset classes in a cost-effective fashion. If you really want to 'take things further' with your finances, you should aim to become one of them.

Getting up to speed on these key concepts may seem like a tall order. You might have read the list above and even wondered what some of it means. Nevertheless, it is not as out of reach as you might think. If you are willing to make the effort to focus your attention on the most important information, you will give yourself a good chance of becoming one of the small minority of investors in the world who have understood all four of the above key concepts and given themselves the best chance of making money on their money as a result.

So, let us deal with each of these concepts and some of the resources you might consider to get you up to speed on them.

The importance of human psychology

It is probably obvious that human psychology has a significant role to play in investment success. It is therefore surprising just how few investors think about it explicitly or spend much time learning about it.

'Behavioural finance' is an area of study within economics and finance that attempts to factor fundamental traits of human psychology into assumptions about how we make investment decisions. Many of these traits are not immediately obvious – in fact, quite a few of them are highly counter-intuitive. This is why many people are often entirely unaware that they are falling foul of such traits when they make poor investment decisions.

The Chartered Institute for Securities & Investment (CISI) textbook for the 'Principles of Investment Risk and Taxation' examination has a section on behavioural finance in which it describes no fewer than *46* psychological biases or theories that can negatively affect our ability to make sensible investment decisions (Wikipedia lists *many* more than even that number).

We have already talked about three of these: *money illusion, anchoring* and the *endowment effect*. As a quick reminder: money illusion refers to our tendency to ignore inflation (particularly real inflation) when assessing the value of something; anchoring concerns how people are inclined to give too much weight to their recent experience (ignoring what actually happens in the long term); and the endowment effect is where individuals demand more for something than they would be willing to pay for it themselves (and are unwilling to acknowledge that their asset is worth less than it was previously). Just being aware of these three biases is a good start.

You will no doubt be relieved that it is not my intention to list and explain dozens of these biases here. This would take up a great deal of space and I don't believe you need to know about them all in detail. Two things are important, however:

- That you understand and acknowledge that psychology has an impact on your ability to invest successfully
- That, as a result, you take the time to read one of the three books I highlight at the end of this section: *Trade Your Way to Financial Freedom* by Dr Van K. Tharp.

Trade Your Way to Financial Freedom should appear in any list of the best investment books of all time. One of the key reasons for this is the excellent job Dr Tharp does in explaining how crucial your psychology and your preconceptions about money are for financial success.

If you have the wrong attitude and preconceptions about money you are unlikely to get ahead financially. This isn't new-age psychobabble; it is just that if you believe that 'the stock market is a casino' or 'investment is very risky', you will never bother to take the time to learn what you need to learn. You will not equip yourself with the knowledge or a plan to get ahead and, like most people, you will never save or invest any money. On the other hand, if you see the incredible things that are possible through investment, you *will* start learning, saving and investing.

'The magic of believing'

Perhaps most important with respect to the psychology of investing is believing that it is possible to make significant returns on your money. Hopefully you remember my sprinter analogy from earlier in the book: when looking at stock market returns, too many people fixate on the returns made by the 'average' fund or share, or on the fact that a particular index has gone sideways or down. But the more you read about the world of investment, the more you realize that there are plenty of investors who consistently make high returns from whom you can learn – or with whom you can invest. As Dr Tharp says:

> Financial freedom is really a new way to think about money ... [It] means that your money working for you makes more money than you need to meet your monthly expenses.

If this sounds unrealistic to you, then the first thing I would say is that there are thousands – if not hundreds of thousands – of people in the world today for whom this is a reality. The only things you need in order to join that group of people are knowledge, belief, time and effort.

The title of the first section of *Trade Your Way to Financial Freedom* is: 'The Most Important Factor in Your Success: You!' We all have different personalities, different attitudes to risk, different work ethics, different commitments. It is important as you get to know more about investing that you choose strategies that fit you personally. This is another key reason why we must think about human psychology in order to achieve investment success.

A key consideration, for example, is how much time you have to devote to running your money. Like most people, when you start on this journey you will have a full-time job. Therefore it would be foolish to choose an approach that required you to monitor financial markets for most of the day. You would need to use an approach that can yield decent results in a few minutes a day, or an hour each weekend perhaps. This is one of the reasons why so many trading courses fail their students – they tend to teach people techniques that require them to spend a huge amount of time sitting in front of screens, which is no use if you have a full-time job, children and so on.

A full discussion of how you might do this is beyond the scope of this book but you will start learning about these things when you immerse yourself in the resources I am about to recommend. For now, please just be aware of the fundamental point that I am making here: psychology and attitude are key.

> If you believe that you can make money from your money, this is an important step on the way to true wealth and financial freedom.

How to be a successful trader in one week

In Chapter 3 we saw examples of some fantastic returns made by conventional professional investors with a reasonably conventional, long-term approach to investing money. I thought it might be worth giving another example of what has been achieved by some folks with no previous knowledge of how to run money and in a very short space of time.

Relatively few people are aware of some of the spectacular results achieved by completely inexperienced traders who are taught how to use a systematic approach to running their money. Many investors have made huge amounts of money impressively quickly doing this. A great example concerns a group of novice traders known as 'Turtles'.

In 1983 two of Chicago's most famous traders made a bet with each other (a bet rumoured to have been part of the inspiration for the 1983 film *Trading Places*). Richard Dennis bet his friend William Eckhardt that he could show anyone how to be a successful trader in only two weeks. They were on holiday at the time and, rather randomly, happened to be visiting a turtle farm in Singapore. Dennis was convinced he could 'raise' traders like the farm-raised turtles, hence the rather strange name they gave the group.

After returning from their holiday, Dennis and Eckhardt put an advert in one of the Chicago papers inviting people to apply to be taught about trading. Within a few weeks they had chosen two small groups of individuals with no previous trading experience. They taught the first group about basic technical analysis and human psychology for two weeks and taught the second group the same lessons in only one week, after honing their message.

What then happened is legendary in trading circles. The Turtles each earned an average return of over 80 per cent per year over the next five years. And the best-performing member of the group, Curtis Faith, who was just nineteen years old when he started as a Turtle, made over 100 per cent per year! As a result, Faith turned $2 million into $31 million in just over four years (remember that, at 100 per cent, $2 million becomes $4 million, then $8 million, then $16 million, then $32 million). How he did it is detailed in his excellent book *Way of the Turtle*.

We are already aware that there are plenty of investment professionals who have made consistently good returns over a large number of years. As we can see, there are also people making spectacular returns after a relatively short period learning about money. One of the most important things these people have in common is their attitude.

As I have already said, rather than obsessing over the statistical 'fact' that it is very difficult to make high returns on your money, it would seem to me that a more enlightened and fruitful approach would be to seek out individuals who have made high returns and to study them and the techniques that made them successful. The following resources will put you squarely on that path.

Resources on human psychology

Here are some of the resources you might consider looking at to help you really understand the importance of human psychology:

- If you take only one action, do take the time to read *Trade Your Way to Financial Freedom* by Dr Van K. Tharp.

Even better, find a little more time and read the other three fantastic books listed below. Remember, there is no hurry, and everything you read will add to your financial skills.

- *Rich Dad, Poor Dad* by Robert Kiyosaki. This book is not specifically about investment or trading. It is a more general book about personal finance. A key message in the book is that 'the poor and the middle class work for money ... the rich have money work for them.' Another point Kiyosaki makes is how poorly education systems around the world prepare people to look after their personal financial situation. You will know by now that these are views I share. *Rich Dad, Poor Dad* has changed the lives of a vast number of people since it was first published, and it is one of the best-selling books on general finance ever written.

- *Think and Grow Rich* by Napoleon Hill. In this section, we have seen how important a person's attitude to money is. People who believe that money is scarce and hard to come by are the least likely to succeed in getting hold of any. Those who believe that it is within their power to become wealthy have a much better chance of becoming wealthy. Napoleon Hill's classic book on this very subject was originally published in the 1930s and has changed the lives of millions of people ever since. *Think and Grow Rich* has the power to improve more than just your financial situation.

- *Way of the Turtle* by Curtis Faith. This book is a fascinating study of what is possible, though I confess there are some sections on specific trading methodology that some people might find a bit off-putting.

So that is human psychology and your attitude to money taken care of. Now, let's see how to get up to speed on top-down analysis by looking at how you might improve your understanding of current affairs, economics and economic history.

Using top-down analysis

As I suggested earlier, once you have a reasonable sum saved you might think about using a proportion of it more proactively. To do this, you will need to come up with ideas about what to do with that percentage of your money.

The first 'filter' for finding these ideas can be described as 'top-down analysis'. This is where you use your knowledge of current affairs, economics, technology and all things financial to identify themes or trends that help you decide where to put your money to work.

We have already looked at two such investment themes: the world as a whole continues to grow and inflation is higher than most people realize. Once you start to look at the world with your 'investor's hat' on, you will, I hope, start to recognize other similar themes. Here are a couple of quick examples ...

Example 1: Growth in the developing world

We have already established that the world's population is growing significantly. At the moment, there are more than 200,000 people being added *per day* to the global population. At the same time, the standard of living in many countries is improving such that hundreds of millions of people in developing nations can now aspire to a 'middle-class' lifestyle in a way previous generations never could.

This has already given us the idea to 'own the world', but if we think in more detail about the implications of this reality we should be able to identify more specific investment themes. For example, the fact there are millions of new mouths to feed in the developing world might be positive for agriculture as a whole.

It will also no doubt be positive for the energy sector and for any company involved in construction in these high-growth economies. Another related theme would be improvement in water or telecom infrastructure. If you stop to think about it, you can brainstorm any number of investment themes that stand to benefit from this global growth.

Example 2: An ageing demographic in the developed world

At the same time that populations are growing and becoming wealthier in most of the developing world, they are doing something rather different in most of the developed world: ageing. In Japan and Europe in particular, an increasing proportion of the population is approaching and passing retirement age. Again, a moment's reflection on this reality should yield some logical conclusions about the sorts of investments that will benefit. We should conclude, for example, that any companies making products for or providing services to the elderly are likely to see the demand for those products and services increase.

As a result, they may well enjoy less of an uphill battle to grow their sales and profits than companies in other sectors, all other things being equal. You probably don't need me to tell you that these might include companies in the healthcare space: those that make drugs or medical devices such as pharmaceutical and biotech firms, or who build or service nursing homes and hospitals.

Your theme-driven investment shopping list

I hope you can see from these two examples how this thinking can yield obvious places to go looking for superior investment returns. Once you start to think like an investor, you will get an intuitive feel for things you believe might give you the best chance of making good returns on your money. Each time you think of something, I suggest you write it down as part of a shopping list of things that you would like to invest in.

Given my own top-down analysis of what is going on in the world at the moment, my personal top ten at the time of writing might look something like this:

1 Precious metals and precious metal mining funds and companies
2 Oil/energy/oil services funds and companies
3 Healthcare, pharmaceutical and biotechnology funds and companies
4 Emerging-market infrastructure: water, railways, automotive, agriculture
5 Potentially explosive frontier markets: Zimbabwe, Mongolia, Burma/Myanmar
6 'Rich' country funds (bonds and shares): Singapore, Qatar, Norway, Canada, Australia
7 The world's best technology companies: Microsoft, Oracle, Intel, Apple
8 The world's best consumer goods companies: P&G, Unilever, etc.
9 The world's best tobacco, gambling and brewing companies ('sin' investing)
10 Clean energy/new energy technologies that don't require government subsidy: uranium, thorium, rare earths, etc.

To be honest, the list of themes that I am keeping an eye on is substantially longer than this as I am constantly getting excited about all sorts of things, but hopefully you can see how helpful it is to start drilling down from the hundreds of thousands of things you might invest in to those that are likely to enjoy a fair wind for structural reasons. Dare I confess that I think it is also actually very good fun working out how to make money from the news?

The 'too hard bucket'

For what it is worth, in the process of thinking about investable themes I will often save myself a great deal of time and effort by completely discarding those that are in what I call the 'too hard bucket'. There are many areas of investment where I believe the individual investment vehicles are just too complicated to analyse with consistent success.

Three examples of this, as far as I am personally concerned, are financial services companies (particularly big banking groups), any company that relies to a great extent on large government contracts (a good example of which would be defence companies) and the whole cryptocurrency/blockchain space. It is entirely possible to make a great deal of money investing in banks if you are very clever and have a deep knowledge of a large number of complex investment ratios, but for the average investor, banks are just too complicated. I feel the same can be said about the cryptocurrency/blockchain space.

An important thing to bear in mind about investment generally is that you should limit the number of things you invest in – I would argue to a maximum of 20 to 30 assets in total. This sort of number gives you the advantages of diversification but also the ability to keep on top of them all. If you own much more than this number, things can become rather complicated.

Given that there are so many things you are able to invest in (if you have your accounts with the right provider), there really is no great loss in deciding to ignore anything that you feel is too complicated. There will always be plenty of options left. For this reason, I am very quick to dismiss any area of investment that I consider too much work to understand and keep on top of. The downside is that you might miss out on spectacular growth in a sector from time to time, but I think this is a small price to pay to avoid the enormous headache of trying to follow a fundamentally complicated and opaque industry sector such as banks or defence companies or an unproven, volatile and risky one such as cryptocurrency/blockchain. Never be afraid to put things in the 'too hard bucket' and move on to something that is easier to understand, especially given how many opportunities there are out there.

To conclude

Building your list of investable themes is a crucial first step. The next and more important step is to work out the specific investment vehicles (funds, shares, etc.) to own within those themes to give you exposure to them. You will also want to do your best to buy those specific vehicles at the right price – that is, a price that gives you the best chance of investment success in the years ahead.

This is where our third key concept comes in: 'bottom–up analysis', of which the two main types are *fundamental* and *technical* analysis. We will look at the basics of these in the next section.

Resources for top-down analysis

Before we move on, let us look at some resources that will help you get a handle on our second key concept as quickly as possible. I recommend the following three action points and resources (in order of importance):

1 **Read *MoneyWeek* magazine.** If you only take one 'further reading' action after finishing this book, subscribing to this magazine is probably the best one to take. It is my heartfelt belief that, if you live in the UK, it is the best weekly financial publication and most likely the best investment you can make in your financial future. By reading *MoneyWeek* you will ensure that you enjoy a constant stream of well-thought-out investment themes, as well as advice on specific investment vehicles such as individual funds and shares. Their brilliant editorial team has been making me money for many years. I think you will be surprised at what an easy read it is – it even has sections on wine, cars and property to lighten the tone. I can't recommend it highly enough. I tend to spend most Saturday mornings reading it over breakfast – which only takes about 20 minutes – a small price to pay in terms of time and effort in my opinion.

2 **Subscribe to some of the many excellent free email services available.** One of the best things about investment today is how much information you can get entirely free of charge. All you need is an Internet connection and an email address. I personally subscribe to dozens of free (and paid) email services and get as many as 30 such emails a day, most of which I read or at least skim. Of course, I am

not suggesting you do the same – I am obviously extremely interested in the subject!

One thing to note is that many of these free email services will inevitably try to sell you their paid subscription products. Many people find this annoying (particularly we cynical Brits who hate such things) but my view is that it is a small price to pay to receive free information. I have subscribed to a number of paid research services over the years and, without exception, they have paid for themselves many times over. The key is ensuring you subscribe to the good ones.

The three services I list below are an excellent starting point, and will provide you with plenty of extremely useful information – entirely free of charge:

- plainenglishfinance.co.uk – I hope you will forgive the self-promotion but I truly believe you should subscribe to our free email service. Unlike many of the other free services, this is not a daily or even monthly email. I send an update from time to time (anywhere between every two to six weeks) to remind you of all the excellent steps you can take to get your finances humming and to highlight anything I think is particularly interesting or important for you to be aware of.

- **Money Morning** – This is *Money Week* magazine's free daily email and I think it is superb. You can subscribe on their website at: moneyweek.com/money-morning-signup

- **Agora Financial, Casey Research and Stansberry & Associates** – These are all first-class, US-based investment research services. If you want to receive their research products, you can pay hundreds or even thousands of pounds to do so, but, fantastically, you can get very useful information from their various free email services. You can find these on their websites:
  o **Agora Financial** (agorafinancial.com/)
  o **Casey Research** (www.caseyresearch.com/)
  o **Stansberry Research** (stansberryresearch.com/)

3 **Read** *The Ascent of Money* **by Niall Ferguson.** Ferguson has been named one of the one hundred most influential people in the world by *Time* magazine. This book is a superb summary of the history of money. It takes you all the way from ancient history to the 2007–9 financial crisis. It is of practical importance for your development as an investor that you have a basic grasp of the history of money and the various financial products. This is the best book for this purpose that I have read to date. For those of you who are not big readers, there is also an accompanying television series which you should be able to find on one of the streaming services.

Bottom-up analysis: how to maximize your chances of buying low and selling high

It is my hope that you will come up with some compelling investment themes relatively quickly once you have started thinking like an investor and are plugged into the wealth of investment information we have looked at above. Now comes arguably the most important part: working out the specific investment vehicles that will give you the best chance of benefiting from your investment themes. This is the hardest part but, I would argue, it can actually be rather fun once you start to get into it.

Bottom-up analysis will also help you to make your big asset allocation decisions because the two main types, fundamental and technical analysis, enable you to work out which of the main asset classes look most interesting at any point in time.

An example theme: oil

Once you have a theme, you need to look for investment vehicles that give you exposure to that theme. Let's use oil as an example. You have decided that it is probably a good idea to have exposure to oil. As the world population grows and becomes more industrialized, there will surely be a higher demand for energy – and oil in particular. You should now make a list of possible investments in the oil space.

Off the top of your head, you will probably immediately think of Shell and BP. You may also realize that you are able to own oil itself, via an ETF for example. A little bit more effort and you might come up with foreign oil firms such as Chevron in the USA or Petrobras, which is a Brazilian company but which trades on the US stock exchange, making it relatively easy to buy through your UK stockbroker (assuming, as ever, that you have the right sort of account). If you are prepared to put in even more effort you might add oil service companies that are experts in drilling or prospecting for oil – there are lots of these in Norway, for example. There will also be ETFs of oil companies and ETFs of oil service companies – that is, a fund where one investment will give you exposure to a basket of companies in the sector.

Although this might sound quite daunting, if you are reading *MoneyWeek* and are plugged into the kinds of free email services I suggested above, you will learn more and more about all sorts of industries as you go along. As ever, I would reiterate that there is no hurry here. Better to get it right than to rush into anything. Do not be afraid to take your time when building your shopping list of themes, funds and companies.

Once you have a reasonable list of possible investments for each of your themes, it is time to think about which investment vehicle or perhaps which two investment vehicles you are going to use to put your money to work in that space. You will do this by subjecting each of the possible investments to some basic fundamental and technical analysis.

Fundamental analysis of shares

Fundamental analysis is when you assess the inherent or fundamental value of an asset in order to work out whether it is cheap or expensive. We discussed certain types of fundamental analysis when we looked at how to value property in Chapter 5, and shares and gold in Chapter 10.

As far as shares are concerned, we might think of fundamental analysis as simply listing all of the things that might affect the true value of a company by adding up all the positives (profits, cash, property, inventory, etc.) and subtracting all the negatives (debt, salaries, all other costs) to get to a number that is the *value* of the company. There are thousands of people (accountants, stockbrokers, fund managers and financial analysts) all over the world doing this job every day with respect to hundreds of thousands of companies.

Working out the fundamental value of a company is essentially what accountants do. At least once a year (although actually four times a year for many companies listed on the stock market) a company publishes its accounts. This will contain almost exactly what I have described above – that is to say, a calculation of the value of the company based on adding up all the positives (profits and assets) and subtracting all the negatives (liabilities).

So far, so simple. The complexity, which keeps so many thousands of people in gainful employment, broadly arises from three sources:

1 Debate about the value of the company's assets: how much a certain factory, office building or brand is worth, for example
2 Expectations of what the value of profits and assets is going to do *in the future*. Financial analysts produce estimates for both of these
3 Debate about what a sensible amount to pay for that value is. This is done using a variety of valuation tools and by comparing companies with each other – something that is called 'peer analysis'.

A very large proportion of the finance industry spends its days thinking about these three complications. We can perhaps illustrate this in further detail if we think about earnings per share again. (Remember we met this idea in Chapter 7 when we looked at shares. Do please go back and have a quick look if you have forgotten the term.)

What we are saying here is that accountants can give us this year's earnings number and asset value reasonably accurately (within reason). The trick is to estimate next year's earnings number and asset value as accurately as possible and then to think about what you should 'pay' for both numbers.

Different types of company have very different fundamental financial metrics. Some companies are capital intensive. This means that they need huge factories and very expensive equipment to do what they do. Examples of these would include automotive, mining, oil, steel and pharmaceutical companies. Other companies, ones that deal with people and ideas for example, need hardly any equipment at all. These would include advertisers and other media firms, lawyers, bankers, software programmers and consultants.

Equally, some companies can grow their sales and profits very quickly, for example a company developing new technology. As recently as just over 15 years ago, iPhones and iPads didn't exist. Today a meaningful percentage of the world's population owns these products – and Apple is now the largest company in history. Apple shares have skyrocketed, as have shares in many of the companies that supply them with the components for their products.

Other businesses find themselves in a market that is dying, sometimes called an 'ex-growth' market. Good examples of these would be Eastman Kodak, the photography company, which filed for bankruptcy in 2012, and HMV in the UK, which suffered from the fundamental decline in shoppers who were buying CDs and DVDs on the high street and entered administration in 2013. You might argue that foreseeing the problems faced by both of these companies wasn't really that difficult for anyone with a keen interest in the world.

The P/E ratio again

Given the differences between companies, the fundamental value you might place on their profits and assets will therefore also be different. If you remember the section on shares from Chapter 7, you will hopefully remember the idea of a P/E ratio – the multiple of a company's profits that an investor is willing to pay to own that share. This is one of the most fundamental ways of assessing a company's value.

All other things being equal, you might imagine that you would be willing to pay quite a high multiple of profits (that is, a high P/E ratio) for a company growing very fast that has no debt and no need to invest in huge factories and machines. And you might want to pay a great deal less (that is, a low P/E ratio) for a company with no growth and large debts. If you find a fast-growing company with great technology on a low P/E ratio, therefore, you will most likely have found a bargain!

The longer you look at investments, the more you will get an intuitive feel for what a company should trade at in terms of fundamental valuation metrics. A dairy company based in only one country and not growing at all should arguably trade on a P/E ratio of around five to ten times its earnings (5–10×). It is likely to be expensive and liable to fall in value if it is trading at 15×, whereas a brilliant global software company with very high profit margins and massive growth potential might even be cheap on 25× earnings. That is to say that you might be willing to pay as much as five times the price, in terms of a multiple of profits, for a company that you think has five times (or more) the prospects of another company.

The PEG ratio

One of my favourite valuation tools in this respect is something called the PEG (price/earnings to growth) ratio. It is worked out by dividing the P/E of a company by its estimated earnings growth. For example: if a company is trading on a P/E of 10× and growing its profits by 10 per cent, you would say it has a PEG ratio of 1×. If that company was trading on a P/E of 20×, the PEG would be 2×. Another company growing at 20 per cent but trading on 10× P/E would have a PEG of 0.5×. The lower the PEG the better, as the number implies you are paying less to 'own' more potential profit growth.

There are a large number of financial ratios and metrics to look at as part of fundamental analysis and they each have their benefits and drawbacks. PEG is just one example and is no exception in terms of having both benefits and drawbacks. The reason I include it here is to show how the tools of fundamental analysis can be quite elegant and often aren't that complicated. At the most basic level they enable you to 'compare apples with apples' when you are trying to find the right company to invest in.

Let us now look at some of the most elementary valuation tools you will want to become aware of in order to give yourself a real head start in choosing a company to invest in.

Using basic valuation tools

Financial analysts use a wealth of financial ratios in their analysis, but in my opinion you can make a perfectly informed assessment of whether a company is cheap or expensive using relatively few valuation tools.

In Chapter 7 we looked briefly at earnings yield, dividend yield and book value. Once you have chosen a theme and made a list of companies you might consider to give you exposure to that theme, the next piece of the jigsaw puzzle is to find out these numbers based on the company's current share price. These are all reasonably simple things to understand and are freely available on websites such as Yahoo or Google Finance – or from your stockbroker's website.

For each company, you should find the current year's P/E, PEG, dividend yield and price-to-book ratio (that is, book value per share). Where possible, you should also find out these numbers for next year. Sometimes you will even be able to get numbers for the year after that but I wouldn't worry too much about those: as you can imagine, forecasts of a company's numbers two years in the future can often be subject to significant revision unless the company has a particularly predictable business model.

Peer group analysis

Once you have these numbers you will be able to perform a very useful, simple analysis of which company might be the best in a given space (sector) by comparing the numbers to each other. This is called 'peer group analysis'. To return to our oil example, we might be trying to decide whether to own Shell or BP (keeping things simple and putting dozens of other companies in our 'too hard bucket').

All you need to do, then, is compare companies in the same space to see which one is the best value. To keep the example simple, if we know that Shell has more attractive financial ratios than BP, this might make us decide that the vehicle we want to own to make a solid long-term investment in our 'oil' theme is Shell. Before you make the decision to buy it, however, you will also need to think about a couple of other things: how Shell's metrics today compare to how they have been historically; and where the stock market as a whole is at the moment.

Historical analysis

So in our oil example so far we have established that:

- oil is probably a good long-term theme
- Shell is probably a great company within that theme
- Shell currently has more attractive valuation metrics than its main rival BP.

This is all useful stuff and moves you closer to your goal of actually pulling the trigger and buying some shares in Shell. An additional factor to consider, however, is how Shell's current valuation metrics compare to those same metrics in the past. Shell might look more attractive than BP at the moment, but what if it is the most expensive it has been in the last 20 years? For example, what if the P/E ratio of Shell going back 20 years has ranged from 5× to 25× and it is now trading at 24.5×? What if Shell's dividend yield has been as low as 1.5 per cent and as high as 6.5 per cent and it is currently 2 per cent? This comparison is known as historical analysis. I hope it is not hard to see that your best chance of buying Shell at the right share price for a long-term investment will be when the valuation metrics are historically attractive as well as being attractive compared to their peer group. If Shell shares are the most expensive they have been for 20 years, then it may not be a good time to buy.

That said, this might not be true if there is a compelling reason for Shell shares to trade very expensively. To give a slightly silly but potentially instructive example: imagine if Shell's scientists were about to announce that they had developed a technology that turns lead into gold. In this instance, you would be forgiven for arguing that the shares now deserve to trade on a higher P/E ratio than in the past. In fact, solving the age-old alchemists' problem would mean that Shell shares should, in theory, suddenly skyrocket and trade on a P/E ratio far higher than ever before.

It is obviously unlikely that Shell will ever discover how to turn lead into gold, but they might announce a huge new oil or gas discovery - either of which might justify their P/E ratio being higher than their peers, and higher than it was before they made the discovery. You will want to be aware of these sorts of *qualitative* differences between companies as well as their financial ratios alone.

Market and sector valuation

Another consideration before actually buying any oil shares is to think about the valuation of both the oil sector at the moment and the stock market as a whole. As I said earlier in this book, it is possible to find valuation metrics such as the P/E ratio or dividend yield for the market as a whole (in this instance we could use the FTSE 100 or S&P 500 P/E ratio) and also for a specific sector (it is possible to find financial ratios for the oil sector as a whole).

A final check we might make before deciding to build a position in Shell would be to see if the market and sector are cheap or expensive historically. This is because share prices are correlated to the value of their sector and the market as a whole. Even though the analysis so far suggests that it is a good time to buy Shell – oil is a great theme; Shell is good value compared to other oil companies; and it is good value historically – you might want to be a little careful of what the oil sector and the market as a whole is doing. For example, if the FTSE 100 and S&P 500 have gone up 20 per cent in the last few months, there is a chance that the market might fall back. When the market falls back, it takes share prices down with it.

However, this is probably the least important analysis you need to perform when thinking about making a long-term investment in a company. If a company looks as if it is fundamentally good value today for all the reasons we have just discussed, it is likely to be a good investment over the long term. Nevertheless, it is still worth doing a quick check to make sure you are not buying in when shares as a whole are extremely expensive. If the market or the sector has gone up a great deal recently and your analysis tells you that this might correct, then you might wait a little longer before buying your shares. Again, there is no hurry here. You have your whole life in which to place your bets.

Fundamental analysis of other asset classes

We have just had a very quick look at the idea of using fundamental analysis to find a good company to invest in. It may be obvious to you that the metrics we used to look at shares cannot be applied to the other asset classes.

> Bonds, property and commodities have their own distinct characteristics and we must evaluate them in a different way as a result.

As such, it is worth saying a little bit about how we might perform a fundamental analysis of each of the other asset classes.

1 BONDS

We looked at the basics of what a bond is in Chapter 7. A bond does not have a P/E ratio or book value. What a bond does have, however, are two fundamentally important metrics: credit quality and yield. The credit quality of a bond is a somewhat subjective assessment of the quality of the bond. This assessment is made by financial analysts at rating agencies, the most famous of which are Moody's, S&P and Fitch. These companies evaluate the financial strength of the company or government that has issued the bond. Once they have done this, they publish a rating, which tells bond investors the quality of the bond. Each of the agencies has its own rating scale. You may have heard a bond described in the press as 'Triple A' (AAA) or read that a certain government's bonds are no longer rated Triple A. This is the top rating on the scale. Each of the rating agencies has its own distinct rating system, and you don't really need to know any more than that.

Yield

The yield is simply the annual percentage return implied by the bond's current price – something we looked at earlier. Bond investors will generally be looking to achieve the highest yield for any given credit rating. If you were to compare two AAA-rated bonds and find that one was yielding 2 per cent and the other 2.2 per cent, all other things being equal you would want to own the one with the higher yield. Of course, this is a highly simplistic analysis, as there is a wide degree of differentiation even between bonds of the same rating. It is these differences that professional bond investors are looking to exploit.

The most important point I would like to make about bonds is that, more than any other main asset class, I believe they are the hardest for the amateur investor to understand and analyse. What I have written above and in Chapter 7 is designed to give you a very basic idea of what they are about, if only so you can understand their terminology a little when you read about them – and also understand more about how government finances work.

I feel strongly that any bond exposure you have in your portfolio should be via bond funds. Direct investment in individual bonds is generally only possible with large sums of money, as most of these products have reasonably large minimum investments and many are only available to professional investors. There are exceptions, particularly for US-based private investors, but I still feel that bond analysis is too complex for the great majority of people. It is only worth learning about direct bond investment in great detail if you have a relatively large amount of money to put to work. For everyone else, I would suggest that whatever bond exposure you have from 'owning the world' with a multi-asset fund will be perfectly sufficient.

2 PROPERTY

We looked in some detail at various ways of valuing property in Chapter 5. To recap: we can think about a property's total return as a function of the assumed net rental yield (after costs, void periods, etc.) plus any assumption you might make for capital growth. This percentage return number can then be compared to return numbers for other asset classes: the interest rate on a current account, the dividend yield (plus expected capital gain) of a share or the yield on a bond, for example.

We also looked at the idea of house prices as a multiple of people's salaries. I like to think of this as the P/E ratio of the property market. In the same way that a P/E of 5× tells us a share is cheaper than a P/E of 10× (at a very basic level), if house prices are currently six times people's salary on average, we know they are more expensive than when they are three times average salary. This is useful information for making big decisions about when property is cheap or expensive versus the other asset classes (again, this is all at a reasonably basic level – you will still want to use other metrics such as demand and supply and the conditions of any local market).

3 COMMODITIES

Just as with bonds and property, we cannot conduct fundamental analysis of commodities using the tools we might use for shares. Gold, oil, wheat, timber and uranium do not produce quarterly earnings numbers or see their price fall when a chief executive has to resign in disgrace.

Fundamental analysis of commodity markets is still possible, however, and there are plenty of individuals and institutions all over the world that spend their time on this. At the simplest level, it involves tracking data on their supply and demand. For metals, analysts all over the world try to assess what mine production is doing and what is happening to inventory levels at various points in the supply chain, and then make estimates about which direction end-demand is going. We have already seen examples of this kind of analysis earlier in the book – when, for example, we talked about how a slowing down in the Chinese economy will have a significant effect on the demand for commodities such as copper, iron ore and coal.

When it comes to the 'soft' (agricultural) commodities, factors to consider would include what is happening to the total amount planted globally of a particular crop and what has happened to the harvest in various parts of the world as a result of the weather (people who love and invest in wine might do this with regard to the global grape crop, for example).

As with bonds, I would argue that it is reasonably hard for the amateur investor to become proficient in the fundamental analysis of commodities. Again, this need not necessarily be a problem. We have already seen how you will gain sufficient commodity exposure from 'owning the world' and 'owning inflation', as described in Chapter 10. If you do decide you want to become more heavily involved in commodities, you will be able to get a wealth of free advice on them from various periodicals and online resources. Finally, I would argue that commodities lend themselves to technical analysis more than many of the other asset classes, particularly the bigger, more liquid ones such as oil or precious metals.

If you are willing to invest a little time in learning about technical analysis, you can start to make a nice return trading the bigger commodities. We will look at this in more detail in the next section.

A note on foreign exchange

There is a large degree of overlap between the FX market and the bond market in terms of fundamental analysis. This is because interest rates (bond yields) and the financial strength of a country are two of the most important factors in the performance of its currency.

As with bonds and commodities, I would stress that the fundamental analysis of foreign exchange is rather specialist and not something the private investor can learn overnight. Again, you will have natural exposure to a wide range of currencies by virtue of owning assets from all over the world, and I would suggest that this is sufficient to give you the asset diversification into foreign exchange that you need.

That said, just as with commodities above, if you have got to the point where you have a reasonably large amount of money and are interested in using some of it to trade more aggressively, there can be great returns to be made in foreign exchange, particularly for the UK-based investor who is able to use a spread-betting account. Just as with commodities, forex also lends itself to technical analysis, which we will look at now.

Technical analysis

Wikipedia defines technical analysis in the following way:

> Technical analysis is a financial term used to denote a security analysis
> discipline for forecasting the direction of prices through the study of
> past market data, primarily price and volume.

To put this in plain English: over a long period of time, academics looking at financial markets worked out a number of methods for predicting where prices in a market would go based on where they had come from.

This may seem quite crazy intuitively but, when you think a little about human nature, it isn't really. If a share or market has been going up steadily then there is a good chance it will continue to do so, if only because of the herd mentality of the investment community. Technical analysis tries to generate rules along these lines to help the investor buy and sell with a high probability of success.

The discipline has been developing for several decades and there is now a bewildering array of techniques and theories available to the investment community with scary names like 'Bollinger bands', 'Donchian channels' and 'exponential moving averages'. When you boil it down, however, technical analysis is really about waiting until other people are investing in something and then jumping on the bandwagon. This can work because the main thing that causes the price of an asset to move is lots of money flowing towards it (up) or away from it (down). Just like fundamental analysis, technical analysis is a huge subject and you could spend a long time learning about it, but it is my firm belief that you don't need to know a great deal in order to improve your ability to invest. Let us look at a couple of technical indicators to give you an example of how simple and powerful technical analysis can be.

1 RELATIVE STRENGTH INDEX (RSI)

Figure 11.1 shows the performance of a London-listed silver ETF.

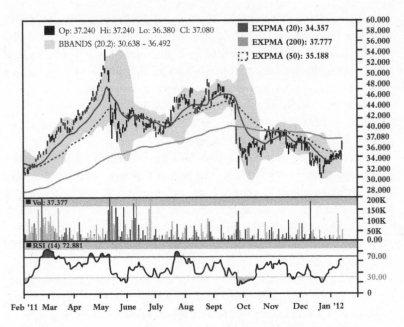

FIGURE 11.1 The performance of a London-listed silver ETF
Source: Barchart.com

This graphic might look a bit complicated but please don't worry; I'm going to explain each section in turn.

The top half or so of the chart plots the daily moves in the price of silver. The middle graphic shows the volume traded (the number of shares of silver which changed hands that day). Days where the bar is light are up days (when the price ends higher than it started) and dark bars are down days. The bigger the bar, the more shares in this fund were traded. As a general rule, if there is big volume it gives you an indication that something is happening in the market, so a big dark bar is (in very basic terms) bad news and a big light bar good news. Most importantly, however, take a look at the bottom graphic with the heading 'RSI (14)'. This is a technical indicator called the 'relative strength index' (RSI). The RSI is simply a mathematical calculation that gives a range of 0–100. You really don't need to understand the detail of how it is calculated; I simply want to look at the relationship between what the RSI is doing and what the price is doing. This is a form of technical analysis.

You can see that the RSI line turns shaded in this chart if it goes below 30 or above 70. Below 30 is what we call 'oversold' and above 70 is 'overbought'. All other things being equal, the RSI tells us that an asset is cheap when it is oversold, so we should think about buying it, and expensive when it is overbought, so we should think about selling it. As such, in this example you would consider buying silver when it went below 30 and consider selling it when it went above 70. I hope you are with me so far!

In reality, someone using RSI would most likely finesse the above strategy based on the RSI going back a few years and look to buy silver when the RSI crosses back up through 30 and sell when it crosses back down through 70. You would also look for times when this happened with a larger volume than normal, given that a big-volume day would be a stronger indicator of a change in trend than a low-volume day.

So let us look at how this strategy, using only one technical indicator, might have served you in the last few years. In Chapter 10 we looked at a number of fundamental reasons why silver might be in a long-run bull market – that is to say, why we might like to have it on our investment shopping list. As always, however, you would ideally buy it when it is cheap and sell it when it is expensive. You must always be thinking about the price at which you buy something once you have decided that it is worth buying thanks to your big-picture analysis.

Following the strategy outlined above, you should be able to see that you would have bought silver in February 2011 when the RSI crossed back above 30. Can you see from the graph that the cost would have been about $31 per share (perhaps use a ruler on the screen or page to help you see what the price is on the graph)? You would then have held it until early May when it crossed back down through 70 and there was heavy volume. You would have been able to sell your position for about $50 per share. That is a 61 per cent return in about three months.

Using the same analysis, you then might have considered buying again at the end of May at about $40 and selling in August at

about \$48 (+20 per cent in three months) and finally buying again
in October at about \$32, in which case you might have thought
about selling again in February 2012, given that silver was above 70
again at about \$37 (+16 per cent since October). In fact, you would
not have been looking to sell your silver since it had not yet crossed
back down through 70. I should perhaps mention that this is not just
theory – this is precisely the analysis I used to trade silver with some
success at the time. To do this, I only needed to follow one share
price, news about one investment (silver) and one broad strategy: the
RSI, with an eye on volumes.

If you think this is an isolated example and something of a freak
it may be instructive to look at some other examples. Figure 11.2
shows the same RSI analysis for the FTSE 100.

Figure 11.3 shows the same again for gold.

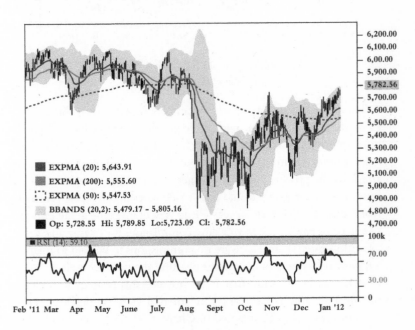

FIGURE 11.2 FTSE 100 daily OHLC chart
Source: Barchart.com

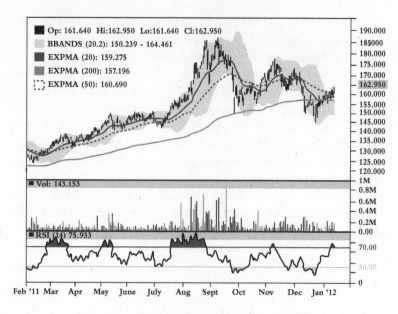

FIGURE 11.3 Gold RSI daily OHLC chart
Source: Barchart.com

I could include plenty of other examples. As with any technical indicator, the RSI is far from perfect, despite how compelling it looks. It does not have a 100 per cent hit rate; however, in recent years it has been a decent tool for timing entry and exit into gold and silver in particular, and it has helped me personally to get a much higher return with just this one strategy than I would have made investing in pretty much any mainstream fund. It is also a very cheap way of investing as the only fees you need to pay are the low dealing commissions for buying and selling a London-listed share. There are no commissions to be paid to financial advisers and a minimal fee structure within the product itself.

It is worth repeating that I did not use this strategy completely blindly. I already had a strong fundamental view on precious metals as an investment, as I explained in Chapter 10. And once I had established that gold or silver was overbought or oversold I would do a little bit more work thinking about volumes and the time of year (both gold and silver have seasonal trends). In addition, I read emails nearly every day from market commentators, some of whom specialize in gold and silver. I would always take their latest opinions and numbers on board as a final check before buying or selling.

Hopefully, this brief example illustrates what can be achieved by using a combination of fundamental and technical analysis. As you can see, such an approach can yield pretty fantastic results over and above obsessing about one or the other alone.

Some of you might be looking at the above and thinking that it all seems rather complicated and time consuming. Rest assured that you will not need to go to this level of detail or put in this amount of time and effort to still have a huge positive impact on your financial situation. It is also clear that this example uses quite old graphs but, as with other similar examples elsewhere in the book, I have not felt the need to update these graphs since the point they make is as valid today as it was back in 2012. I just wanted to use this as an example to illustrate what can be achieved with a little effort and an open mind.

2 FORMULA-BASED TREND FOLLOWING/MOVING AVERAGES

Another example of a simple but consistently successful technical strategy is the use of formula-based trend following of some kind.

Trend following simply takes a current (or recent average) price of an asset and compares it to a historical average price. If the current (or recent average) price is above the chosen historical average price then the investor remains invested in that asset. If the current price, is found to be below the relevant historical average, then the investor sells out of the asset and switches those funds into cash (or something similarly defensive). As an example, the methodology might be to take the price that a stock market (or any other market for that matter) closed at yesterday and compare it to the average price that stock market has closed at over the last 50, 100 or 200 trading days. Or it might take the average price the stock market has closed at for the last 20 trading days and compare it to the average price over the last 200 days.

Some longer-term strategies even compare the average price over the last 30 weeks versus the last 50 weeks. (Readers who have a copy of second edition of this book may recall that I looked at the work of a British financial author and hedge fund manager called Mark Shipman who has used this approach very successfully for many years.)

Some incredibly short-term currency traders might even compare the last ten minutes against the previous hour, for example. There is no hard-and-fast rule and many different methods can work.

The important idea here is that if an asset starts falling, at a certain point the trend following signal will tell you to switch out of that asset and into cash. The level at which you would do this is based on a strict, disciplined, consistent and rules-based process. Equally, when the price of that asset starts to rise again, you would reinvest in it.

This methodology is proven in practice and tested over more than one hundred years with different assets and in different countries and, applied sensibly, can have a very significant effect on protecting against big falls in all markets and improving returns.

Evidence that formula-based trend following works ...

... IN STOCKMARKETS

It isn't difficult to show just how powerful trend following can be, given the evidence of history across many markets in many regions of the world. Figures 11.4 and 11.5 illustrate the point.

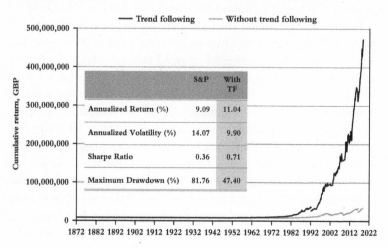

FIGURE 11.4   S&P: January 1872 – September 2018
Source: Professors Andrew Clare and Steven Thomas and Dr James Seaton
(Solent Systematic Investment Strategies)

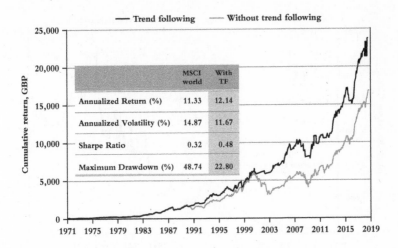

FIGURE 11.5 MSCI world: January 1971 – September 2019
Source: Professors Andrew Clare and Steven Thomas and Dr James Seaton
(Solent Systematic Investment Strategies)

Figure 11.4 shows just how powerful an impact basic trend following has had over the very long term in the US stock market, going back as far as 1872! Figure 11.5 shows the same for world stock markets as a whole since 1971. Please take a moment to consider the numbers in the pull-out boxes. For example, over 145 years the use of simple trend following has improved annual performance by more than 2 per cent a year, reduced volatility by over 4 per cent and the maximum drawdown from 81.76 to 47.40 per cent. This has an enormous impact on wealth generation over time.

... AND IN OTHER ASSET CLASSES

Amazingly enough, trend following can be similarly effective when used in other asset classes. Figures 11.6 and 11.7 show the significant improvements in returns and reduction in volatility and drawdown by using trend following in both the commodities and property markets. These charts and numbers show us how extraordinarily powerful a tool trend following can be for investment.

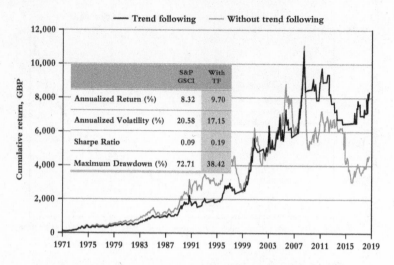

FIGURE 11.6 Commodities: January 1971 – September 2019
Source: Professors Andrew Clare and Steven Thomas and Dr James Seaton
(Solent Systematic Investment Strategies)

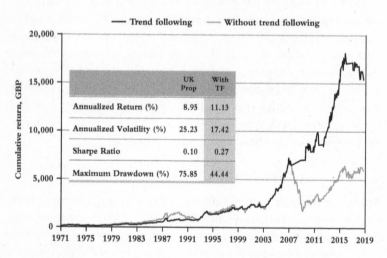

FIGURE 11.7 Quoted UK property: January 1971 – September 2019
Source: Professors Andrew Clare and Steven Thomas and Dr James Seaton
(Solent Systematic Investment Strategies)

When people like Mark Shipman started using these sorts of trend-following approaches to investment, they had to calculate the moving averages themselves – initially with a pen and paper but then with a computer and their own software or complicated Excel spreadsheets. Today you are able to find this sort of information on dozens – probably hundreds – of websites for free. This is another example of the point I made in Chapter 3: that today's financial products and information sources are better than ever before. The fact that you can learn how to find the RSI or moving average for thousands of possible investments entirely free of charge is a huge development in investment, and gives you tools that an investor from twenty or more years ago could only dream of.

I highlight these sorts of strategies purely to show you what is possible today using free information and with a relatively small amount of effort on your part. I would hope that you have found these two examples of technical analysis sufficiently compelling to want to learn more. This being the case, let us now look at some resources you might use to do so.

Resources for fundamental analysis

- As ever, there are literally thousands of books you could read to learn about *fundamental analysis*. To really get to grips with the subject you should probably read a few of them but it is my belief that you will get a pretty good idea about things and most likely get quite inspired about investment generally if you read just this one, at least just to get you started: *One Up On Wall Street* by Peter Lynch. As one of the most famous American investors of all time, Lynch made just short of 30 per cent per year for 13 years while running the Fidelity Magellan Fund. This book shows you how, with a little bit of knowledge, you have a very good chance of making a better return on your money than many professional investors – and I highly recommend it as a result.

- *MoneyWeek* magazine again! If you subscribe to *MoneyWeek* you will begin to get a feel for how fundamental analysis works, as there are weekly columns teaching you about these things. There are also good video tutorials on the *MoneyWeek* website.

There are plenty of other books which will help you to learn more about fundamental analysis listed in the bibliography.

Resources for technical analysis

- *Big Money, Little Effort* by Mark Shipman. If you only read one book to inspire you about technical analysis, I recommend this one. My other reason for choosing this book is that it is a very easy and quick read. It communicates important and compelling points in easy-to-understand language. A few minutes of reading will reward you with some eureka moments and a tangible moneymaking strategy.
- Free online technical analysis. There are many sites that enable you to conduct technical analysis for a wide variety of assets. When you get more comfortable with using a little bit of technical analysis, barchart.com and stockcharts.com are good places to start.

4 Arranging your financial affairs with third parties

Using the best third parties is key when taking things further with your investments. If you arrange your financial affairs effectively with them, you will be able to to do the following.

1 Invest cheaply in all asset classes

Happily, we can dispatch this last section very quickly as we already looked at the best way to arrange your affairs when we learned how to optimize your financial accounts in Chapter 6. We also looked very briefly at spread betting at the end of that chapter. At this point I would like to stress that if you want to 'take things further' with investment and try to make money from your money, you should really consider learning about spread betting.

As I have already said, spread betting can be a very dangerous thing to do if you have not educated yourself about it enough – but, if you really are committed to making money from your money, it is one of the best ways to achieve your goal of being able to invest cheaply in all asset classes.

Within a spread betting account, you are able to take long and short positions on a huge range of shares, bonds, commodities and currencies and the gains you make will be tax-free. You are also able to run positions worth a multiple of the money you have to start with and to build watch lists for your themes. All of these facts make spread betting extremely powerful if you know what you are doing.

If you are interested in learning about spread betting, then one good place to start is to read *The Naked Trader's Guide to Spread Betting* by Robbie Burns. There are also tutorial videos on *MoneyWeek*'s website, and you might also consider having a look at www.ig.com. IG is the UK's biggest spread-betting company (I have an account with them), and there is some great information about spread betting on their website, as you might expect.

2 Receive a constant stream of possible investment ideas

Again, we have already taken care of this requirement by virtue of the resources recommended in this chapter. If you subscribe to *Money-Week* and the free email services I have outlined, you will be getting quality investment ideas on a regular basis. There are paid services too, but if you have already followed the suggestions in this chapter, you should be pretty well covered without having to spend a penny.

In summary

So that is it for our chapter on taking things further. To be honest, key concept 4 (third parties) is somewhat surplus to requirements, given that we have learned most of the points it makes already. 'Repetition is the mother of invention', however, and one of the most important themes of *How to Own the World* is that you have never been in a stronger position than you are today to take advantage of investing in financial assets.

I wish you the very best of luck learning about investment – and making a huge difference to your life as a result.

Conclusion

'Tell 'em what you're going to tell 'em. Tell 'em. Tell 'em what you told 'em.'

Paul White, first director of CBS News, paraphrasing
Dale Carnegie

The quote above is well-known advice for making a presentation, and I think it is also useful in a book like *How to Own the World*. If you have come this far then I congratulate you heartily. Your financial knowledge is now quite possibly better than that of a large proportion of the population – including many finance professionals, economists and politicians (dare I say most politicians!).

I hope you feel that you have learned enough to make a real and lasting difference to your financial affairs and, by extension, to your entire life.

Given my belief in the above quote, I thought it might be useful to summarize what we have learned. I would hope that by now you are up to speed on the following crucial points:

- You can and should invest your money.
- You must understand what is happening in the world today, particularly given the pension predicament we all face.
- Even despite this pension predicament, you are capable of arranging your own affairs so that it needn't worry you.
- You can do a better job than many professionals, particularly because if you do you will avoid their fees and quite possibly end up with better financial arrangements, too.
- You need to learn about and benefit from the incredible power of compound interest.
- Today's financial accounts, products and sources of information are the best they've ever been – if you know where to go.

- You can benefit from the fact that the world will continue to grow economically (barring a major war or similar crisis – in which case, investment performance might be the least of your concerns!).
- You can actually benefit from the fact that there is high *real* inflation in the world.
- You can always find the money you need to invest, particularly if you are willing to change your living arrangements if you're spending too much on them.
- You can set up your own personal financial accounts to benefit from providers who are far better than the more mainstream financial services firms – and save on costs and increase the range of things you can invest in as a result.
- The various asset classes you might invest in aren't as complicated as you may previously have believed.
- Making a financial plan is an important step on your road to financial success.
- You can make superior returns with the relatively simple approach of 'owning the world' and 'owning inflation'. Learning how to do this is no harder than learning how to drive.
- Once you have a reasonable amount of money, you can aspire to learning much more about investment. Doing so can yield spectacular results in the long term.

I hope you have enjoyed the book and that you feel excited and empowered about what is possible with your money as a result.

The final point I would like to make is that I very much hope you join the Plain English Finance community by subscribing to our free email. This book is, by its very nature, a static source of information. Obviously, finance is an incredibly dynamic subject. By subscribing you will ensure that you are kept in touch with some of the most important news and developments in finance in the months and years ahead. (I would highlight that this is not one of those annoying daily emails. I only write something every few weeks when I think there is something reasonably interesting to say.)

So that is it. I thank you for taking the time to read the book and I wish you the very best for your future. If you are able to take control of your financial affairs, I have every confidence that it will yield wonderful results for every area of your life.

Happy investing!

Andrew Craig

Bibliography

Antopolous, Andreas M. *Internet of Money,* vol. 1. CreateSpace Independent Publishing Platform, 2016 [ebook].

———. *Internet of Money,* vol. 2. CreateSpace Independent Publishing Platform, 2017 [ebook].

Arnold, Glen. *Financial Times Guide to Investing: The Definitive Companion to Investment and the Financial Markets.* Harlow, England: Pearson Financial Times/Prentice Hall, 2010.

———. *Financial Times Handbook of Corporate Finance: A Business Companion to Financial Markets, Decisions & Techniques.* New York: Pearson Financial Times, 2010.

Bakan, Joel. *The Corporation: The Pathological Pursuit of Profit and Power.* New York: Free Press, 2005.

Bartholomew, James. *The Welfare State We're In.* London: Politico's, 2006.

Bastiat, Frederic. *The Law.* Lightning Source, 2007.

Berman, Morris. *The Twilight of American Culture.* New York: Norton, 2006.

Bernstein, Stefan. *Commodities in a Day.* Hawkhurst: Global Professional, 2009.

Bjergegaard, Martin, and Jordan Milne. *Winning without Losing: 66 Strategies for Succeeding in Business While Living a Happy and Balanced Life.* Pine Tribe, 2014.

Blum, William. *Rogue State: A Guide to the World's Only Superpower.* Monroe: Common Courage, 2005.

Boettke, Peter J. *Living Economics: Yesterday, Today, and Tomorrow.* Oakland: Independent Institute, 2012.

Bolton, Anthony. *Investing against the Tide: Lessons from a Life Running Money.* London: Financial Times/Prentice Hall, 2009.

————, and Jonathan Davis. *Investing with Anthony Bolton: Anatomy of a Stock Market Winner.* Petersfield, Hants: Harriman House, 2006.

Bonner, William. *Dice Have No Memory: Big Bets and Bad Economics from Paris to the Pampas.* Hoboken: John Wiley & Sons, 2011.

————, and Addison Wiggin. *Empire of Debt: The Rise of an Epic Financial Crisis.* Hoboken: John Wiley & Sons, 2006.

————, and Lila Rajiva. *Mobs, Messiahs, and Markets: Surviving the Public Spectacle in Finance and Politics.* Hoboken: John Wiley & Sons, 2007.

Bootle, R. P. *The Trouble with Europe: Why the EU Isn't Working, How It Can Be Reformed, What Could Take Its Place.* London: Nicholas Brealey, 2015.

Borthwick, Mark. *Pacific Century: The Emergence of Modern Pacific Asia.* Boulder: Westview, 2007.

Bostrom, Nick. *Superintelligence: Paths, Dangers, Strategies,* repr. edn. Oxford: Oxford University Press, 2016.

Botsman, Rachel, and Roo Rogers. *What's Mine Is Yours: The Rise of Collaborative Consumption.* New York: Harper Business, 2010.

Bower, Tom. *The Squeeze: Oil, Money and Greed in the 21st Century.* London: HarperPress, 2009.

Bradfield-Moody, James, and Bianca Nogrady. *The Sixth Wave.* London: ReadHowYouWant.com, 2010.

Browne, Harry. *Fail-safe Investing: Lifelong Financial Security in 30 Minutes.* New York: St. Martin's Griffin, 2001.

Brussee, Warren. *The Second Great Depression.* Bangor: Booklocker.com, 2005.

Bryson, Bill. *Notes from a Small Island.* London: Black Swan, 1996.

Bueno de Mesquita, Bruce. *Prediction: How to See and Shape the Future with Game Theory.* London: Vintage, 2010.

Burniske, Chris, and Jack Tatar. *Cryptoassets: The Innovative Investor's Guide to Bitcoin and Beyond.* New York: McGraw-Hill Education, 2017.

Burns, Robbie. *The Naked Trader: How Anyone Can Make Money Trading Shares.* Petersfield: Harriman House, 2007.

———. *The Naked Trader's Guide to Spread Betting: How to Make Money from Shares in Up or Down Markets.* Petersfield: Harriman House, 2010.

Buzan, Tony. *The Speed Reading Book.* London: BBC, 1997.

Carnegie, Dale. *How to Win Friends and Influence People.* London: Vermilion, 2006.

Carson, Rachel. *Silent Spring.* Boston, MA: Houghton Mifflin, 2002.

Carswell, Douglas. *The End of Politics and the Birth of iDemocracy.* London: Biteback, 2012.

Casey, Douglas R. *Crisis Investing: Opportunities and Profits in the Coming Great Depression.* New York: Stratford Press, 1980.

Cassidy, John. *Dot.con: How America Lost Its Mind and Money in the Internet Era.* New York: Perennial, 2003.

Chancellor, Edward. *Devil Take the Hindmost: A History of Financial Speculation.* New York: Farrar, Straus and Giroux, 1999.

Chang, Ha-Joon. *23 Things They Don't Tell You about Capitalism.* New York: Bloomsbury, 2011.

———. *Bad Samaritans: The Myth of Free Trade and the Secret History of Capitalism.* New York: Bloomsbury, 2008.

———. *Economics: The User's Guide.* New York: Penguin, 2014.

Chace, Callum. *The Economic Singularity.* Three Cs, 2016 [ebook].

Chomsky, Noam, and David Barsamian. *Imperial Ambitions: Conversations on the Post-9/11 World.* New York: Metropolitan, 2005.

Chomsky, Noam, John Schoeffel, and Peter R. Mitchell. *Understanding Power: The Indispensable Chomsky.* London: Vintage, 2003.

Coates, John. *The Hour between Wolf and Dog: Risk-Taking, Gut Feelings and the Biology of Boom and Bust.* London: Fourth Estate, 2012.

Conway, Mark R., and Aaron N. Behle. *Professional Stock Trading: System Design and Automation.* Waltham: Acme Trader, 2003.

Craig, David. *Squandered: How Gordon Brown Is Wasting over One Trillion Pounds of Our Money.* London: Constable, 2008.

Csikszentmihalyi, Mihaly. *Creativity: Flow and the Psychology of Discovery and Invention.* New York: HarperCollins, 1996.

Dalio, Ray. *Principles.* New York: Simon & Schuster, 2017.

Dampier, Mark. *Effective Investing: A Simple Way to Build Wealth by Investing in Funds.* Petersfield, Hants: Harriman House, 2015.

Davidson, James Dale, and William Rees-Mogg. *Blood in the Streets: Investment Profits in a World Gone Mad.* New York: Summit, 1987.

———. *The Great Reckoning: Protect Yourself in the Coming Depression.* New York: Simon & Schuster, 1993.

———. *The Sovereign Individual.* New York: Touchstone, 1999.

Davies, Ewan. *Made in Britain,* rev. edn. London: Abacus, 2012.

De Botton, Alain. *Status Anxiety.* London: Penguin, 2005.

Deffeyes, Kenneth S. *Beyond Oil: The View from Hubbert's Peak.* New York: Hill and Wang, 2005.

Dennis, Felix. *How to Get Rich.* London: Ebury, 2007.

Dent, Harry S. *Demographic Cliff: How to Survive and Prosper during the Great Deflation Ahead,* repr. edn. London: Penguin, 2015.

——— *The Great Depression Ahead: How to Prosper in the Crash following the Greatest Boom in History.* New York: Free Press, 2009.

Diamandis, Peter H., and Steven Kotler. *Abundance: The Future Is Better than You Think.* New York: Free Press, 2012.

————. *Bold: How to Go Big, Create Wealth, and Impact the World.* New York: Simon & Schuster, 2015.

Diamond, Jared. *Guns, Germs, and Steel: The Fates of Human Societies.* New York: W. W. Norton & Company, 2005.

————. *Collapse: How Societies Choose to Fail or Survive.* London: Penguin, 2006.

————. *The Third Chimpanzee: The Evolution and Future of the Human Animal.* New York: HarperCollins, 1992.

Dicken, Peter. *Global Shift: Reshaping the Global Economic Map in the 21st Century.* New York: Guilford Press, 2003.

Dobelli, Rolf. *The Art of Thinking Clearly.* London: Sceptre, 2017.

Doyen, Robert, and Meg Elaine Schneider. *Making Millions for Dummies.* Hoboken: John Wiley & Sons, 2009.

Einhorn, David. *Fooling Some of the People All of the Time: A Long Short Story.* Hoboken: John Wiley & Sons, 2008.

Elder, Alexander. *The Complete Trading for a Living: The Legendary Approach to Trading.* New York: John Wiley & Sons, 2006.

Ellenberg, Jordan. *How Not to Be Wrong: The Power of Mathematical Thinking. London:* Penguin, 2015.

Estrada, Javier. *Finance in a Nutshell: A No-nonsense Companion to the Tools and Techniques of Finance.* London: Financial Times/Prentice Hall, 2005.

Faber, Mebane T. *The Ivy Portfolio: How to Invest Like the Top Endowments and Avoid Bear Markets.* Hoboken: John Wiley & Sons, 2011.

Faith, Curtis M. *Way of the Turtle: The Secret Methods that Turned Ordinary People into Legendary Traders.* New York: McGraw-Hill, 2007.

Feierstein, Mitch. *Planet Ponzi: How Politicians and Bankers Stole Your Future.* London: Bantam Press, 2012.

Ferguson, Niall. *The Ascent of Money: A Financial History of the World.* New York: Penguin, 2008.

———. *The Cash Nexus: Money and Power in the Modern World, 1700–2000*. New York: Basic Books, 2001.

———. *Civilization: The West and the Rest*. London: Allen Lane, 2011.

———. *High Financier: The Lives and Time of Siegmund Warburg*. New York: Penguin, 2010.

Fergusson, Adam. *When Money Dies: The Nightmare of the Weimar Hyper-Inflation*. London: Old Street Publishing, 2010.

Ferriss, Timothy. *The 4-hour Work Week: Escape the 9–5, Live Anywhere, and Join the New Rich*. London: Vermilion, 2007.

———. *Tools of Titans: The Tactics, Routines, and Habits of Billionaires, Icons, and World-Class Performers*. London: Vermilion, 2016.

Fischer, David Hackett. *The Great Wave: Price Revolutions and the Rhythm of History*. New York: Oxford University Press, 1996.

Fisher, Philip A. *Common Stocks and Uncommon Profits and Other Writings*. New York: John Wiley & Sons, 2003.

Fitz-Gerald, Keith. *Fiscal Hangover: How to Profit from the New Global Economy*. Hoboken: John Wiley & Sons, 2010.

Franken, Al. *Lies and the Lying Liars Who Tell Them: A Fair and Balanced Look at the Right*. New York: Dutton, 2003.

Freeman-Shor, Lee. *The Art of Execution: How the World's Best Investors Get It Wrong and Still Make Millions*. Petersfield, Hants: Harriman House, 2015.

Frieden, Jeffry A., and David A. Lake. *International Political Economy: Perspectives on Global Power and Wealth*. New York: St. Martin's Press, 1987.

Friedman, Thomas L. *The World Is Flat: A Brief History of the Twenty-First Century*. New York: Farrar, Straus and Giroux, 2006.

Frisby, Dominic. *Bitcoin: The Future of Money?* London: Unbound, 2014.

———. *Life after the State*. London: Unbound, 2013.

Fukuyama, Francis. *The End of History and the Last Man*. New York: Free Press, 1992.

———. *Trust: The Social Virtues and the Creation of Prosperity*. New York: Free Press, 1996.

Funnell, Warwick, Jane Andrew, and Robert E. Jupe. *In Government We Trust*. London: Pluto Press, 2009.

Galbraith, Kenneth. *The Affluent Society*. London: Penguin, 1991.

———. *The Great Crash 1929*. London: Penguin, 1992.

Garrett, Garet. *A Bubble That Broke the World*. Boston, MA: Little, Brown, 1932.

Getty, J. Paul. *How to Be Rich*. New York: Jove Books, 1983.

Gladwell, Malcolm. *Blink: The Power of Thinking Without Thinking*. New York: Little, Brown, 2005.

———. *David and Goliath: Underdogs, Misfits, and the Art of Battling Giants*. Penguin, 2014.

———. *Outliers: The Story of Success*. New York: Little, Brown, 2008.

———. *The Tipping Point: How Little Things Can Make a Big Difference*. Boston MA: Back Bay Books, 2002.

Goleman, Daniel. *Emotional Intelligence: Why It Can Matter More Than IQ*. New York: Bantam Press, 2006.

Goodman, Leah McGrath. *The Asylum: The Renegades Who Hijacked the World's Oil Market*. New York: William Morrow & Company, 2011.

Gough, Leo. *How the Stock Market Really Works: The Guerrilla Investor's Secret Handbook*. London: Financial Times/Prentice Hall, 2001.

Graham, Benjamin, and Jason Zweig. *The Intelligent Investor: The Definitive Book on Value Investing*. New York: HarperBusiness, 2003.

Green, Alexander. *The Gone Fishin' Portfolio: Get Wise, Get Wealthy – and Get on with Your Life*. Hoboken: John Wiley & Sons, 2010.

Greenblatt, Joel. *You Can Be a Stock Market Genius: Uncover the Secret Hiding Places of Stock Market Profits.* New York: Simon & Schuster, 1999.

Greene, Robert, and Joost Elffers. *The 48 Laws of Power.* London: Profile Books, 2002.

Griffis, Michael, and Lita Epstein. *Trading for Dummies.* Hoboken: John Wiley & Sons, 2009.

Haakonssen, Knud. *Adam Smith: The Theory of Moral Sentiments. Cambridge:* Cambridge University Press, 2002.

Hagstrom, Robert G. *The Warren Buffet Way: Investment Strategies of the World's Greatest Investor.* New York: John Wiley & Sons, 1995.

Hale, Tim. *Smarter Investing: Simpler Decisions for Better Results.* Harlow: Financial Times/Prentice Hall, 2006.

Harari, Yuval Noah. *Sapiens: A Brief History of Humankind.* New York: Vintage, 2015.

———. *Homo Deus: A Brief History of Tomorrow.* New York: Vintage, 2017.

Harbour, Jeremy. *Go Do!: For People Who Have Always Wanted to Start a Business.* Chichester: Capstone, 2012.

Hawken, Paul. *The Ecology of Commerce: A Declaration of Sustainability.* New York: HarperBusiness, 2010.

Hayek, Friedrich von. *The Road to Serfdom: Text and Documents.* Chicago: University of Chicago, 2007.

———. *A Tiger by the Tail: A 40-years' Running Commentary on Keynesianism by Hayek.* London: Institute of Economic Affairs, 1972.

Hazlitt, Henry. *Economics in One Lesson: 50th Anniversary Edition.* Little Rock: Laissez Faire, 1996.

Heinberg, Richard. *The Party's Over: Oil, War and the Fate of Industrial Societies.* Gabriola: New Society, 2003.

Hill, Napoleon. *Think and Grow Rich*. Los Angeles: Highroads Media, 2008.

Hobbes, Thomas. *Leviathan*. New York: Pearson Longman, 2008.

Hobsbawm, Eric. *Industry and Empire: From 1750 to the Present Day*. New York: The New Press, 1999.

Huntington, Samuel Phillips. *The Clash of Civilizations and the Remaking of World Order*. New York: Free Press, 2002.

Hutton, Will. *The State We're In*. London: Vintage, 1996.

———. *The World We're In*. London: Abacus, 2007.

Ivins, Molly. *Who Let the Dogs In?: Incredible Political Animals I Have Known*. New York: Random House, 2004.

Jackson, Tim. *Prosperity without Growth: Economics for a Finite Planet*. London: Earthscan, 2010.

James, Oliver. *Affluenza*. London: Vermilion, 2008.

———. *Britain on the Couch: How Keeping up with the Joneses Has Depressed Us since 1950*. London: Vermilion, 2010.

———. *The Selfish Capitalist: Origins of Affluenza*. London: Vermilion, 2008.

Johnson, Luke. *Start It Up: Why Running Your Own Business is Easier Than You Think*. Portfolio Penguin, 2011.

Kahn, Michael N. *Technical Analysis Plain and Simple: Charting the Markets in Your Language*. Upper Saddle River: FT Press, 2010.

Kahneman, Daniel. *Thinking, Fast and Slow*. London: Penguin, 2011.

Kawasaki, Guy, and Peg Fitzpatrick. *The Art of Social Media: Power Tips for Power Users*. Portfolio Penguin, 2014.

Kay, J. A. *The Truth about Markets: Their Genius, Their Limits, Their Follies*. London: Penguin, 2004.

Keen, Steve. *Debunking Economics: The Naked Emperor of the Social Sciences*. Annandale: Pluto Australia, 2001.

Kelly, Kevin. *The Inevitable: Understanding the 12 Technological Forces That Will Shape Our Future,* rep. edn. London: Penguin, 2017.

Kennedy, Paul. *The Rise and Fall of the Great Powers: Economic Change and Military Conflict from 1500 to 2000.* New York: Random House, 1987.

Kerr, James M. *Legacy.* London: Constable, 2013.

Keynes, John Maynard. *The General Theory of Employment, Interest, and Money.* BN Publishing, 2008.

Kiyosaki, Robert T. *Rich Dad, Poor Dad: What the Rich Teach Their Kids about Money That the Poor and Middle Class Do Not!* New York: Warner Business, 2000.

Klein, Naomi. *No Logo: No Space, No Choice, No Jobs.* New York: Picador, 2010.

Kroijer, Lars. *Investing Demystified: How to Invest without Speculation and Sleepless Nights.* London: FT Publishing International, 2013.

Kunstler, James Howard. *The Long Emergency: Surviving the Converging Catastrophes of the Twenty-First Century.* New York: Atlantic Monthly, 2005.

Lanchester, John. *Whoops!: Why Everyone Owes Everyone and No One Can Pay.* London: Allen Lane, 2010.

Lee, John. *How to Make a Million Slowly: My Guiding Principles from a Lifetime of Successful Investing.* London: FT Publishing International, 2013.

Lefèvre, Edwin. *Reminiscences of a Stock Operator.* Hoboken: John Wiley & Sons, 2006.

Levitt, Steven D., and Stephen J. Dubner. *Freakonomics: A Rogue Economist Explores the Hidden Side of Everything.* New York: William Morrow & Company, 2006.

———. *Superfreakonomics.* Moosic, PA: HarperCollins Canada, 2009.

Lewis, Michael. *The Big Short: Inside the Doomsday Machine.* New York: W. W. Norton & Company, 2010.

————. *Flash Boys: A Wall Street Revolt.* Penguin, 2015.

————. *Liar's Poker: Rising through the Wreckage on Wall Street.* New York: W. W. Norton & Company, 2010.

————. *The New New Thing: A Silicon Valley Story.* New York: Penguin, 2001.

Lieven, Anatol, and John Hulsman. *Ethical Realism: A Vision for America's Role in the World.* New York: Pantheon, 2006.

Lovelock, James. *The Revenge of Gaia: Earth's Climate in Crisis and the Fate of Humanity.* New York: Basic Books, 2007.

Lowenstein, Roger. *When Genius Failed: The Rise and Fall of Long-term Capital Management.* New York: Random House, 2000.

Luce, Edward. *The Retreat of Western Liberalism.* New York: Little, Brown, 2017.

Lynch, Peter, and John Rothchild. *Beating the Street.* New York: Simon & Schuster, 1993.

————. *One Up on Wall Street: How to Use What You Already Know to Make Money in the Market.* New York: Simon & Schuster, 2000.

Lyons, Gerard. *The Consolations of Economics: How We Will All Benefit from the New World Order.* Faber & Faber, 2015.

MacDonald, Michael, and Christopher Whitestone. *The Silver Bomb: The End of Paper Wealth Is upon Us.* CreateSpace, 2012.

Machiavelli, Niccolò. *The Prince.* London: Penguin, 2003.

Mackay, Charles. *Extraordinary Popular Delusions.* New York: Dover Publications, 2003.

McKenna, Paul. *I Can Make You Rich.* New York: Bantam, 2008.

McLean, Bethany, and Peter Elkind. *The Smartest Guys in the Room: The Amazing Rise and Scandalous Fall of Enron.* New York: Portfolio, 2004.

Mainelli, Michael, and Ian Harris. *The Price of Fish: A New Approach to Wicked Economics and Better Decisions.* London: Nicholas Brealey, 2014.

Mallaby, Sebastian. *More Money than God: Hedge Funds and the Making of a New Elite.* New York: Penguin, 2010.

―――. *The World's Banker: A Story of Failed States, Financial Crises, and the Wealth and Poverty of Nations.* New York: Penguin, 2006.

Marcus Aurelius. *Meditations.* London: Penguin, 2006.

Markusen, James R., James R. Melvin, Keith E. Maskus and William H. Kaempfer. *International Trade: Theory and Evidence.* Boston, MA: McGraw-Hill, 1995.

Marx, Karl, and Friedrich Engels. *The Communist Manifesto.* London: Penguin, 2002.

Marz, Eduard. *Joseph Schumpeter: Scholar, Teacher, and Politician.* New Haven: Yale University Press, 1991.

Mauldin, John. *Bull's Eye Investing: Targeting Real Returns in a Smoke and Mirrors Market.* Hoboken: John Wiley & Sons, 2004.

―――, and Jonathan Tepper. *Endgame: The End of the Debt Supercycle and How It Changes Everything.* Hoboken: John Wiley & Sons, 2011.

Mayer, Christopher W. *World Right Side Up: Investing across Six Continents.* Hoboken: John Wiley & Sons, 2012.

Mill, John Stuart. *On Liberty and Other Essays.* Oxford: Oxford University Press, 1991.

Mill, John Stuart, and Jeremy Bentham. *Utilitarianism and Other Essays.* Harmondsworth: Penguin, 1987.

Mobius, Mark. *The Little Book of Emerging Markets: How to Make Money in the World's Fastest Growing Markets.* Singapore: John Wiley & Sons Singapore, 2012.

Monnery, Neil. *Safe as Houses?: A Historical Analysis of Property Prices.* London: London Partnership, 2011.

Moody, James, and Bianca Nogrady. *The Sixth Wave: How to Succeed in a Resource-Limited World.* North Sydney: Random House Australia, 2010.

Moore, Michael. *Dude, Where's My Country?* New York: Warner Books, 2003.

———. *Stupid White Men, and Other Sorry Excuses for the State of the Nation!* New York: ReganBooks, 2001.

Moore, Rob. *Money: Know More, Make More, Give More.* London: John Murray Learning, 2018.

More, Thomas. *Utopia.* London: J. M. Dent, 1994.

Mount, Ferdinand. *The New Few: A Very British Oligarchy.* London: Simon & Schuster, 2012.

Moyo, Dambisa. *Winner Take All: China's Race for Resources and What It Means for the World.* New York: Basic Books, 2012.

Naish, John. *Enough: Breaking Free from the World of More.* London: Hodder & Stoughton, 2008.

Needleman, Lionel. *The Economics of Housing.* Staples Press, 1965.

Oldfield, Richard. *Simple but Not Easy: An Autobiographical and Biased Book about Investing.* London: Doddington Publishing, 2007.

Olen, Helaine. *Pound Foolish,* repr. edn. London: Portfolio, 2019.

Olsen, Jeff. *The Slight Edge,* 3rd rev. edn. Lancaster, UK: Gazelle, 2013.

O'Neil, William J. *The How to Make Money in Stocks Complete Investing System: Your Ultimate Guide to Winning in Good Times and Bad.* New York: McGraw-Hill, 2011.

O'Shaughnessy, James P. *What Works on Wall Street: The Classic Guide to the Best-Performing Investment Strategies of All Time.* Maidenhead: McGraw-Hill, 2011.

Pape, Scott. *The Barefoot Investor: Five Steps to Financial Freedom in Your 20s and 30s.* Chichester: Capstone 2006.

Parker, Christopher. *Harriman's Book of Investing Rules: The Do's and Don'ts of the World's Best Investors.* Petersfield, Hants: Harriman House, 2017.

Penn, Mark J., and E. Kinney Zalesne. *Microtrends: The Small Forces Behind Tomorrow's Big Changes.* New York: Twelve, 2007.

Perkins, John. *Confessions of an Economic Hit Man.* New York: Plume, 2006.

Piketty, Thomas, and Arthur Goldhammer. *Capital in the Twenty-First Century.* Harvard University Press, 2014.

Pilger, John. *The New Rulers of the World.* London: Verso, 2003.

Porritt, Jonathon. *Capitalism as if the World Matters.* London: Earthscan, 2005.

Ramsey, David. *Total Money Makeover,* repr. edn. Nashville: Thomas Nelson, 2013.

Rand, Ayn. *Atlas Shrugged.* London: Penguin, 2007.

Reich, Robert B. *Supercapitalism.* New York: Vintage, 2008.

Rickards, James. *Currency Wars: The Making of the Next Global Crisis.* New York: Portfolio, 2011.

———. *Death of Money: The Coming Collapse of the International Monetary System.* New York: Portfolio, 2014.

———. *New Case for Gold.* New York: Portfolio, 2016.

Ridley, Matt. *The Rational Optimist: How Prosperity Evolves.* New York: Harper Collins, 2010.

Robbins, Anthony. *Money: Master the Game: 7 Simple Steps to Financial Freedom.* Simon & Schuster, 2014.

Roberts, J. M., and Odd Arne Westad. *The New Penguin History of the World.* London: Penguin, 2007.

Robin, Vicki. *Your Money or Your Life: 9 Steps to Transforming Your Relationship with Money and Achieving Financial Independence: Revised and Updated for the 21st Century,* 2nd edn. New York: Penguin, 2008.

Robinson, Lee. *The Gathering Storm.* Monaco: Derivatives Vision, 2010.

Rockefeller, Barbara. *Technical Analysis for Dummies*. Hoboken: John Wiley & Sons, 2011.

Rogers, Jim. *Adventure Capitalist: The Ultimate Road Trip*. Chichester: John Wiley & Sons, 2004.

———. *A Bull in China: Investing Profitably in the World's Greatest Market*. Hoboken: John Wiley & Sons, 2009.

———. *A Gift to My Children: A Father's Lessons for Life and Investing*. Chichester: John Wiley & Sons, 2009.

———. *Hot Commodities: How Anyone Can Invest Profitably in the World's Best Market*. New York: Random House, 2007.

———. *Investment Biker: Around the World with Jim Rogers*. New York: Random House, 2003.

Rosefielde, Steven, and Daniel Quinn Mills. *Masters of Illusion: American Leadership in the Media Age*. Cambridge: Cambridge University Press, 2007.

Rosling, Hans, and Ola Rosling. *Factfulness: Ten Reasons We're Wrong about the World – And Why Things Are Better Than You Think*. London: Sceptre, 2018.

Roubini, Nouriel, and Stephen Mihm. *Crisis Economics: A Crash Course in the Future of Finance*. New York: Penguin, 2010.

Rousseau, Jean-Jacques. *A Discourse on Equality*. London: Penguin, 2003.

———. *The Social Contract*. Harmondsworth, Penguin: 1975.

Sachs, Jeffrey. *Common Wealth: Economics for a Crowded Planet*. New York: Penguin, 2008.

———. *The End of Poverty: Economic Possibilities for Our Time*. New York: Penguin, 2005.

———. *The Price of Civilization: Reawakening American Virtue and Prosperity*. New York: Random House, 2011.

Sampson, Anthony. *The Seven Sisters: The Great Oil Companies and the World They Shaped*. New York: Viking, 1975.

Sandel, Michael J. *What Money Can't Buy: The Moral Limits of Markets*. New York: Farrar, Straus and Giroux, 2012.

Sardar, Ziauddin, and Merryl Wyn Davies. *Why Do People Hate America?* Cambridge: Icon Books, 2003.

Schiff, Peter D. *The Real Crash: America's Coming Bankruptcy – How to Save Yourself and Your Country.* New York: St. Martin's Press, 2012.

———, and John Downes. *Crash Proof 2.0: How to Profit from the Economic Collapse.* Hoboken: John Wiley & Sons, 2009.

———, and Andrew J. Schiff. *How an Economy Grows and Why It Crashes: A Tale.* Hoboken: John Wiley & Sons, 2010.

Schilit, Howard, and Jeremy Perler. *Financial Shenanigans*, 3rd edn. New York: McGraw-Hill Education.

Schlosser, Eric. *Fast Food Nation: The Dark Side of the All-American Meal.* New York: Perennial, 2002.

———. *Reefer Madness: Sex, Drugs, and Cheap Labor in the American Black Market.* Boston, MA: Houghton Mifflin, 2003.

Schwager, Jack. *Hedge Fund Market Wizards: How Winning Traders Win.* Hoboken: John Wiley & Sons, 2012.

——— *Market Wizards: Interviews with Top Traders.* Columbia: Marketplace, 2006.

Sculley, John. *Moonshot!: Game-changing Strategies to Build Billion-dollar Businesses.* Rosettabooks, 2014.

Sethi, Ramit. *I Will Teach You to be Rich,* rev. edn. New York: Workman, 2019.

Shaxson, Nicholas. *Treasure Islands: Tax Havens and the Men Who Stole the World.* London: Bodley Head, 2011.

Shiller, Robert J. *Finance and the Good Society.* Princeton: Princeton University Press, 2012.

Shipman, Mark. *Big Money, Little Effort a Winning Strategy for Profitable Long-Term Investment.* London: Kogan Page Publishers, 2008.

——. *The Next Big Investment Boom: Learn the Secrets of Investing from a Master and How to Profit from Commodities.* London: Kogan Page Publishing, 2008.

——. *EQ vs IQ: The Reason Why Not Every Intelligent Trader or Investor Is Rich.* CreateSpace, 2014.

Siegel, Jeremy J. *Stocks for the Long Run: The Definitive Guide to Financial Market Returns and Long-Term Investment Strategies.* New York: McGraw-Hill, 2008.

Silver, Nate. *Signal and the Noise: The Art and Science of Prediction.* London: Penguin, 2013.

Simmons, Matthew R. *Twilight in the Desert: The Coming Saudi Oil Shock and the World Economy.* Hoboken: John Wiley & Sons, 2005.

Slater, Jim. *The Zulu Principle: Making Extraordinary Profits from Ordinary Shares.* London: Orion, 1992.

Smith, Adam: *The Theory of Moral Sentiments.* Cambridge: Cambridge University Press, 2002.

——. *The Wealth of Nations.* London: Penguin, 1999.

Smith, David. *The Age of Instability: The Global Financial Crisis and What Comes Next.* London: Profile, 2010.

Smith, James. *Zero to £1 Million: My Stock Market Lessons and Techniques.* CreateSpace, 2016.

Smith, Roy C., and Ingo Walter, *Street Smarts: Linking Professional Conduct with Shareholder Value in the Securities Industry.* Brighton, MA: Harvard Business School Press, 1997.

Smith, Terry. *Accounting for Growth: Stripping the Camouflage from Company Accounts.* London: Century Business, 1992.

Soros, George. *The Age of Fallibility: The Consequences of the War on Terror.* New York: PublicAffairs, 2006.

——. *The Alchemy of Finance.* Hoboken: John Wiley & Sons, 2003.

————. *The Bubble of American Supremacy: Correcting the Misuse of American Power.* New York: PublicAffairs, 2004.

————. *The Crash of 2008 and What It Means: The New Paradigm for Financial Markets.* New York: PublicAffairs, 2009.

————. *The Crisis of Global Capitalism: Open Society Endangered.* New York: PublicAffairs, 1998.

————. *On Globalization.* New York: PublicAffairs, 2002.

————. *Open Society: Reforming Global Capitalism.* New York: PublicAffairs, 2000.

————. *Soros on Soros: Staying Ahead of the Curve.* New York: John Wiley & Sons, 1995.

————. *Underwriting Democracy.* New York: Free Press, 1991.

St. Clair, Jeffrey. *Grand Theft Pentagon: Tales of Corruption and Profiteering in the War on Terror.* Monroe: Common Courage, 2005.

Stanley, Thomas J., and William D. Danko. *The Millionaire next Door: The Surprising Secrets of America's Wealthy.* Atlanta: Longstreet, 1996.

Stiglitz, Joseph E. *Globalization and Its Discontents.* New York: W. W. Norton & Company, 2003.

————. *The Price of Inequality.* New York: W.W. Norton, 2012.

Strauss, William, and Neil Howe. *The Fourth Turning: An American Prophecy.* New York: Broadway, 1998.

Sullivan, Paul. *The Thin Green Line: The Money Secrets of the Super Wealthy.* New York: Simon & Schuster, 2015.

Sun Tzu. *The Complete Art of War.* Boulder: Westview, 1996.

Suskind, Ron. *The Way of the World: A Story of Truth and Hope in an Age of Extremism.* New York: Harper, 2008.

Sutherland, *Stephen. Liquid Millionaire: How to Make Millions from the Up and Coming Stock Market Boom.* Milton Keynes: AuthorHouse, 2008.

Swensen, David. *Pioneering Portfolio Management,* 2nd edn. New York: Free Press, 2009.

Taleb, Nassim. *Antifragile: Things that Gain from Disorder.* London: Penguin, 2013.

———— *The Black Swan: The Impact of the Highly Improbable.* New York: Random House, 2010.

————. *Fooled by Randomness.* London: Penguin, 2007.

Tannehill, Morris, and Linda Tannehill. *The Market for Liberty: Is Government Really Necessary?; Is Government Our Protector ... or Our Destroyer?* New York: Laissez Faire, 1984.

Templar, Richard. *The Rules of Wealth: A Personal Code for Prosperity.* Harlow: Pearson/Prentice Hall Business, 2007.

————. *The Rules of Work: A Definitive Code for Personal Success.* Harlow: Pearson/Prentice Hall Business, 2010.

Tharp, Van K. *Super Trader: Make Consistent Profits in Good and Bad Markets.* New York: McGraw-Hill, 2011.

————. *Trade Your Way to Financial Freedom.* New York: McGraw-Hill, 2007.

Thiel, Peter A., and Blake Masters. *Zero to One: Notes on Startups, or How to Build the Future.* Virgin Books, 2015.

Toffler, Alvin. *Future Shock.* Toronto: Bantam Books, 1971.

————. *Powershift: Knowledge, Wealth, and Violence at the Edge of the 21st Century.* New York: Bantam Books, 1990.

Toffler, Alvin. *The Third Wave.* Toronto: Bantam Books, 1981.

Turk, James, and John A. Rubino. *The Collapse of the Dollar and How to Profit from It: Make a Fortune by Investing in Gold and Other Hard Assets.* New York: Doubleday, 2007.

Vaitilingam, Romesh. *Financial Times Guide to Using the Financial Pages.* Harlow: Financial Times/Prentice Hall, 2006.

Vanhaverbeke, Frederik. *Excess Returns.* Petersfield, Hants: Harriman House, 2014.

Vonnegut, Kurt. *A Man Without a Country.* New York: Random House, 2007.

Wapshott, Nicholas. *Keynes Hayek: The Clash That Defined Modern Economics.* New York: W. W. Norton & Company, 2011.

Webb, Merryn Somerset. *Love Is Not Enough: A Smart Woman's Guide to Making (and Keeping) Money.* London: Harper Perennial, 2008.

Weiner, Eric J. *The Shadow Market: How a Group of Wealthy Nations and Powerful Investors Secretly Dominate the World.* New York: Scribner, 2010.

Weissman, Richard L. *Mechanical Trading Systems: Pairing Trader Psychology with Technical Analysis.* Hoboken: John Wiley & Sons, 2005.

Wiggin, Addison. *The Demise of the Dollar ... and Why It's Even Better for Your Investments.* Hoboken: J. Wiley & Sons, 2008.

———. *The Little Book of the Shrinking Dollar: What You Can Do to Protect Your Money Now.* Hoboken: John Wiley & Sons, 2012.

———, and Justice Litle. *Gold: The Once and Future Money.* Chichester: John Wiley & Sons, 2006.

Index

Acknowledgements

This book is dedicated in loving memory of my mother, Mrs Gillian Craig (1949–2017).

It is also dedicated to ...

... my long-suffering and wonderfully supportive wife, Rachel

... our gorgeous little daughter, Ella, who 'helped' with this third edition at my feet in the office at home

... Neville, Michael and Joanna, respectively my father, brother and sister

... Timothy James Peacock, COO of Plain English Finance, without whom this book wouldn't exist

... my cousin Mary Ramsden, about which the same can be said

... Dimitri Goulandris, Roderick Collins, Alan Back, Professors Steve Thomas and Andrew Clare, and Dr James Seaton

... to Brian Guckian, David Holdsworth, Jonathan Fry, Mike Dobson and Virgil Wolf – you all know why ...

... Iain Campbell and Jenny Campbell (no relation) and the rest of the team at John Murray Learning for keeping us on track!

... Adam Gauntlet, our literary agent at Peters Fraser and Dunlop

... and to Ioni Appelberg, with thanks for your invaluable input on all things Bitcoin

... to everyone else who has contributed to Plain English Finance and *How to Own the World* in the last few years and to every single person who has taken the time to read the book already in either of the previous editions ... and particularly those who have taken the time to post a review!

If you enjoyed *How to Own the World* – are you ready to take things further?

We hope you got a great deal out of reading this book and feel more confident about saving and investment than you did before you read it!

If you want to take the next steps on your road to financial freedom, please do consider joining thousands of like-minded people on a similar journey by subscribing to our free email list.

Unlike many other similar email services, ours is categorically not an annoying daily bombardment! We only write something every 2-4 weeks when we feel we have something helpful to say.

You just need to enter your name and email address in the box at the bottom of the landing page of our website: www.plainenglishfinance.co.uk

If you're even more interested in getting your finances humming, then please consider joining our Plain English Finance Community: https://plainenglishfinance.co.uk/community-support

Finally – each year, Andrew speaks at various industry events and conferences.

If you're interested in booking Andrew to speak to your organisation about owning the world – do please send an email to: hello@plainenglishfinance.com

Until then – Happy investing!